Critical Topics in an Aging Society

Editorial Adviser, Toni C. Antonucci, PhD

- *Using Technology to Improve Care of Older Adults*
  Diane Chau, MD, FACP, and Thomas F. Osborne, MD, Editors
- *Homeless Older Populations: A Practical Guide for the Interdisciplinary Care Team*
  Diane Chau, MD, and Arnold P. Gass, MD, FACP, Editors
- *The New Politics of a Majority-Minority Nation: Aging, Diversity, and Immigration*
  Fernando M. Torres-Gil, PhD, and Jacqueline L. Angel, PhD
- *Social Isolation in Later Life: Strategies to Bolster Health and Well-Being*
  Lenard W. Kaye, DSW, PhD, and Cliff Singer, MD, Editors
- *Elder Justice, Ageism, and Elder Abuse*
  Lisa Nerenberg, MSW, MPH

Elder Justice, Ageism, and Elder Abuse

Lisa Nerenberg, MSW, MPH, has been actively involved in the field of elder abuse prevention and aging for almost 35 years. She was the founding director of the San Francisco Consortium for Elder Abuse Prevention, which piloted the nation's first elder abuse multidisciplinary team and other widely replicated services. She is the founding director of the California Elder Justice Coalition, which was created in 2012 to provide a voice from the field in policy development.

Nerenberg is on the faculty of City College of San Francisco, where she teaches classes on health and aging, elder abuse, and ageism and adultism. She also helped create the Elder Advocate Specialist Community Health Worker certificate within the school's Department of Health Education.

She has presented at hundreds of professional forums in the United States and worldwide, testified before Congressional committees, served on governmental advisory committees, and written extensively about elder abuse and related issues. *Elder Abuse Prevention: Emerging Trends and Promising Strategies* (2008) describes what agencies, communities, tribes, states, and national organizations can do to prevent abuse, treat its effects, and ensure justice.

Elder Justice, Ageism, and Elder Abuse

Lisa Nerenberg, MSW, MPH

SPRINGER PUBLISHING COMPANY

Springer Publishing Company, LLC
11 West 42nd Street
New York, NY 10036
www.springerpub.com
http://connect.springerpub.com

Acquisitions Editor: Sheri W. Sussman
Compositor: Exeter Premedia Services Private Ltd.

ISBN: 978-0-8261-4756-1
ebook ISBN: 978-0-8261-4757-8
DOI: 10.1891/9780826147578

21 22 23 / 5 4 3 2

Library of Congress Cataloging-in-Publication Data

Names: Nerenberg, Lisa, author.
Title: Elder justice, ageism, and elder abuse/Lisa Nerenberg, author.
Other titles: Critical topics in an aging society.
Description: New York, NY: Springer Publishing Company, LLC, [2019] |
  Series: Critical topics in an aging society | Includes bibliographical
  references.
Identifiers: LCCN 2018049515| ISBN 9780826147561 | ISBN 9780826147578 (e-book)
Subjects: | MESH: Elder Abuse—legislation & jurisprudence | Elder
  Abuse—prevention & control | Ageism—legislation & jurisprudence |
  Ageism—prevention & control | Social Justice | Public Policy | Aged |
  United States
Classification: LCC HV6626.3 | NLM WA 33 AA1 | DDC 362.6/82—dc23
LC record available at https://lccn.loc.gov/2018049515

Lisa Nerenberg: https://orcid.org/0000-0003-3612-0058

Contents

Foreword

The beauty of this important book lies in its conclusion. Ms. Nerenberg drives home the message that we desperately need a national elder justice agenda to make sure that we have the right policies in place to provide an inclusive and value-driven approach to addressing elder mistreatment. Wouldn't that be wonderful? We know it's possible because this illuminating book takes us through the background and trajectory of the elder justice framework and what is needed for it to further evolve and finally meet the needs of older adults. From the Declaration of Independence through the Constitution and our Bill of Rights, the notion of justice is at the very heart of our societal values. Why, then, does it seem so difficult to apply our principles of justice to older adults? This book provides the road map that has led us to our current dilemmas and offers the path forward to a truly just society for all. Elder justice is far more than the eradication of elder abuse, although that would be a new world order. True elder justice lies in eliminating all the facets of society that systematically exclude older adults from their basic human rights: ageism, paternalism, and, in some cases, frank discrimination.

I am glad Ms. Nerenberg has given of herself to create this much needed guide for what we must do to ensure a society that demands elder justice.

Terry Fulmer, PhD, RN, FAAN
President of The John A. Hartford Foundation

Preface

Justice has been on my mind a lot in the past few years as the field of elder abuse prevention, the focus of my career, has rebranded itself and adopted the label of elder justice. This is seen in the Elder Justice Act of 2010, which was championed by the Elder Justice Coalition, and followed by the creation of the Elder Justice Coordinating Council, the Elder Justice Roadmap, and the Elder Justice Caucus in the U.S. House of Representatives. All focus on preventing abuse.

This change in terminology feels natural and reflects a natural evolution in thinking. Many in the fields of aging and elder abuse prevention have come to recognize how the effects of poverty, discrimination, and trauma accumulate and intermingle as we age. These "social determinants" shape our health and susceptibility to disease and disability. As Harvard epidemiologist Nancy Krieger explains, "We carry our histories in our bodies. How could we not?" (California Newsreel, 2008, para. 2). Social determinants also influence the likelihood of being mistreated, neglected, or treated unfairly.

Perhaps those in the field of aging have a greater appreciation of the links between social justice and aging policy. They are apparent in milestones like the Social Security Act, which was enacted during the Depression when the poverty rate for older Americans was over 50%. The Older Americans Act and Medicare were created against the backdrop of the civil rights movement and, as Stanford and Rivas (2017) point out, "older adults' fingerprints are all over the history of the Civil Rights Movement" (para. 5). Civil rights and aging policy were inextricably linked.

To me, the recasting of elder abuse as elder justice seems incomplete. It casts freedom from abuse as *a* right, yet fails to explain how abuse fits into the broader scheme of justice and human rights. I wrote this book to explore that failure.

But then the ground began to shift. The 2016 presidential election happened and, in its aftermath, innumerable challenges developed to justice and

rights. The book is not an attempt to make sense of these events or to anticipate their outcomes for aging policy and practice. It is too early for that as the
fates of key programs and fundamental rights lie in the balance.

What is germane is the intense interest in justice and human rights that
these developments have ignited. Suddenly, everyday Americans are pas-
sionately arguing about whether healthcare is a right. Justice and human
rights are being debated in town halls, on college campuses, and in high
schools. Justice and human rights seem to be on everybody's mind.

These developments provide a context for defining and advancing elder
justice, and an animating force for change. Not only do older Americans,
their allies, and advocates have an enormous stake in the outcomes, these
groups can also play a role in shaping them. To do so, advocates need to
define elder justice writ large (beyond its current boundaries) and explore
the opportunities it presents. Our voices need to be heard, not in competition
with others, but to share what we know about how injustice plays out across
the life span and to support the rights of people of all ages.

I turned to our field's history and its leaders and trailblazers for insights
and inspiration; explored what America's founders meant by justice and
where their aspirations left off and laws began; and looked at how the United
Nations and international groups view human rights and apply them to
older people.

The book also reflects a confluence of factors in my own life. A decade ago,
I started meeting with colleagues to discuss systemic obstacles to elder abuse
prevention, which led to the creation of the California Elder Justice Coalition
(CEJC) to provide a forum for exploring issues and solutions. Over the years,
we discussed disparities in older people's access to protective services, victim assistance, and support services, which came into particularly sharp
relief during the recession of 2008 as resources were cut, leaving more elders
vulnerable. We discussed threats to autonomy, privacy, and liberty, some of
which we were complicit in. Some were troubled by the increasing dominance of criminal justice approaches to abuse, which seemed to overshadow
protections for the rights, preferences, and needs of victims. We drew from
our own work and enlisted others to broaden the dialogue through summits, roundtable discussions, a blueprint, and a set of elder justice principles,
which are contained in Chapter 11.

As a teacher of aging policy, public health, ageism, and elder abuse in a
school that is deeply committed to human rights and social justice, the imper-
ative to teach from that perspective is clear. My dual paths of teacher and
advocate further came together in 2018 as I helped launch an Elder Advocate
Community Health Worker certificate program.

Recently, the National Committee for the Prevention of Elder Abuse disbanded after more than 30 years. Under the leadership of Rosalie Wolf and a dedicated membership of advocates, researchers, and service providers from multiple disciplines, the organization helped lay the foundation for research and practice today. The national office of the Gray Panthers, a grassroots advocacy group that condemned ageism and aligned with other social justice groups, also closed its doors in recent years, passing the torch to state and local chapters to carry on. It is troubling and ironic that forums like these are disbanding as the need for allies, advocates, and leadership intensifies.

New forums are needed to fill these voids. Toward that end, the CEJC has launched a National Elder Justice Academy, and I am working with a dynamic team of leaders of other state elder justice coalitions to start a national organization. Both, I hope, will provide opportunities for new leaders to emerge, retired colleagues to re-engage (free from employer-imposed constraints against speaking out), and others committed to elder justice to work together.

I offer this book as a contribution to that effort, to be debated or negated, or to simply serve as a jumping off point for discussion. It is my hope that it generates new ideas and reimagines the tried and true. Toward these ends, I have offered a basic introduction to some of the foundational principles and vocabularies of human rights, public health, aging services, elder abuse, ageism, and ethical and legal concepts. I believe that to be effective, we need to be conversant in them all.

Some suggest that elder justice is a fad or a repackaging of what we have been doing all along. It can become that if we let it. But the paradigm offered here can ground our work in basic principles enshrined in the Constitution and Universal Declaration of Human Rights. For as long as these values and the institutions that protect them endure, elder justice is secure.

Others have expressed skepticism that adopting a broader view of elder justice will require vast changes in what we do, intrude on other disciplines, or place us in competition with other constituencies. I believe that elder justice can do the opposite. It can help us connect the dots to provide a clearer view of how disciplines intersect and diverge and lend clarity to our roles. It unites professionals with advocates, service providers with those they serve, and our fields' pioneers with newcomers. It provides a unifying vision and shared goals.

I have suggested that it is perhaps time to amend the Elder Justice Act to better reflect "elder justice writ large." When I float the idea to colleagues, however, it is generally met with skepticism; they see it as a monumental lift with huge potential for unintended consequences. Kathy Greenlee, former

Secretary of Aging, who was largely responsible for implementing the law, suggests instead the need for a cultural shift, a change in how we think about elder justice (K. Greenlee, personal communication, April 16, 2018). She also points to the power of self-advocacy and the need to break down barriers between professionals and advocates and between the young and old. In this respect, we have an advantage over other constituencies—the fortunate among us will all be old someday.

Writing the book has been exhausting and enriching. I have been inspired by what others have achieved, disheartened by challenges and setbacks, and humbled to consider what remains to be done. The year I had to write it soared by at breakneck speed and I apologize in advance for omissions and shortchanging critical topics and considerations. The Elder Justice Agenda, which I present in Chapter 12, is skewed toward elder abuse and healthcare (the topics I know best), when other critical threats to older people's rights demand attention; however, I believe that the concepts and approaches contained in the Elder Justice Agenda can be readily applied to other challenges. I invite others to fill in the gaps and look forward to continuing the conversation.

ACKNOWLEDGMENTS

I am deeply indebted to the many friends and colleagues who made this book possible. For the many hours of conversation and interviews, I thank Georgia Anetzberger, Bill Benson, Kathy Greenlee, Jeffrey Hall, Nina Kohn, Paula Mixson, Janey Skinner, Charles Sabatino, Susan Somers, and Pam Teaster. My sincere thanks also go to those who reviewed chapters and shared their expertise and insights, including Suzanne Anderson, John Dussich, Terri Fulmer, Eileen Goldman, Frederick Hertz, Naomi Karp, Nina Kohn, Mary Joy Quinn, Carol Sewell, and Pam Teaster.

Many thanks go to the current and past members of the California Elder Justice Coalition's Steering Committee, including Suzanne Anderson, Donna Benton, Christine Damonte, Molly Davis, Nicole Fernandez, Nicole Howell, Adria Navarro, Jill Nielsen, Shawna Reeves, Gloria Sanchez, Jean Schuldberg, and Carol Sewell. The depth of these individuals' knowledge, empathy, savvy, finesse, and generosity has never ceased to amaze me.

My deep appreciation also goes to my colleagues at City College of San Francisco (CCSF), an enormously talented and innovative group of educators, and, in particular, to Robin Roth, Tim Berthold, Phoebe Vanderhorst, Annie Sze, and Beth Freedman, who taught me how to teach and, by example, how it is done with skill and empathy. I am grateful to my students at CCSF for sharing their stories and asking the right questions, including and perhaps especially those I could not answer that spurred me on to learn more. I am delighted by their eagerness to discuss social justice and the rich insights they bring to the discussion.

I am also indebted to Dan Woodard, whose wisdom, integrity, patience, generosity, and sense of humor sustain me always.

I am most indebted to Sheri W. Sussman at Springer Publishing Company for, once again, giving me this opportunity.

REFERENCES

California Newsreel. (2008). Unnatural causes. . . Is inequality making us sick? [Interview transcript]. Retrieved from https://www.unnaturalcauses.org/assets/uploads/file/krieger_interview.pdf

Stanford, E. P., & Rivas, E. E. (2017, May). Where do older adults fit in the evolution of civil rights in America? *Aging Today*, pp. 1–14. Retrieved from https://www.asaging.org/blog/where-do-older-adults-fit-evolution-civil-rights-america

1

Introduction and Overview

TRUTH, JUSTICE, AND THE AMERICAN WAY

The concept of justice is deeply entrenched in America's psyche. As children, we pledge allegiance to a flag that stands for liberty and justice for all. In school, we recite the "self-evident" truth that all men are created equal, with inalienable rights to life, liberty, and the pursuit of happiness. Generations of Americans can recite the icon Superman's oath to uphold "truth, justice, and the American way." But where do these ideas come from?

The preamble to the Declaration of Independence, written in 1776 and foreshadowing the basic principles the country was founded on, came from classic liberal theory, which has little to do with today's liberalism and its increasingly narrow set of political goals and ideologies. Classic liberal theory is associated with the Enlightenment and holds that moral values and principles are not just individual or religious matters, but rather apply to political, social, and economic institutions (Almgren, 2018). They are untethered to political parties.

The classic liberal philosopher John Locke asserted that all men were entitled to "life, liberty, and the pursuit of estate (property)." He further called for equality under the law, freedom of religion, freedom of speech, freedom of the press, the right to assemble, the right to petition the government for redress of grievances, and the right to bear arms.

These concepts were obviously on Thomas Jefferson's mind when he wrote the Declaration of Independence. In replacing Locke's "right to estate" with the nebulous "right to happiness," Jefferson sidestepped the matter of slavery, which treats humans as property, and his own ownership of slaves. Clearly, the rights our founders proclaimed were far from self-evident or inalienable. At best, they were aspirational.

© Springer Publishing Company DOI: 10.1891/9780826147578.0001

The Constitution, passed in 1787, spelled out what the new government could do but not what it couldn't. Fearful that it would become too powerful and resort to the overreach that had given cause to their revolution, the founders added the Bill of Rights to assert what Jefferson explained as "what the people are entitled to against every government on earth, general or particular, and what no just government should refuse." They included the freedom of speech, the press, religion, the right to protection against violence, due process, and freedom from warrantless searches and seizures. The Constitution's first 10 amendments became law in 1791, with others added later. How they apply to elder justice is explored in Chapter 7.

Throughout American history, policy makers and citizens continued to argue about justice and rights: what they were, who they applied to, and how to protect them. Martin Luther King is often credited with saying "the arc of the moral universe is long, but it bends toward justice." King was actually paraphrasing the 19th century abolitionist Theodore Parker, who was referring to the trajectory of the antislavery movement, which serves as a poignant reminder that the arc of justice is not a smooth one. Although the Constitution was amended to abolish slavery in 1865 through the Thirteenth Amendment, slavery was reignited during Reconstruction, and, in 1948, when the newly formed United Nations (UN) adopted the Universal Declaration of Human Rights, U.S. representatives carved out exceptions to provisions barring racial discrimination since not all states had yet ratified the Amendment (see Chapter 5).

Human rights are not limited to those protected by laws. Philosophers and religious leaders point to moral rights that reflect a wide range of ideologies, which have fluctuated in prominence over time. Divergent ideologies about rights and justice have animated politics, fueled movements, and provoked wars and uprisings. Today, they are at the core of debates about entitlement programs and safety net services. They fuel the Black Lives Matter, Me Too, and Never Again movements. They are reflected in conflicts over immigration and tax and entitlement reform. Calls for universal single-payer healthcare echo back to the Depression, reigniting debate over the fundamental question of whether healthcare is or should be a right.

This book assumes that advocates for older people can increase their effectiveness by achieving a clearer understanding of Americans' not-so-self-evident nor inalienable rights. It explores how social justice and human rights principles have applied to older adults in the past and are viewed today. It examines how the interests of older adults compare to and are intertwined with those of other groups. In essence, it frames elder justice as the intersection between aging policy and policy that promotes human rights and justice.

ORGANIZATION AND CHAPTER OVERVIEW

Chapters 2 through 5 describe historical antecedents and precedents for elder justice and suggest how human rights and social justice principles have been embedded in what has traditionally been referred to as "aging policy." These chapters look at other policies that significantly affect older people but do not fall under that rubric. They further explore ageism and its role in policy. Taken together, they offer two models or approaches that can guide the development of elder justice: the public health model and proposals for an international convention on the rights of older people.

Chapters 6 through 10 consider how elder justice principles can be applied. As examples, they focus on how individual rights and social justice apply to elder abuse prevention, to the justice system, in the consumer context, at the end of life, and with respect to people with diminished mental capacity. They also look at equity across generations and among older people.

Chapters 11 and 12 look ahead. Chapter 11 calls for a new paradigm of elder justice and offers a rationale for why one is needed. Chapter 12 builds on other chapters to demonstrate how elder justice might translate into practice, training, policy, public awareness and engagement, and research.

CHAPTER 2: ELDER JUSTICE WRIT LARGE AND SMALL: A HISTORY

The terms "elder rights" and "elder justice" have been largely appropriated by the field of elder abuse, which has applied them narrowly to policies and programs that address elder and dependent adult abuse and mistreatment. But "aging policy" in the United States is grounded in social justice principles and goals that go back to the country's founding. Chapter 2 explains how Social Security, Medicare, Medicaid, Supplemental Security, the Older Americans Act, and the Elder Justice Act have advanced individual rights and social justice.

Chapter 2 also explores how discrimination against older people has been addressed, explicitly, through measures like the Age Discrimination in Employment Act, and by policies that protect older people as members of other groups. This includes laws and regulations that protect people with disabilities, residents of institutions, consumers, crime victims, prison inmates, and others.

CHAPTER 3: AGEISM: "ISM" OR ISN'T IT?

Today, the term "ageism" typically conjures up images of demeaning greeting cards and television sitcoms. But Robert Butler, the Pulitzer Prize winning expert on aging who coined the term, had a more expansive view. He believed that ageism accounts for the disregard for older people's rights seen in public policy. He saw it in the failure of institutions to address the needs of older people or protect their rights, citing as evidence government's failure to protect older people against mistreatment or to enforce nursing home regulations. He saw it in the lack of attention to older people in disaster preparedness plans and in the institutional ageism that leaves many older people impoverished and vulnerable.

Although Butler and others saw ageism as standing alongside other "isms"—other forms of injustice and discrimination—it never achieved their traction. Chapter 3 explores why. It suggests that age acts as an intensifier of other "isms" and interacts with them through the process of "intersectionality."

CHAPTER 4: "HEALTH JUSTICE IS SOCIAL JUSTICE": A PUBLIC HEALTH PERSPECTIVE

While today's heated debate about healthcare exposes widespread disagreement as to whether healthcare is or should be a right, in the field of public health it is a given. Public health seeks to achieve optimal health for everyone, employing the "ecological model" to identify and respond to individual, interpersonal, community, and societal factors that pose health risks to entire populations. In addition to targeting the traditional culprits—pathogens, pollutants, unhealthy lifestyles, and genetic dispositions—public health is increasingly focusing on the "social determinants" of disease, disability, and premature death. These include factors like poverty, discrimination, social exclusion, and where people live and work.

Public health focuses on preventing, rather than treating, health problems by identifying and eliminating or reducing "risk factors" that predispose people to get sick in the first place. The approach is in sharp contrast to the medical model that dominates America's healthcare system today and directs the lion's share of public funds toward hospitals, nursing homes, and costly treatments and drug therapies. Chapter 4 proposes that public health be included as a key component of elder justice, providing an alternative or complement to the medical model that is more compatible with social justice goals.

CHAPTER 5: ELDER JUSTICE ON THE GLOBAL STAGE

When the Universal Declaration of Human Rights (UN General Assembly, 1948) was drafted in the dark shadows of two world wars, they were intended to be universal; that is, they applied to everyone. Yet one by one, advocates for oppressed and disadvantaged groups called for special measures to reaffirm and protect their rights through treaties, declarations, reports, and targeted programs. Advocates for older people have followed suit.

Today, multiple entities within the complex and sprawling UN infrastructure, in partnership with nongovernmental organizations (NGOs), are addressing age from the perspectives of human rights, public health, and social development; and are identifying ageist biases and disparities in policies that target older people. They are further exploring how older people are impacted by "mainstream" policies that affect everyone with respect to such diverse challenges as climate change, migration and immigration, criminal justice reform, war, and natural disasters, through a process that is sometimes referred to as "mainstreaming" and employing "affirmative action" (AA) to address them. "Mainstreaming" involves ensuring that age equity and the needs and perspectives of old people are reflected in policy development, research, advocacy/dialogue, legislation, resource allocation, and planning, implementating, and monitoring of programs and projects. "Affirmative action" is sometimes referred to as positive discrimination in favor of older people through institutional preferences to compensate for past inequalities. These efforts are coalescing in proposals for an international "convention" (a type of treaty that spells out the rights of specific groups) to protect the rights of older people. Chapter 5 considers how these efforts can help shape the emerging elder justice movement in the United States and lead to more expansive, comprehensive, and cohesive approaches to policy, programs, and practice.

CHAPTER 6: ELDER ABUSE AS A THREAT TO ELDER JUSTICE

Although freedom from elder abuse is broadly recognized today as a core principle of elder justice, some abuse prevention policies and programs have been criticized from their inception for being ageist, paternalistic, or antithetical to human rights principles. Mandatory elder abuse reporting laws, in particular, are seen by some as a threat to old people's rights to privacy and self-determination. Involuntary interventions like guardianship, which is sometimes used to prevent particularly egregious abuse, have also come under fire.

Framing elder abuse as a matter of justice and rights requires that abuse prevention advocates respond to these criticisms by examining how well elder abuse prevention policies and programs align with social justice principles and goals. Chapter 6 suggests areas that may be problematic and the potential challenges they pose to individual rights. It also looks at elder abuse prevention policies, programs, and interventions from the point of view of fairness, or the extent to which they are available to everyone who needs them.

CHAPTER 7: SEEKING JUSTICE THROUGH THE JUSTICE SYSTEM

Myriad statutory, procedural, and technological innovations have been made in the criminal and civil justice systems to increase access to courts and legal services for older people and people with disabilities. Advocates have championed accessible courtrooms, due process protections in guardianship, enhanced protections for victims of abuse, vertical prosecution, enhanced penalties for predators and those who exploit vulnerabilities, and forensics research and innovations.

Despite this progress, glaring disparities exist in access. In particular, those who are poor or of limited means ("nonaffluent") are likely to go unrepresented or inadequately represented. Other barriers include thresholds on losses in financial elder abuse crimes that fail to acknowledge the harm that small losses can have on those with limited resources. Many older crime victims do not receive restitution, victim assistance, or compensation. Chapter 7 further exposes challenges to the rights of the increasing numbers of incarcerated older people and those on parole and probation.

CHAPTER 8: . . . AND JUSTICE FOR ALL: PARITY AND FAIRNESS

"Distributive justice" refers to fairness in access to resources, protection, rights, and opportunities. Chapter 8 applies the principle to older adults from two perspectives: (a) intergenerational equity, or fairness toward older people vis-à-vis other age groups, and (b) fairness among older people. Examples of the former include the preponderance of protective service resources that go to children compared to vulnerable adults. Disparities among elders result, to a great extent, from discrimination and historical injustices and oppression that began earlier in life, carrying into old age.

Chapter 8 proposes to rectify intergenerational inequities by adopting an "across the life span" approach to allocating resources for health, social, legal, and protective services. It further urges policy makers and program developers to design policies and programs to reflect America's demographic profile, trends, and the special needs of different age groups. In addition to ensuring greater fairness, the approach combats the counterproductive "generations at war" narrative, which some suggest has been intentionally propagated for political gain. The chapter further calls for programs for older people to acknowledge challenges and barriers faced by older people of color; women; lesbian, gay, bisexual, transgender (LGBT); immigrants; and other socially and economically disadvantaged groups.

CHAPTER 9: CONSUMER CHOICE: THE POWER AND PERILS

At the beginning of the 21st century, advocates and providers of long-term care began referring to health and long-term care patients as "consumers" and introducing "consumer choice" options into health and long-term care. This reframing of care users as consumers would seem to suggest that these individuals are entitled to the rights and privileges afforded to consumers in other markets, yet what these rights encompass remains unclear. Chapter 9 explains what consumer rights are and suggests how they might apply in long-term care. It considers obstacles that older consumers with physical and cognitive disabilities may face as well as barriers imposed by the markets themselves, such as the failure of healthcare to respond to *market forces* that are supposed to drive prices down and lead to new and improved products.

Chapter 9 further considers changes in the long-term care market, such as the shift from once-dominant charitable and nonprofit entities to the proliferation of large, for-profit hospitals, nursing homes, and community-based long-term care programs like the Program of All-Inclusive Care for the Elderly (PACE). It highlights critical challenges such as the lifting of consumer protections contained in the Patient Protection and Affordable Care Act[1] and the epidemic of consumer fraud.

CHAPTER 10: ELDER JUSTICE IN ILLNESS, DEATH, AND BEYOND

Perhaps nowhere are challenges to human rights and justice more pronounced than at the end of life. By the age of 85, nearly half of older adults experience some level of cognitive impairment, which may jeopardize their ability to make such deeply value-laden personal decisions as how they want to live (and die), who they want to make decisions for them if the need arises, and to whom they want to leave assets and possessions.

Chapter 10 calls attention to common violations of individual rights at the end of life such as the disregard of advance directives like "living wills" and "do not resuscitate" orders. It highlights the perils of these instruments, which were created to preserve autonomy but can be weaponized to exploit.

---

[1] Also referred to as the Affordable Care Act, the ACA, or "Obamacare."

The highly controversial rights of individuals to control their own deaths and enlist others to help them are also explored. The chapter suggests how the "right to life" takes on new meaning in light of technological innovations that seek to extend life to previously unimaginable lengths and their implications for individual and collective rights. It also explores the implications of its corollary—the "right to die."

CHAPTER 11: MOVING FORWARD

Chapter 11 calls for a new paradigm of elder justice that is based on the principles of human rights and social justice as they apply to older people. It builds on and reinforces past progress, revisits old assumptions and unfulfilled promises, and identifies new needs and challenges.

The chapter lays the groundwork for an elder justice agenda by suggesting the need for a new conceptual framework and elements to include. It builds upon principles of human rights and justice and employs public health methods to identify needs and suggest solutions. It connects the dots among existing policies and practices, building on those that have proven successful and rejecting those that have not.

CHAPTER 12: AN ELDER JUSTICE AGENDA

The final chapter brings it all together by proposing an Elder Justice Agenda. It summarizes recommendations made throughout the book and organizes them into categories: practice, training, policy, public awareness and engagement, and research. It further suggests steps and actions for getting started.

The agenda is neither complete nor definitive. Rather, it is offered to stimulate discussion, debate, problem solving, collaboration, and innovation. It is further provided to inspire thought leaders and those new to the field of aging and abuse prevention to share perspectives. It provides opportunities for critics and advocates to be heard, and young and old to join together to tackle today's unprecedented challenges and shape the future of an aging America.

REFERENCES

Almgren, G. (2018). *Health care politics, policy, and services: A social justice analysis* (3rd ed.). New York, NY: Springer Publishing.

UN General Assembly. (1948). *Universal declaration of human rights* (217 [III] A). Paris, France: Author. Retrieved from http://www.un.org/en/universal-declaration-human-rights

2

Elder Justice Writ Large and Small: A History

INTRODUCTION

Public policy bearing the labels of *elder rights* and *elder justice* is scant and only recently appeared on the scene. Elder rights first appeared in an amendment to the Older Americans Act (OAA) in 1992 (Title Seven), and elder justice appeared in the Elder Justice Act (EJA) as part of the Patient Protection and Affordable Care Act (ACA) of 2010. Both terms are narrowly defined and refer almost exclusively to protections against abuse, neglect, and exploitation.

But justice is not just about abuse. Since America's founding, older people have benefitted from a wide range of programs and policies that sought to advance social justice. These include programs to:

- Reduce poverty and ensure financial security in retirement
- Provide health and long-term care
- Provide social support
- Enhance independence and autonomy for those with chronic diseases and disabilities
- Reduce disparities
- Prohibit discrimination in the workforce, housing, healthcare, and other settings
- Prevent violence, abuse, and exploitation

Aging policy in the United States clearly reflects principles of liberal theory, as espoused by Locke and adapted by America's founders. *Distributive justice*, which refers to fairness in society's distribution of resources and opportunities, is reflected in programs like Social Security, created in 1935 at the height of the Great Depression, when the poverty rate of older Americans

© Springer Publishing Company DOI: 10.1891/9780826147578.0002

was over 50% (Social Security Administration, 2018). Considered to be among the most fundamental and consequential federal programs impacting older Americans, it was designed as a first step toward achieving *old-age insurance* as part of President Franklin D. Roosevelt's New Deal to bring stability and mobility to the workforce and ensure retirement income. In policy parlance, Social Security is an *income maintenance* or *income security* program because it provides financial relief in the form of payments for basic expenses. Because workers pay into the program through payroll taxes, it is considered to be an earned benefit that retirees, their survivors, and dependents have a right to. They may also be referred to as *insurance, entitlement,* or *contributory* programs.

About 62 million people, or more than one in every six U.S. residents, are collecting Social Security benefits today (Center on Budget and Policy Priorities, 2018), and the poverty rate for older Americans is about 9.2% (Fontenot, Semega, & Kollar, 2018). However, this figure is considered by many to underestimate elder poverty because it fails to reflect such factors as the high proportion of their incomes that older people pay in out-of-pocket medical expenses and variations in the cost of housing across the country, which significantly impact many elders. In 2011, the government released a new Supplemental Poverty Measure (SPM) that adjusts for these added expenses and, when applied to older people, increases the rate to 13.7%. The measure has not, however, replaced official rates. Experts believe that eliminating Social Security today would more than triple the poverty rate for older Americans, bringing it back to 40% (Center on Budget and Policy Priorities, 2018).

As described in Chapter 8, poverty rates are significantly higher for certain groups that are more dependent on Social Security. Although Social Security was never intended to completely finance retirements but to serve as a supplement to pension plans and savings, it is the sole source of income for many and has a greater impact on women and older people of color (see Chapter 8).

HEALTHCARE

Controversy has surrounded the right to healthcare from as far back as the turn of the 18th century, when an English physician and scientist, Edward Jenner, who had created a vaccine for smallpox, was summoned by the then president Thomas Jefferson to vaccinate his relatives, neighbors, and slaves at Monticello (Gawande, 2017). The mortality rate for smallpox at the time was around 30%, which had prompted England, France, and Denmark to start vaccination programs. As a proponent of limited federal government, Jefferson was hesitant to replicate the European programs, hoping states would do so. In 1813, when it was clear that the states were not going to act, Congress passed the Vaccine Act. Americans who wanted the vaccine could get it, making it what popular surgeon and health commentator Atul Gawande considers to be the country's first healthcare entitlement for the general population. He credits the act with saving thousands of lives and raising the nation's life expectancy (Gawande, 2017).

Roosevelt considered adding healthcare to the Social Security Act but decided against it because he feared it would sink the bill in light of the intense opposition it provoked. Instead, his administration took a different approach. During World War II, when a huge part of the workforce was off fighting and there was a labor shortage, a wage freeze was imposed to keep labor costs down. Responding to employers who were having trouble attracting workers, the administration gave corporate tax breaks to companies that offered insurance to their workers. During the 1940s and 1950s, more workers were brought into the private system through this indirect form of government assistance, thereby establishing a private, employment-based healthcare system—the only one in the world.

In 1945, President Truman called for the creation of a national health insurance fund to be run by the federal government. The proposal was introduced to Congress in the form of a Social Security expansion bill that was known as the W-M-D bill in reference to its cosponsors in Congress, Senators Robert Wagner and James Murray and Representative John Dingell. The proposal was quickly met by strident opposition from the American Medical Association (AMA), which launched the most expensive lobbying effort that had ever been mounted, branding the plan as "un-American" and "socialized medicine" (Zelizer, 2015). The AMA further charged that Truman's administration consisted of "followers of the Moscow party line." The organization worked closely with conservatives in Congress to kill the measure (Hacker, 2015).

In President Lyndon Baines Johnson's (LBJ's) Great Society Programs, introduced in 1964 and 1965, Medicare established near universal medical and healthcare for older workers, and Medicaid established a health program for people of all ages. Unlike Medicare, which workers earned the right to, Medicaid is a means-tested, needs-based program; that is, it only covers those who are unable to work as the result of certain disabilities and who have no other source of income. The OAA and the Civil Rights Act were also established at this time, marking this period as an enduring watershed for healthcare, civil rights, and older Americans.

Congressman Claude Pepper, who worked with LBJ for Medicare's passage, wanted Medicare to align even more closely with social justice goals by covering long-term care for those with chronic illnesses, conditions, or disabilities. In particular, he wanted to see long-term care provided in the community as opposed to nursing homes (the program only paid for short-term stays in a nursing home and short periods of home-based services following hospital stays).

Medicaid provided long-term care, but originally only covered care in nursing homes. Later it was extended to cover long-term services and supports in the community under some circumstances. Pepper's last major aging initiative before he died in 1989 was a failed attempt to include in-home and community-based services as benefits in the Medicare program. The bias for institution-based medical care over home- and community-based programs persists today (see Chapter 3).

Although President Nixon, who followed LBJ, was a critic of Great Society programs, his administration made concessions for the working, or "deserving," poor, which included older Americans, people with disabilities, and children. In 1972, Congress enacted Supplemental Security Income (SSI). Like Social Security, SSI is an *income maintenance* or *income security* program. Like Medicaid, it is *means-tested* (based on need).

The distinction between entitlement and means-tested programs is significant from a political perspective. Entitlement programs enjoy broad public support whereas means-tested programs are considered "welfare" and are much less popular and more vulnerable politically. Most Americans believe that entitlements are a right but are more skeptical of welfare programs, which are considered to be handouts.

AGING SERVICES

The OAA, another Great Society program, set up a national service delivery system to enable older Americans to remain in their homes and communities for as long as possible. OAA services include home delivered and congregate meals, information and referral, in-home care, adult day centers, caregiver support services, health and wellness programs, transportation, legal assistance, elder abuse prevention, caregiver support, a program for older workers, and adult day care. It established the federal Administration on Aging (AoA), state units on aging (SUAs), and area agencies on aging (AAAs, or "triple-As") to administer OAA programs. It also included the Long-Term Care Ombudsman Program (LTCOP), which trains volunteers to monitor patient care in nursing homes. OAA programs further target services to isolated seniors and older Native Americans and create employment opportunities. OAA programs are universal in that they are available to everyone over the age of 60, regardless of income or assets (with the exception of the older worker program, which has income criteria and is available to those over the age of 55).

Elder rights language was added to the OAA in 1992, when Title VII was added. Although Title VII advanced some elder rights goals, it fell far short of creating a well-defined or comprehensive program. The amendment defined "elder rights" narrowly, focusing on the rights of older people to be free from abuse and extending protections solely to "vulnerable" older people, which refers to people who have physical or cognitive disabilities.

Title VII brought together four advocacy programs: (a) the LTCOP; (b) a small program addressing elder abuse and neglect (including funds for the National Center on Elder Abuse); (c) legal aid for older adults; and (d) a program to let older people know about insurance and public benefits programs, help them sign up, and advocate on their behalf if problems arise. Title VII also encourages SUAs to collaborate with other legal services programs.

By equalizing access to healthcare and targeting those in greatest need, Great Society programs advance the social justice goal of distributive justice. The services also speak to the "right to life," a right that the founders never defined.

One interpretation of the right to life comes from Martha Nussbaum, a prominent liberal philosopher of law and ethics, who contends that freedom depends on people's functional capacity—what they are able to do and to be. Functional capacity, in turn, determines the kind of lives people are able to lead and the opportunities they are able to take advantage of. Nussbaum has identified 10 central human capabilities that are required in a free society. The *right to life*, included among them, is defined as "being able to live a life of normal length; not dying prematurely, or before one's life is so reduced as to be not worth living." Other human capabilities that are required in a free society are the *right to bodily health*, which includes being adequately nourished and sheltered, and the *right to bodily integrity*, which refers to moving freely from place to place and being protected against assault (Almgren, 2018).

COMBATTING DISCRIMINATION

The Civil Rights Act, also passed in 1965, had a significant, and sometimes underappreciated, impact on older people. In barring federally funded programs from discriminating against people based on their race, color, or national origin, the act dealt a significant blow to racial segregation and discrimination in hospitals and health facilities and in the broader medical establishment.

The Civil Rights Act, of course, also banned discrimination in education, employment, housing, lending, and voting. Although it was intended to protect all Americans, its failure to do so prompted subsequent movements to demand the rights of women, people with disabilities, Native Americans, Blacks, and others. Many of these movements continue today and are gaining renewed momentum.

Another antidiscrimination law that benefits older people was the Age Discrimination in Employment Act of 1967, which prohibited employment discrimination against persons 40 years of age or older. A provision added in 1986 prohibited mandatory retirement in most sectors.

Protections against age-based discrimination are also highlighted in a wide range of other laws that apply to diverse situations and settings. Examples include the Disaster Relief and Emergency Assistance Act, which bans discrimination in relief operations on the grounds of race, color, religion, nationality, sex, *age*, or economic status, and the Equal Credit Opportunity Act, which prohibits creditors from discriminating against credit applicants on the basis of race, color, religion, national origin, sex, marital status, *age*, or because they receive public assistance. Other laws that do not specifically mention older people are frequently invoked by aging advocates, as is the case with the National Voter Registration Act of 1993, which was created to encourage eligible citizens to register to vote but does not explicitly mention older people. It is often cited when older people, especially nursing home residents, face obstacles. Chapter 3 discusses the extent to which laws have succeeded in ending discrimination.

Among the most consequential antidiscrimination laws for older people is the Americans with Disabilities Act (ADA) of 1990, which prohibits discrimination on the basis of disability in employment, state and local government, public accommodations, commercial facilities, transportation, and telecommunications. It covers people with physical or mental impairments and mental illnesses that substantially limit their daily activities.

Among the discriminatory practices described in the ADA is employers' failure to "reasonably accommodate" workers with disabilities (e.g., taking steps to make work settings more accessible), and requiring employers to provide unpaid leave for medical treatment. The ADA's impact on older people was significantly expanded as the result of the landmark 1999 Olmstead Supreme Court decision (*Olmstead v. L. C.*, 1999), which did not even involve older people.

THE OLMSTEAD SUPREME COURT DECISION

In 1995, the Atlanta Legal Aid Society filed a lawsuit on behalf of two women in a state psychiatric hospital. Both had developmental disabilities; in addition, one had been diagnosed with schizophrenia, and the other with a personality disorder. Both women had been voluntarily admitted to the hospital.

Professionals working with the women determined that both were capable of living in the community with help, and they were eventually released. However, their lawyers argued that the facility's failure to immediately release them once it had been deemed appropriate to do so was a violation of their civil rights under the ADA. Georgia community mental health officials countered that they could not provide the services that the women needed.

The court sided with the women, ruling in a six–three decision that they had been unjustifiably retained, which constituted discrimination and was in violation of the ADA. The court went on to say that people with disabilities could not be unnecessarily segregated and must receive services in the most integrated settings possible. In essence, the decision extended the ADA's "reasonable accommodation" standard beyond the workplace and applied it to long-term care settings.

The impact was profound and sweeping. The U.S. Department of Health and Human Services (HHS) Secretary notified governors of the decision and directed them to develop plans, with stakeholder involvement, to ensure that individuals with disabilities received services in the most integrated settings appropriate to their needs. The Health Care Financing Administration (the precursor of the Centers for Medicare and Medicaid Services [CMS]) and the Office of Civil Rights (OCR) within HHS further directed state Medicaid directors to work with the federal government to develop plans and let them know that OCR would be evaluating their compliance with the ADA and the Olmstead decision. States were told to respond to nursing home residents' requests for reviews to determine if they were capable of living in the community and ombudsmen were directed to help residents seek reviews and file complaints for failures to comply.

The Olmsted decision also fueled the "consumer choice" movement, which cast users of community-based long-term care as "consumers" and created more opportunities for them to exercise choice and direct their own care (see Chapter 9). This includes programs like "Money Follows the Person," which was created to enable states to rebalance Medicaid long-term care funds from institutional to community-based care and help nursing home residents move back into their homes and communities. Under

"Medicaid voucher programs," some older people can purchase services or assistive devices or make home modifications to enable them to remain at home. Some permit consumers to hire friends, neighbors, and family members as personal care attendants rather than having licensed home care agencies provide care.

The impact was impressive. Prior to Olmstead, 75% of Medicaid long-term care dollars paid for institutional care, while just 25% paid for care at home (Gordon, 2015). Fifteen years after the decision, nearly half of all Medicaid long-term care spending went to care at home.

The federal government took other steps that reflected the Olmstead decision, many of which are overseen today by the Administration for Community Living (ACL), which was created by HHS in 2012 to bring together programs serving older people with those serving adults with disabilities. These include the AoA, the Administration on Intellectual and Developmental Disabilities (AIDD), and the HHS Office on Disability.

ACL encourages AAAs and Independent Living Centers (ILCs) to help people remain in the community through measures like home modifications (e.g., grab bars, ramps, and door levers that make it possible for older adults to leave a nursing facility, or avoid one in the first place).

Another step ACL has taken to maximize older consumers' choice and control is to promote the use of advance directives, including living wills and powers of attorney. It has further suggested the following guidelines for service providers to protect consumers' rights:

1. People need to be informed and have the opportunity to express their preferences.
2. Service providers must respect those preferences and place individual choices at the center of treatment decisions—whether the decision involves avoiding unwanted treatments or providing services that an individual does want.
3. Service providers should honor individuals' choices, help manage their symptoms, and provide needed emotional and spiritual supports to them and their families.

Despite these successes, some had hoped that the Olmstead decision would go further in eliminating Medicaid's institutional bias, pointing out that Medicaid's statutory framework still made it easier to get coverage for institutional, as opposed to home based, care (Carlson & Coffey, 2010).

WOMEN'S RIGHTS AND OLDER WOMEN

In light of the fact that the majority of elders are women, older women are significantly affected by women's rights and antiviolence laws. Failed efforts to enact an equal rights (for women) amendment to the Constitution go back to the 1920s and were reignited in 1970, which culminated in the passage of an amendment by both chambers of Congress in 1972. Although it never achieved the required ratification by 38 states, most states enacted their own equal rights amendments.

Congress has enacted other measures to protect specific rights for women. Among those of greatest consequence for older women are laws prohibiting workplace discrimination since older women are disproportionately represented among the poor, which is due in large part to workplace discrimination and barriers they faced earlier in life. The gendered nature of poverty is even greater among older women of color.

Older women have also benefitted from the Violence Against Women Act (VAWA), which was enacted in 1994 to combat violence by men toward their wives and intimate partners. VAWA criminalized domestic violence, sexual assault, stalking, and violations of protective orders; made gender-motivated crimes a violation of federal civil rights law (42 U.S.C.A. § 13981); enhanced privacy protections for victims; and provided support for shelters, research, and education for judges, police, and others. In 1999, the act was amended to include the Older Women's Protection From Violence Act, which resulted in improved access to domestic violence services for older women, targeted outreach, and the expansion of eligibility requirements to enable older women who faced violence from sons and daughters, as well as from intimate partners, to benefit.

COMBATTING ABUSE AGAINST ELDERS AND VULNERABLE ADULTS

Public policy and programs to protect older and vulnerable adults against abuse, neglect, and exploitation followed a different track. Adult Protective Services (APS) was created by Congress in 1952 as part of a package of services originally defined as "welfare" under the Social Security Act and administered by the Department of Health, Education, and Welfare (HEW). It provided a safety net of social and legal services for adults who could not meet their own needs and who lacked formal or informal supports to assist. It also provided help to victims of abuse, neglect, and exploitation (Bonnie & Wallace, 2003).

As noted earlier, the terminology is important. Programs with the "welfare" stigma do not enjoy the popularity that programs like Social Security and Medicare, which are considered to be earned benefits, do. Despite the fact that APS was converted from a "means-tested" to a "universal" program in 1979, and the changing of its parent organization's name from HEW to HHS, the program has never been popular in the eyes of the public.

In the early 1960s, Congress made matching funds available for states to establish protective units and funded six demonstration projects to explore models for delivering APS. One of the most frequently cited findings of the projects comes from a study led by Rose Blenkner of the Benjamin Rose Institute that showed that APS clients were more likely to die prematurely or to be placed in institutional care than those who received traditional services (Blenkner, Bloom, Wasser, & Nielsen, 1971).[1]

Despite these disturbing findings, Title XX of the Social Security Act was passed in 1974, authorizing APS services to adults 18 years of age and older who were experiencing abuse, neglect, or exploitation or were unable to care for themselves, regardless of their incomes or assets (Mixson, 2010). The Omnibus Reconciliation Act of 1981 (P.L. 97-35) amended Title XX to change protective service funds from a matching grant to a "block grant."

Block grants reflect the philosophy of New Federalism, which seeks to transfer power from the federal government to states by giving them lump-sum allocations and broad discretion in how to implement programs. Federalists claim that the approach fosters innovation and reduces waste, while opponents counter that block grants are simply a pretense for cost cutting since the grants are typically less than what the federal government had been paying for the programs directly.

Under block grant funding, states decide how to use APS and other Title XX funds, which often involves apportioning them among competing programs for children and adults (Lynch, 2016). APS typically fares poorly. Thirty-seven states use part of their Social Services Block Grant (SSBG) funds to support APS and, for some, it is the only federal money supporting APS.

Dramatic disparities between funding for child and elder abuse were among the issues addressed in a series of Congressional hearings on elder abuse that began in the late 1970s. In 1978, Congressman Mario Biaggi, who had been an architect of the Child Abuse Prevention and Treatment Act, chaired a Subcommittee on Human Services Select Committee on Aging

---

[1] A reanalysis of the data was conducted in 1976, which did not refute the findings, but showed that social casework did not actually cause harm (Berger & Pilivan, 1976).

hearing on the topic, and that same year, Congressman Claude Pepper, chair of the Subcommittee on Health and Long-Term Care of the House Select Committee on Aging, also began a series of hearings around the country, which continued through the following year (Bonnie & Wallace, 2003).

In the absence of federal funding and direction, states took what Bergman (1991) called a "follow the leader approach" to developing APS programs. One by one, they enacted mandatory reporting laws that were patterned after child abuse reporting programs, with APS designated as the entity to investigate and respond to reported cases (for more on states' responses to elder abuse and the APS role in the response, see Chapter 6).

The federal government continued to hold hearings on elder abuse through the 1980s and 1990s, referring to the problem as "a hidden problem," "a national disgrace," a "tragedy," a "secret shame," and a "national epidemic." The hyperbole failed to yield legislation or funding, however, and one committee member summed up the stretch of inactivity as the "decade of shame." The hearings did, however, lead to funding for research and demonstration grant programs to test models of service delivery and to establish the National Center for Elder Abuse. Both were administered by the AoA.

THE EJA AND THE ACA

A major milestone in elder justice came in 2010, with the enactment of the EJA as part of the ACA. Despite the expansive scope suggested by the title, the EJA focused almost exclusively on elder abuse, establishing the structure for a coordinated federal response to the problem. It contains provisions to:

- Improve and enhance APS programs
- Enhance the LTC Ombudsman Program
- Receive reports of crimes in long-term care facilities

HHS assumed responsibility for implementing the EJA, with the ACL playing a key role. It has integrated ACA and EJA provisions and priorities into its mission, highlighting linkages and relationships among the social justice goals of the OAA, the individual rights and consumer choice provisions of the ADA and the Olmstead decision, the ACA's focus on health equity, and the EJA's commitment to eliminating abuse, neglect, and exploitation of vulnerable adults and older people. Under the leadership of former Assistant Secretary of Aging Kathy Greenlee, the ACL further committed to countering ageism by focusing on functional challenges and needs rather than chronological age in assessing needs. ACL has also acknowledged the role of social and economic factors (determinants) in creating disparities by advancing policy and programs to improve the lives of underserved groups. It has further promoted consumer choice in long-term care through programs that encourage innovation and help aging and disability organizations function more effectively in the health and long-term care marketplaces.

The EJA also established an Elder Justice Coordinating Council to oversee its implementation and develop recommendations for the HHS and Congress. It includes representatives from HHS, the Department of Justice, the Consumer Financial Protection Bureau, the Social Security Administration, the Corporation for National and Community Service, the Federal Trade Commission, the Department of the Treasury, the Department of Veterans Affairs, the Postal Inspection Service, the Department of Labor, the Department of Housing and Urban Development, and the Securities and Exchange Commission. The Attorney General of the United States is a permanent member. Every 2 years, the council is required to submit a report to Congress on its accomplishments and activities. The reports include updates on what the council has done and progress made by its members.

Funding has been slow in coming and extremely limited. Although the EJA passed in 2010, its first funding didn't come until 2015 when Congress appropriated just $4 million for a new Elder Justice Initiative. Although this has gradually increased to $12 million in 2018, it remains well below the $25 million that was originally requested by the Administration. The funds have been used to develop a national APS data collection system, research and demonstration projects, and to support state APS systems, including the National APS Resource Center and voluntary consensus guidelines for state APS systems.

The ACA's contributions to elder justice go well beyond the provisions contained in the EJA. Primary among these is the expansion of Medicaid, which increased access to healthcare for millions of Americans of all ages and succeeded in narrowing disparities in access (Griffith, Evans, & Bor, 2017).

CONCLUSION

Clearly, the Social Security Act, the OAA, the ACA, the EJA, and the Olmstead decision form the foundation of elder rights and elder justice policy. But myriad other policies and programs have implications for elder rights and elder justice. They range from policies and programs addressing opioid addiction, to voting rights, to immigration policy. Identifying and addressing them all is beyond the scope of this book and beyond the scope of any single discipline or network. It is a task left to advocates, activists, consumers, and service providers in multiple fields with diverse perspectives. The chapters that follow suggest models and approaches for doing so and make the case for why a unifying vision or paradigm of elder justice is needed.

REFERENCES

Almgren, G. (2018). *Health care politics, policy, and services: A social justice analysis* (3rd ed.). New York, NY: Springer Publishing.

Berger, R., & Pilivan, I. (1976). The effect of casework: A research note. *Social Work, 21,* 205–207. doi:10.1093/sw/21.3.205

Bergman, J. (1991). Testimony of James Bergman. Elder abuse: What can be done? Hearing before the Subcommittee on Human Services of the Select Committee on Aging. 102nd Cong. 1st Sess. 92–95, 92–120. Washington, DC: U.S. Government Printing Office. Committee Publication No. 102–808.

Blenkner, M., Bloom, M., Wasser, E., & Nielsen, M. (1971). A research and demonstration project of protective services. *Social Casework, 52,* 483–499.

Bonnie., R. J., & Wallace, R. B. (Eds.). (2003). *Elder mistreatment: Abuse, neglect, and exploitation in an aging America.* Washington, DC: National Academies Press.

Carlson, E., & Coffey, G. (2010). *10-plus years after the* Olmstead *ruling: Progress, problems, and opportunities.* Washington, DC: National Senior Citizens Law Center. Retrieved from http://aucd.org/docs/policy/community_living_supports/Protecting%20 the%20Rights%20of%20Low-Income%20Older%20Adults%2010-Plus%20Years%20 After%20the%20Olmstead%20Ruling.pdf

Center on Budget and Policy Priorities. (2018). Policy basics: Top ten facts about Social Security. Retrieved from https://www.cbpp.org/research/social-security/policy -basics-top-ten-facts-about-social-security

Gawande, A. (2017, October 2). Is health care a right? *The New Yorker.* Retrieved from https://www.newyorker.com/magazine/2017/10/02/is-health-care-a-right

Gordon, F. (2015). ADA at 25: Aging advocates celebrate partnership and progress [Issue brief]. *Justice in Aging.* Retrieved from http://justiceinaging.org/wp-content/ uploads/2015/06/ADA-at-25_Aging-Advocates-Celebrate-Partnership-and -Progress.pdf

Griffith, K., Evans, L., & Bor, J. (2017). The Affordable Care Act reduced socioeconomic disparities in health care access. *Health Affairs, 36*(8), 1503–1510. doi:10.1377/ hlthaff.2017.0083

Fontenot, K, Semega, J. L., & Kollar, M. A. (2018, September). Income and poverty in the United States: 2017. *Current Population Reports.* Retrieved from https://www.census. gov/content/dam/Census/library/publications/2018/demo/p60-263.pdf

Hacker, J. S. (2015, June 9). Out of balance: Medicare, interest groups, and American politics [Blog post]. Retrieved from http://www.asaging.org/blog/out-balance-medicare -interest-groups-and-american-politics

Lynch, K. (2016). *Social Services Block Grant: Background and funding.* Retrieved from https:// fas.org/sgp/crs/misc/94-953.pdf

Mixson, P. M. (2010). Public policy, elder abuse, and adult protective services: The struggle for coherence. *Journal of Elder Abuse & Neglect, 22*(1–2), 16–36. doi:10.1080/08946560903436148

Olmstead v. L. C. (98-536) 527 U.S. 581 (1999).

Social Security Administration. (2018). Fast facts & figures about Social Security, 2018. Retrieved from https://www.ssa.gov/policy/docs/chartbooks/fast_facts/2018/index.html

Zelizer, J. E. (2015, February 15). How Medicare was made. *The New Yorker*. Retrieved from https://www.newyorker.com/news/news-desk/medicare-made

Ageism: "Ism" or Isn't It?

INTRODUCTION

In coining the term "ageism," Pulitzer Prize–winning aging expert Robert Butler was adding another "ism" to the lexicon that today includes racism, sexism, classism, ableism, heterosexism, anti-Semitism, and anti-Arabism. The common theme is that each establishes defined norms or standards of rightness used to judge people. Those who do not meet the standard are subject to exclusion, bias, exploitation, marginalization, oppression, and violence.

Butler clearly saw the parallels. He first used the term publicly during a 1969 interview with the young *Washington Post* reporter Carl Bernstein (think Watergate) about a proposed plan to convert an apartment complex into public housing for poor older adults in Chevy Chase, Maryland (Achenbaum, 2015; Butler, 1969). Community members opposed the plan, and Bernstein asked Butler if he thought racism was to blame as older African Americans were likely to be included among the tenants. Butler responded that he believed ageism, more than racism, was at play and that it was the thought of people with canes "cluttering" up the neighborhood that was enraging the neighbors.

Butler also believed that ageism and cross-generational antipathy were at play during the political clashes that erupted in the 1960s and continued through the 1970s and 1980s. He attributed the clashes surrounding the 1968 Democratic National Convention to "the elements of a counterrevolution by the middle-aged against both the young and the old" (Butler, 1969, p. 243). It was during those decades that the concept of the "generation gap" and the notion that the young and old were pitted against each other in competition for scarce resources took hold.

Among the first to embrace and promote the new term was Maggie Kuhn, who founded the Gray Panthers in 1970 after being forced to retire from a job she loved when she turned 65 (Sanjek, 2009). Like Butler, Kuhn saw ageism as a form of social injustice and a violation of human rights akin to the other "isms." She shared Butler's view that ageism was responsible for discrimination in the workplace and healthcare as well as for the poor care provided by nursing homes. She, too, saw ageism being espoused by antiwar activists and human rights advocates.

Kuhn and her followers saw the problem in even broader terms. The Gray Panthers supported a universal single-payer healthcare system, fought for gay rights, aligned with the antiwar movement, actively participated in campaigns for a nuclear freeze, and fought against U.S. intervention in Central America and apartheid in South Africa. They aligned with other social justice activists, taking their name from the Black Panthers, which had been formed to combat police brutality and gone on to create health clinics, kids' breakfast programs, and other social service programs in inner cities. The two groups were united in more than name only. They collaborated on Project SAFE (Seniors Against a Fearful Environment) in Oakland, California, a program in which Black Panthers escorted seniors who lived in dangerous neighborhoods on errands and to appointments.

Roger Sanjek (2009) described the Gray Panthers' solidarity with other movements as "part of an endlessly creative effort to muddle society's expectations and open up new possibilities for how groups like older adults and inner-city African Americans could interact with each other." Gray Panthers wanted more than simply to secure more rights and resources for their "interest group." They sought to change the way the public viewed older adults and, beyond that, the social role people were expected to play at every stage of life.

Kuhn recognized the group's power to legitimize other movements through compelling media images of old people carrying signs and defying authority. She appeared on the Phil Donahue and Johnny Carson shows and made headlines by committing to "do something outrageous every day."

The Panthers used traditional political channels as well, working with members of Congress, including Ron Dellums, Claude Pepper, Paul Wellstone, and activists such as Ralph Nader on nursing home reform, ending age discrimination in the workplace, and promoting long-term care insurance and services to help older people lead independent lives.

The Gray Panthers had 60,000 financial contributors at the height of its power in the early 1980s. Although membership dropped after Kuhn's death in 1995, the group continued to respond to new issues and forge new partnerships, engaging in social initiatives like the Occupy Wall Street movement (Brown & Hollister, 2012). By 2014, however, membership had dropped to 15,000 and, in 2015, the national office closed (Wallis, 2014). Board members launched the National Council of Gray Panther Networks to take its place by supporting local Gray Panther networks through action alerts and maintaining a presence on Facebook (R. Block, personal communication, May 22, 2018).

HISTORY

Although many attribute ageism to today's youth-obsessed culture, it is deeply rooted in history. Butler pointed out that old age tended to be valued in primitive societies but eroded as the population of old people increased and economic conditions worsened:

> Older persons often provided knowledge, experience, and institutional memory that was of adaptive–even survival–value to their societies. Although nomadic groups in various parts of the world abandoned the old and disabled when safety and security were at stake, overall older people were venerated. However, as the number and percentage of older persons, especially the frail and demented, increased, the perception grew that they were burdens to their families and society. It became widespread as societies shifted from agrarian economies, where older men had traditionally owned the land, to industrialized economies, when work was no longer centered in the home and older persons lost authority. (Butler, 2006, p. 1)

Historian Jill Lepore agrees that ageism is linked to demographics: "When elders are rare, they are valued, but as their ranks swell, they become less so" (Lepore, 2011). This theory does not bode well in light of the "aging tsunami" that looms large today. Despite the best efforts of advocates to suppress the term, it prevails, fueling anxiety about the cataclysmic threat it portends.

Lepore also believes that ageism shaped how age and aging have been studied and described historically and that the field of geriatrics was, from the start, infused with ageism. She writes:

> The word "geriatrics" was coined, in 1909, by a New York doctor, an Austrian immigrant named I. N. Nascher. As the story goes, Nascher was making rounds one day when the attending physician, discussing an elderly woman who was very ill, diagnosed her ailment as "old age." "What can be done about it?" Nascher asked. "Nothing," he was told. Not long after, Nascher wrote an article called "Why Old Age Ends in Death." He thought it might not have to. (2011, para. 26)

The view that old age is a disease that can and should be *treated* is alive and well today in Silicon Valley and other high-tech enclaves where technocrats and venture capitalists are investing fortunes in efforts to prevent old age and death. Oracle founder Larry Ellison has unabashedly proclaimed his wish to live forever and donated more than $430 million to antiaging research. He has said, "Death makes me very angry. Premature death makes me angrier still" (as cited in Cha, 2015). Billionaire entrepreneur and venture capitalist Peter Thiel has a similarly combative view: "I've always had this really strong sense that death was a terrible, terrible thing. . . . Most people end up compartmentalizing and they are in some weird mode of denial and acceptance about death, but they both have the result of making you very passive. I prefer to fight it" (Cha, 2015, "The 'Great Enemy'"). Larry Page, cofounder of Google, started the health venture start-up Calico (the California Life Company) with the aim of "curing" death (Cha, 2015).

The pouring of large sums of money into antiaging technologies by private enterprises has some ethicists worried, fearing that their efforts are driven more by personal ethos (hubris, say some) than the public good. Government regulation and oversight to protect the public's interest is, in fact, anathema to many antiaging titans.

AGEISM AND ADULTISM

Defining ageism poses challenges. To begin with, there is confusion and inconsistency surrounding the terms "adultism" and "ageism." "Adultism" suggests that adults are the norm and most valued age group in society. Those who are not adults—youth and old people—are less valued and visible and occupy second-class status. The term, therefore, can apply to discrimination and prejudice against both old and young, and is, in fact, used that way by some. Others use the term "ageism" the same way—to describe discrimination against both old and young. Butler's use of the term "ageism" to refer exclusively to old people has clearly taken hold in popular culture in the United States, with the lesser known "adultism" typically applied to children and youth. In this book, ageism refers to discrimination and injustices against the old.

Using the term in this way separates discrimination against elders from discrimination against children and youth. The latter addresses such issues as the failure of schools to keep children safe, widespread abuses in the juvenile justice and foster care systems, child trafficking and other forms of exploitation, and lack of economic and social opportunities for high-risk youth. Although some object to viewing ageism in relation to injustices against children and youth in light of past missteps in equating elder abuse with child abuse in public policy, "across the life span" perspectives on age-based discrimination are not uncommon in the academic arena. Discrimination against old and young are juxtaposed in curricula, journals, and discourse, with respect to discrimination in the workplace, healthcare, housing, and public benefits programs. Members of both groups may face challenges in defending their rights to make decisions for themselves and therefore have a stake in how the legal system assesses and addresses decision-making capacity.

Comparisons of discrimination against the young and old also highlight the way in which the government withholds or extends rights to those whose capacity or judgment is in question and when those entrusted to act on their behalf violate that trust. Public entities are permitted to intervene in the lives of both children and incapacitated adults under the legal principle of *parens patriae,* which is Latin for "parent of his or her country." Courts and public agencies are frequently criticized as ageist or adultist in their use of *parens patriae* with respect to both groups.

THE FACES OF AGEISM

Butler (2006) described ageism in three realms: (a) stereotypes and prejudices against older adults, (b) discrimination against individuals, and (d) institutional practices and policy that disadvantage older adults or perpetuate discrimination.

Americans have generally focused on the first two, a tendency that is perhaps best explained by what researchers at the FrameWorks Institute, a communications research and consulting firm, attribute to Americans being "more likely to rely on little-picture explanations that reduce the problem [discrimination] to the everyday interactions of a few outlier individuals with ill-will in their hearts" (Sweetland, Volmert, & O'Neil, 2017, p. 12). The observation comes from one of several reports issued as part of a collaborative venture commissioned by leaders from eight national aging organizations in 2012 to explore how the public views older adults. The project has yielded articles, toolkits, workshops, and presentations on "reframing aging" to combat ageism and other negative or counterproductive perceptions about age and older adults.

Institutional ageism refers to biases that are embedded in public policy and institutions. It includes policies, rules, and practices that discriminate against older people or that subordinate their rights and interests to those of other groups. The lack of attention to the needs, concerns, and rights of older people has also been attributed to ageism.

Ageism can be intentional or inadvertent. Intentional ageism has been blamed for such horrific acts of violence and exploitation as those seen in the disturbing spate of videos of older people being beaten or sexually abused in nursing homes that have appeared on the Internet in recent years (Ornstein, 2015).

Unintentional, or inadvertent, expressions of ageism, on the other hand, are carried out without awareness that they are biased or discriminatory (Anti-Ageism Taskforce at the International Longevity Center, 2006). It may result from *implicit bias*, which refers to negative associations people hold but are not aware of. Examples include such common statements as "I love talking to old people," which may seem innocuous. Yet if "old people" were replaced with Blacks, gays, or Jews, few would deny its cringeworthiness.

Variations on this theme include *positive ageism*, which assumes that old people as a group are happier and wiser than the young (Palmore, 1999). These terms also suggest homogeneity among old people. As Chonody and Teater (2016) point out, "There is nothing about age per se that makes individuals better conversationalists or even better at giving good advice" (p. 12). They point to studies showing that while old people do report being sought after for their wisdom, many do not view the stereotype favorably.

Scholars and researchers have tried to measure ageism in various ways. Some have assumed that ageism is grounded in misperceptions about older people and attempted to measure those misperceptions (Achenbaum, 2015). Others have attempted to find out how people think regarding racism and sexism (Palmore & Manton, 1973). In recent years, researchers have studied the impact of negative attitudes about age held by older people and their healthcare providers on their health. Much of the research has been criticized for methodological problems, some stemming from controversies over definitions. Early attempts to create *equity indices* (or yardsticks) for measuring ageism encountered myriad barriers (Achenbaum, 2015).

ELDER ABUSE

Although the report card acknowledges the alarming scope and seriousness of individual acts of violence, exploitation, and emotional abuse that stem from personal animus against the old, much of its focus is on institutional ageism. This includes society's apparent tolerance of abuse and failure to devote reasonable resources to preventing it and holding offenders accountable. Chapter 7 provides ample examples, including the failure to fund the Elder Justice Act (EJA), lax enforcement of nursing home regulations, and the lack of a comprehensive plan or strategies to combat abuse.

Ageism is also apparent in how certain forms of abuse are viewed and responded to. Fraud and scams that target old people, for example, which can be devastating, are often discounted or explained away as lapses in old people's judgment, their assumed penchant for politeness toward strangers, or greed. These stereotypes belie the true nature of these crimes, some of which are committed by organized criminal organizations and pose significant threats to public safety and security. Terrorist experts Perri and Brody (2011) describe the link between scams targeting older Americans and terrorism:

> Terrorists derive funding from a variety of criminal activities ranging in scale and sophistication from low-level crime to organized fraud or narcotics smuggling, or from state sponsors and activities in failed states and other safe havens. Some of the fraud schemes include but are not limited to, credit card fraud, bank fraud, mortgage fraud, charitable donation fraud, insurance fraud, identity theft, money laundering, immigration fraud, and tax evasion. (p. 46)

Despite the seriousness of these crimes, much of the scant public funding devoted to their prevention goes to "just say no" campaigns that are reminiscent of the "just say no [to drugs]" approaches of the 1960s and 1970s. In both cases, the focus is on victims' behavior rather than criminal conduct and suggest that victims bear the brunt of the blame. There is little evidence to suggest that the approach has been effective in either case.

Ageism is also frequently blamed for what some consider paternalism in elder abuse reporting and response systems, which were patterned after those designed to protect children and assume that older victims, like children, are unable or unwilling to seek help on their own.

ABUSE IN NURSING HOMES

Perhaps nowhere is ageism more evident than in society's failure to protect residents of nursing homes and residential care facilities for the elderly (RCFEs). These failures are evidenced by facts like these:

- Each year 1 to 3 million serious infections occur in long-term care facilities with as many as 380,000 people dying as a result (Centers for Disease Control and Prevention [CDC], 2017).
- A CNN investigative report found that more than 1,000 nursing homes were cited for mishandling or failing to investigate or prevent alleged cases of rape, sexual assault, and abuse between 2013 and 2016—nearly 100 were cited multiple times. At least a quarter were allegedly perpetrated by aides, nurses, and other staff members (Ellis & Hicken, 2017).

- Forty-two percent of U.S. nursing homes have "chronic deficiencies," defined as three or more repeat citations for the same safety standard (Mollot & Demissie, 2017).
- One third of residents who went to a nursing home for short-term care were harmed, and almost 60% of that harm was preventable and likely to be attributable to poor care (Levinson, 2014).

What is perhaps most disturbing is the failure of government regulatory entities to hold facilities accountable for substandard care, abuse, or neglect. Although infractions can lead to Medicare and Medicaid withholding funding or closing homes, penalties for infractions are not vigorously enforced and financial penalties are too low to prompt real change. Homes that are forced to close often reopen under different names. The situation is getting worse, with enforcement actions against nursing homes decreasing. From 2015 to 2016, the total federal fines collected decreased by nearly 10% (from $57,242,134 to $51,613,644).

Few cases of abuse in facilities are prosecuted, and of those that are, most involve offenses by line staff rather than operators who hold the real power needed to institute change and reforms. Residents' and their advocates' ability to sue homes for abuse and neglect has been diminished by "arbitration clauses" that many homes require residents to sign as a condition of admission. In the fall of 2016, new nursing home regulations were implemented that bar federally funded facilities from requiring residents to sign the clauses; however, the new rule has been blocked in court, making its future uncertain. As if preventing abuse in nursing homes did not pose challenges enough, they may pale in comparison to stopping abuse in the other settings that make up the residential care continuum, which are largely unregulated.

AGEISM IN HEALTHCARE

When age itself is viewed as a disease, it is not surprising that ageism pervades the medical system. Much has been written about how biases toward older people have led to both under- and overtreatment (Lachs, 2010; Ouchida & Lachs, 2015). Older people are less likely to receive health and medical services across the care spectrum from preventive interventions to cancer treatments. They are less likely to be immunized against many diseases, including some that are likely to be contracted in old age, and less likely to be screened for common illnesses and conditions, reducing the prospects for early diagnosis and treatment. The assumption that older adults are not sexually active prevents some health and medical care providers from asking about sexually related problems or to screen for them.

When care providers believe that pain, fatigue, cognitive impairment, depression, and anxiety are inevitable in old age, they are less likely to explore the causes of or treat the symptoms of these conditions. This is particularly true when it comes to pain, which is often dismissed or minimized. The stereotype that old people are set in their ways and unable to change is believed to discourage mental health providers from diagnosing and treating psychological disorders.

On the other hand, health and medical care providers may overtreat older patients if they view natural and expected changes of aging as diseases and perform costly, painful, or debilitating procedures that offer few benefits.

Ageist attitudes held by old people themselves have also been shown to negatively affect their health. Dr. Becca Levy of the Yale School of Public Health found that people with positive views of aging live an average of 7.6 years longer than those with negative views (Levy, Slade, Kunkel, & Kasl, 2002). It might be assumed that when older people view pain, depression, anxiety, and other problems as inevitable, they may be discouraged from seeking help.

Ageism further pervades service delivery and financing. It is embedded in Medicare and Medicaid, which favor medical approaches that focus on "treating" old people as opposed to maintaining quality of life, autonomy, independence, and security. A notable example is the fact that Medicare provides for hospitalization and acute care but fails to provide long-term services and supports (LTSS) for those with chronic illnesses and conditions, including case management, homemakers, home health aides, personal care, adult day health services, rehabilitation, respite care, and other services for caregivers, which focus on preserving autonomy and independence. Medicare only provides home care following medical treatment.

Although Medicaid provides LTSS for some people with chronic illnesses and disabilities, it too has a built-in medical bias as evidenced by the fact that states that receive Medicaid are required to provide nursing home services but not home and community care, despite the fact that these services can potentially circumvent the need for more costly institutional care and are more closely aligned with personal autonomy and independence.

The ageist "age as disease" perspective even extends to end-of-life decisions and care. When old age is seen as an illness that ends in death, death, too, becomes a medical matter. Physicians exercise outsized control in such deeply personal and value-laden decisions as when to stop treatment, when guardians or other surrogates are needed, when hospice and other end-of-life care will be authorized, and if and under what circumstances people can be helped to end their own lives. This is despite the fact that physicians are not required to receive training in the principles of legal and ethical decision making.

This has changed to some extent with the hospice and "right to die" movements leading to shifts in thinking about death. They reject the medicalization of death, focusing instead on preserving the quality of dying people's lives and their autonomy and dignity. But even these are physician driven. Medicare reimbursement for hospice is authorized after two physicians have determined that a person's death is imminent, and treatment is futile. States' "right to die" laws also require that physicians attest to the imminence of death and the futility of treatment, underplaying the dying person's values, choice, and control. In other words, end-of-life care is prescribed when medical care fails or becomes futile. Only then do patients earn the right to die.

Changes to financing and consumer rights in long-term care are also putting more control into the hands of those service users (see Chapter 9). Medicaid waiver programs have allowed states to develop home- and community-based services, and the Patient Protection and Affordable Care Act promotes nonmedical approaches to disease prevention (Koh & Sebelius, 2010; see Chapter 9).

Combatting ageism in healthcare will require changes at the individual and institutional levels. Training for health professionals needs to focus on quality of life, independence, and autonomy. It also needs to reflect changing values and attitudes about death and dying. At the institutional and system levels, combatting ageism will require moving away from service delivery systems that over-rely on physician-driven care toward value-based and client-driven approaches. It will require changing public perceptions of old age and physical decline as diseases that can or should be prevented to recognizing them as stages of life with their own challenges and rewards that can be enhanced with supports and services rather than through cures and fixes.

Bill Thomas, a geriatrician who founded the Eden Alternative and Green House Projects and calls himself a "nursing home abolitionist," perhaps offers the most compelling argument for rejecting the call to "cure old age": "Such a hope, while understandable, ignores the possibility that there is something vital and true to be grasped and then savored with the distinctly human experience of growing old" (Thomas, 2004, p. 31).

Reducing ageism in healthcare will require reexamining how resources are allocated to Medicare and Medicaid and reexamining public policy related to end of life. Older people and their families will need information and guidance to help them make informed decisions about their health and medical care.

AGEISM IN THE WORKPLACE

When Facebook founder Mark Zuckerberg famously said, "Young people are just smarter," he was not alone in his thinking. A 2015 Harris Poll found that 65% of baby boomers rated themselves as being the "best problem-solvers and troubleshooters" in the work setting, with only 5% of millennials agreeing and 54% calling the boomers the "biggest roadblocks" (Workfront, 2015, p. 28). As Achenbaum (2015) has pointed out, the tables have turned on baby boomers. The generation that once mocked old people now faces job discrimination.

Ageism in the workplace has historically referred to discrimination against job applicants in hiring and, in the case of employees, discrimination in promotions, discharges, compensation, or the terms, conditions, or privileges of employment on the basis of age. It can also refer to failures to provide older workers with updated training and opportunities for advancement.

In 1967, Congress enacted the Age Discrimination in Employment Act (ADEA) of 1967, which made it illegal to discriminate against workers aged 40 and older. It applied to those seeking new jobs and current workers. The act allows workers or applicants in companies with 20 or more employees to sue employers for back pay and future losses resulting from discrimination. Although the law marked a milestone, it had unintended consequences. As Yoffe (2011) points out, the law seems to have fueled enthusiasm for enacting mandatory retirement laws by those who feared having to address the unpleasantness of having to fire older workers who were no longer fit to work. Congress responded by abolishing mandatory retirement through amendments to the ADEA in 1986.

Despite these efforts, age-based discrimination remains among the top categories of discrimination addressed by the federal Equal Employment Opportunity Commission (EEOC), making up almost 20% of its caseload (Palmer, 2017). Many of these complaints and others made to state entities that address discrimination are filed against high-tech firms. A survey of Silicon Valley firms conducted by *USA Today* in 2016 found that of the 90 age-related discrimination complaints filed to the California Department of Fair Employment and Housing for investigation or to request the right to sue, Hewlett-Packard was named most often (in 11 claims), followed by Apple (9), Google (8), Oracle (7), and Genentech (7). Yahoo, Intel, LinkedIn,

Facebook, Tesla Motors, and Twitter were also named. Most claims were for wrongful termination, while a lesser number of complaints cited discriminatory hiring or promotion practices (Swartz, 2016).

In the absence of mandatory retirement and in light of antidiscrimination laws, employers have gotten sneaky. *Forbes* blogger Deborah Jacobs (2013) describes ways companies ditch older employees, which include eliminating jobs, layoffs (often through restructuring), isolating older workers, offering retirement packages with incentives to take early retirement, cutting job duties, denying promotions, and "suddenly stupid" tactics, which is when employers suddenly begin finding fault with older workers' performance. Job postings for "recent college graduates" or applicants who "enjoy the pressures of the job" and can "fit in with a young team" are also common.

Older workers are particularly likely to experience workplace discrimination during market downturns and recessions and are less likely to be hired and rehired (Lipnic, 2018). In the introduction to a 2018 EEOC report on progress made since ADEA, author Victoria Lipnic notes:

> A 54-year-old worker who may have lost his job in early 2008 at the beginning of the Great Recession is now 64 years old. The average unemployment duration for a 54-year-old was almost a year, and it may have taken that person two or three years to find a new job. Further, that new job may not have been on a par with the one he had before. To make up for that financial loss, he will likely need to work longer than originally planned. (p. 1)

Increases in reports have also been attributed to more older workers wanting to or having to work longer; a spike in mergers and restructuring in which companies lay off tens of thousands of workers; and evolving skill sets that have marginalized some workers and put a premium on others.

Clearly, ageism is not the only reason employers want to shed older workers. Some older workers develop physical or cognitive impairments that seriously compromise their performance but lack the insight or will to leave jobs on their own. Allowing them to continue can be costly to businesses and create liabilities, although employers may have genuine compassion toward them. The problem has fallen into the laps of human resource professionals. Articles in the journals for human resource professionals are increasingly addressing issues like how to coach older workers out of the workforce without incurring liability. In these instances, human resource professionals and supervisors are encouraged to work with employees to find alternative jobs within the institution or make changes in their hours or responsibilities to help them cope better and enable employers to retain workers with valuable skills and experience.

Researchers have also begun to explore bullying against older workers by younger coworkers. Bullying includes preventing older workers from getting their work done, verbal abuse, threatening conduct, intimidation, and humiliation (Brownell, 2014). Some states have enacted "healthy workplace" bills that address workplace harassment, bullying, and abusive work environments on the basis of age, race, disability, and sex. The statutes allow employees who are subjected to abusive work environments to sue both their employers and alleged bullies for monetary damages (Habinsky & Fitzgerald, 2011). Some further shift responsibility for addressing harassment from employees to employers by shielding employers who have and enforce antiharassment policies from liability. For an individual to collect damages, the laws require victims to prove harm; this is shown by evidence collected from licensed health professionals that victims experienced harm to their health as a result of the harassment.

DISASTER PREPAREDNESS

The shocking heat-related deaths of 12 nursing home residents in 2017 more than 2 weeks after Hurricane Irma had knocked out the home's air conditioning and left residents in sweltering heat led to public outrage and calls for investigations. Similar outcries occurred in 2005, upon discovering that 75% of those killed by Hurricane Katrina were over the age of 60, and in the aftermath of the September 11, 2001, terrorist attacks, when animal protection workers were on the scene rescuing pets well before adult protective service workers. Similar failures in emergency response have occurred in other parts of the world. In 2011, 56% of those who died in the Great East Japan Earthquake and Tsunami were 65 and older despite the fact that older people comprised just 23% of the population.

Public outrage following events like these have typically led to epidemiological studies of high-risk populations, and subsequent inadequate reforms. A 2012 CDC report pointed out three primary gaps and limitations in disaster preparedness for older adults: (a) Strategies used to identify vulnerable older adults across the country have not been evaluated, (b) there is no consensus on the best way to identify and protect older adults, and (c) gaps exist in legal mandates to protect older adults (Centers for Disease Control and Prevention, 2012).

The CDC report offers strategies for improving disaster relief to older people in the community (it did not look at those in institutions). Among the needs addressed are planning for the delivery of services, medications, medical equipment, and other materials needed to support older adults during emergencies. The report also highlights the need for officials, planners, and emergency responders to know where older adults are located and how they might be adversely affected by different types of emergencies. Specific needs that are identified include (a) geographic information system (GIS) mapping technology to coordinate information about the locations of vulnerable older adults, community resources, and potential hazards; (b) registries to track medical equipment, transportation, or evacuation assistance and older adults needing help; and (c) shelter intake procedures to identify older adults who need special help.

The challenges involved in providing disaster relief to people in nursing homes are even greater. In 2016, the Centers for Medicare and Medicaid Services (CMS) released revisions to federal regulations on emergency preparedness in 17 healthcare settings, including hospitals, nursing facilities, home health agencies, transplant centers, and kidney dialysis centers. The regulations address five primary areas: emergency plans, facility procedures, communication plans, training and testing, and emergency power systems. Federal, state, and local governments should take additional steps to ensure adequate preparation for the natural disasters that inevitably will envelop nursing facilities and other healthcare providers in years to come.

Subsequent to their release, the advocacy organization Justice in Aging issued *Why Many Nursing Facilities Are Not Ready for Emergency Situations: Seven Recommendations to Address Current Law's Gap* (Carlson, 2017), which criticizes the new regulations as being excessively vague and not broad enough in scope. It recommends that: (a) the federal government clearly requires emergency generators sufficient to maintain safe temperatures; (b) federal and/or state governments should require advance coordination among facilities, other healthcare providers, and relevant government agencies; (c) federal and/or state governments should require contractual arrangements for evacuation procedures; (d) local communities should maintain relevant information on an ongoing, community-wide basis; (e) government agencies or provider associations should develop resources to assist in emergency plan development; (f) federal and/or state governments should require review of emergency plans by knowledgeable agencies or persons; (g) knowledgeable agencies or persons should be enlisted to review emergency plans; and (h) federal surveyors should assess meaningful sanctions for violations of emergency preparedness requirements.

Ensuring disaster relief for older people at the international level is a monumental task, with international aid organizations predicting that the number of people over the age of 60 worldwide will reach 1.4 billion by 2030, with nearly three quarters living in developing countries where the impact of climate change is expected to be most severe. The World Health Organization (WHO) projects that in 2030, 38,000 older people will die from heat exposure alone (Beard, Officer, & Cassels, 2015).

In preparation, the United Nations (UN) Office for Disaster Risk Reduction and Help Age International has collaborated on projects to ensure that older people are included in disaster risk reduction work. The Disaster Risk and Age Index, which ranks countries based on the disaster risk faced by older people, provides feedback to countries and policy makers on how they are doing with respect to age-inclusive disaster plans, and identifies where changes are needed.

The two organizations also collaborated to produce Charter 14, which details special considerations for old people in disaster risk management. They range from involving older people in the planning process; specialized warning and evacuation plans; specialized supplies, including medications; access to emergency cash and retirement funds; affordable disaster insurance; and accessible rest centers and shelters.

MEDIA AND MARKETING

Perhaps the most familiar signs of ageism come in the form of media's portrayals of old people (or the lack of). Studies on the frequency, content, and tone of media portrayals of aging are rare and predominantly negative. Jessica Walker, the founder of Aging Watch, a website that tracks ageism in the media, describes five portrayals (www.agingwatch.com):

1. Elders are portrayed as helpless victims.
2. Elders who defy negative stereotypes are presented as bizarre and comical.
3. Growing old is equated with inevitable deterioration and decline.
4. Elders are demonized as a group.
5. Elders are underrepresented and ignored.

Media analysts and researchers have explored how media users translate what they see and use it to shape their lifelong perceptions (Milner, Van Norman, & Milner, 2012). They have found that children internalized age-based stereotypes before they are personally relevant to them and thereafter accept them unconditionally and uncritically. Later, when they start thinking about themselves as aging, they act in ways consistent with the stereotypes.

Research also suggests that negative stereotypes of old people in the media affect individuals' attitudes and public discourse (Milner et al., 2012). It suggests that ageist perceptions negatively impact peoples' self-esteem, self-efficacy, and resilience. Little is known about how negative media portrayals of old people shape political attitudes toward old people.

Not surprisingly, efforts to portray older people more positively have come from businesses courting the lucrative aging market. Many focus on changing attitudes about beauty and sex appeal. One ad in the campaign, called "Withered or Wonderful?" featured a 95-year-old model and asked readers to respond to the question "Will society ever accept old can be beautiful?" Viewers were invited to log on to the campaign website and cast their votes. This ad was a huge success from a marketing perspective, with Dove claiming a 700% rise in product sales in the United Kingdom (where the marketing effort originated) and 600% in the United States within the first 2 months of the campaign's launch (Brodbeck & Evans, 2007; Millard, 2009).

The Dos Equis "Most Interesting Man in the World" campaign featured an older man with gray hair and laugh lines who is sophisticated, adventurous, and sexual (Abrams, 2014), suggesting that his appeal stemmed from his experience and knowledge. The ad achieved near cult status on the Internet.

The FrameWorks Institute looked beyond beauty and sex appeal to consider how the media shapes attitudes about aging that have policy implications (O'Neil & Haydon, 2015). They note that the media typically represents older adults in one of two ways: (a) as frail, diseased, cognitively impaired, and in need of constant care; or (b) as active, healthy, and independent. While the former reinforces pervasive negative stereotypes of vulnerability, the latter, surprisingly, is also unproductive from an advocacy perspective, as it equates successful aging to lifestyle and consumption choices (e.g., eating well and exercising) and fails to acknowledge the importance of social supports and overcoming structural barriers—it suggests that older people who are not thriving are themselves to blame. The report suggests communication strategies to increase public support for policies and programs that benefit older people and encourage them to get involved in promoting change.

AGE AND OTHER ISMS

Ageism's relationship to other isms is frequently acknowledged, often in the context of "intersectionality," a term that is widely used by social justice advocates and academics and refers to the interplay of various forms of discrimination and their cumulative impact. Butler and Kuhn acknowledged links between ageism, racism, and sexism; Achenbaum has noted discrimination based on sexual identity and orientation and dementia; and Applewhite talks about "the double whammy of ageism and sexism." Others have described double or triple jeopardy in reference to the interplay of age, race, and gender.

Policy makers, too, have acknowledged these relationships and taken steps to ensure that they are reflected in policy and programs. In 2016, the Administration for Community Living, in acknowledging that year's theme for the UN International Day of Older Persons, issued the statement: "It is important to recognize that ageism is not experienced in the same way for all older adults. Gender, ethnicity, disability, care dependency, sexual orientation, gender identity, and HIV status can intersect with age and have a compounding effect on social opportunity, access to services, and quality of life" (Walker, 2016, para. 6).

The Law Commission of Ontario went further in describing the interplay of factors that need to be considered in public policy impacting older adults:

The concept of ageism must be able to reflect and integrate the fact there are differences in income, education, sexual orientation, gender, area of geographic residence, their family and marital status, immigration and citizenship status, race and ethnic origin, and mental, physical, or intellectual disabilities. It will be important to consider the cumulative effect of other "isms", and the extent to which ageism may simply be later life sexism in disguise. (Spencer, 2009, p. 10)

The FrameWorks Institute researchers explored public perceptions about ageism and its links to other forms of discrimination. They found that although Americans think ageism is important and that it is a matter of human rights, they do not see it as being on par with racism, sexism, and other forms of oppression (Sweetland et al., 2017). Others have noted that while at certain times in history old people and those with disabilities have been singled out for violence and exploitation—they were among those exterminated by the Nazis—they have not been the targets of the level of hatred that led to slavery, mass genocide, mass incarceration, the denial of citizenship, deportation, and political disenfranchisement experienced by other groups. Ageism, therefore, does not generate the same sense of moral outrage as other forms of discrimination. Ashton Applewhite, who has written extensively about ageism, puts it this way: "Why insist on adding another 'ism' to the list when so many higher-profile forms of discrimination, racism in particular, rightfully demand bandwidth?" (Applewhite, 2017, para. 2).

AGEISM IN PUBLIC POLICY AND POLITICS

Governments and courts use a variety of means to protect individuals against ageism, some of which were described earlier in this chapter. They include anti–age discrimination laws, due process protections in guardianship proceedings, and, in a few states, older adults being included among those protected in hate crime laws.

The Anti-Ageism Taskforce of the International Longevity Center (2006) took a more expansive view in addressing ageism in public policy and programs, suggesting that ageism thrives in the following situations:

1. In the absence of comprehensive national health insurance and pension systems, employers confront high costs that increase as workers grow older, discouraging employers from hiring and retaining older workers.
2. In the absence of adequate lifelong continuing education that encourages and supports enhancement of job skills and development of new skills that keep pace with the job market, it is difficult for older workers to acquire the skills employers seek.
3. In the absence of an effective national health promotion and disease prevention program, and a modest investment in biomedical and behavioral research, conditions such as frailty and dementia among older people result in avoidance and uneasiness about old age, reinforcing stereotypes (p. 3).

Bob Blancato and Meredith Ponder (2015) blame ageism for the American failure to fund LTSS; failure to adequately address the needs of older caregivers (including those who are the primary caregivers of children); lack of attention to end-of-life decisions and care; lack of involvement by older people in research studies; and failure to ensure an adequate supply of people trained in gerontology and geriatrics.

Blancato and Ponder also suggest that the slow pace of long-term care reform may reflect people's denial about getting old or their rejection of the idea that it will happen to them. This may account for the fact that only half of Americans over the age of 40 believe that "almost everyone" is likely to require long-term care, and just 25% believe they will fall into that category, despite the fact that over 70% of people over the age of 65 will, in fact, require care (Tompson et al., 2013).

CONCLUSION

Combatting ageism requires going beyond discussions about antiaging products and offensive greeting cards to dialogue about human rights and dignity. It needs to begin by identifying the impact of ageism in everyday life but demands going further to view ageism as a structural problem requiring systemic and institutional remedies and consider how it is reflected in, and perpetuated by, public policy. It may be the starting point for developing a conceptual framework for elder justice policy and practice (see Chapter 11).

The International Longevity Center's report card is still relevant today and can heighten understanding about ageism's role in diverse aspects of life. It needs to be updated, however, to reflect today's unprecedented challenges, which include escalating clashes over entitlement programs, emergent technologies that potentially give wealthy elites an edge on immortality, and the impact of climate change, mass migration, immigration, and cybersecurity on older people.

REFERENCES

Abrams, S. (2014, January 23). What the most interesting man in the world can teach marketers. Retrieved from http://adage.com/article/guest-columnists/interesting-man-world-teaches/291102

Achenbaum, W. A. (2015, October 19). A history of ageism since 1969 [Blog post]. Retrieved from http://asaging.org/blog/history-ageism-1969

Age Discrimination in Employment Act, 29 U.S.C. §§ 621–634 (1967).

Anti-Ageism Taskforce at the International Longevity Center. (2006). *Ageism in America.* New York, NY: International Longevity Center–USA. Retrieved from http://aging.columbia.edu/sites/default/files/Ageism_in_America.pdf

Applewhite, A. (2017, January 18). Building an anti-ageism movement: The time is now. *Forbes*/Next Avenue. Retrieved from https://www.forbes.com/sites/nextavenue/2017/01/18/building-an-anti-ageism-movement-the-time-is-now/#299265b01a9a

Beard, J., Officer, A., & Cassels, A. (Eds.). (2015). *World report on ageing and health.* Geneva, Switzerland: World Health Organization. Retrieved from http://apps.who.int/iris/bitstream/10665/186463/1/9789240694811_eng.pdf

Blancato, R., & Ponder, M. (2015, October 20). The public policies we need to redress ageism [Blog post]. Retrieved from http://asaging.org/blog/public-policies-we-need-redress-ageism

Brodbeck, M., & Evans, E. (2007). Dove campaign for real beauty case study. Retrieved from https://www.scribd.com/document/138664858/Dove-Campaign-for-Real-Beauty-Case-Study

Brown, S., & Hollister, B. (2012, May 23). Gray Panthers join in, speak out about putting profits over people [Blog post]. Retrieved from http://www.asaging.org/blog/aging-outrage-and-occupy-movement

Brownell, P. (2014). Ageism in the workplace. In C. Franklin (Ed.), *Encyclopedia of social work.* Oxford, UK: National Association of Social Workers Press and Oxford University Press. doi:10.1093/acrefore/9780199975839.013.844

Butler, R. N. (1969). Age-ism: Another form of bigotry. *The Gerontologist, 9*(4), 243–246. doi:10.1093/geront/9.4_part_1.243

Butler, R. N. (2006). Combating ageism: A matter of human and civil rights. In Anti-Ageism Taskforce at the International Longevity Center (Ed.), *Ageism in America* (pp. 1–5). New York, NY: International Longevity Center–USA. Retrieved from https://aging .columbia.edu/sites/default/files/Ageism_in_America.pdf

Carlson, E. (2017). Why many nursing facilities are not ready for emergency situations: Seven recommendations to address current law's gaps [Issue brief]. *Justice in Aging.* Retrieved from http://www.justiceinaging.org/wp-content/uploads/2017/10/ WHY-MANY-NURSING-FACILITIES-ARE-NOT-READY-FOR-EMERGENCY -SITUATIONS.pdf?eType=EmailBlastContent&eId=b57801d5-9367-4939-b269 -eeaca1b9543e

Centers for Disease Control and Prevention. (2012). *Identifying vulnerable older adults and legal options for increasing their protection during all-hazards emergencies: A cross-sector guide for states and communities.* Atlanta, GA: U.S. Department of Health and Human Services.

Centers for Disease Control and Prevention. (2017). Nursing homes and assisted living (Long-Term Care Facilities [LTCFs]). Retrieved from https://www.cdc.gov/longterm care/index.html

Cha, A. E. (2015, April 4). Tech titans' latest project: Defy death. *The Washington Post.* Retrieved from https://www.washingtonpost.com/sf/national/2015/04/04/tech

Chonody, J. M., & Teater, B. (2016). Why do I dread looking old?: A test of social identity theory, terror management theory, and the double standard of aging. *Journal of Women and Aging, 28*(2), 112–126. doi:10.1080/08952841.2014.950533

Ellis, B., & Hicken, M. (2017, February 22). Sick, dying and raped in America's nursing homes. Retrieved from http://www.cnn.com/interactive/2017/02/health/nursing -home-sex-abuse-investigation

Habinsky, J., & Fitzgerald, C. M. (2011, January 21). Office bully takes one on the nose: Developing law on workplace abuse. *New York Law Journal.* Retrieved from http:// workplaceviolencenews.com/2011/01/21/office-bully-takes-one-on-the-nose -developing-law-on-workplace-abuse

Jacobs, D. L. (2013, November 3). 11 sneaky ways companies get rid of older workers [Blog post]. Retrieved from https://www.forbes.com/sites/deborahljacobs/2013/ 11/03/11-sneaky-ways-companies-get-rid-of-older-workers/#795281e86d0e

Koh, H. K., & Sebelius, K. G. (2010). Promoting prevention through the Affordable Care Act. *New England Journal of Medicine, 363*(14), 1296–1299. doi:10.1056/NEJMp1008560

Lachs, M. (2010). *Treat me, not my age: A doctor's guide to getting the best care as you or a loved one gets older.* New York, NY: Penguin Group.

Lepore, J. (2011, March 14). Twilight. *The New Yorker.* Retrieved from http://www.new yorker.com/magazine/2011/03/14/twilight-jill-lepore

Levinson, D. (2014). *Adverse events in skilled nursing facilities: National incidence among Medicare beneficiaries* (OEI-06-11-00370). Washington, DC: U.S. Department of Health and Human Services. Retrieved from http://oig.hhs.gov/oei/reports/oei-06-11-00370 .pdf

Levy, B. R., Slade, M. D., Kunkel, S. R., & Kasl, S. V. (2002). Longevity increased by positive self-perceptions of aging. *Journal of Personality and Social Psychology, 83*(2), 261–270. doi:10.1037//0022-3514.83.2.261

Lipnic, V. A. (2018). *The state of age discrimination and older workers in the U.S. 50 years after the Age Discrimination in Employment Act (ADEA).* Retrieved from https://www.eeoc .gov/eeoc/history/adea50th/upload/report.pdf

Millard, J. (2009). Performing beauty: Dove's "Real Beauty" campaign. *Symbolic Interaction, 32*(2), 146–168. doi:10.1525/si.2009.32.2.146

Milner, C., Van Norman, K., & Milner, J. (2012). The media's portrayal of ageing. In J. R. Beard, S. Biggs, D. E. Bloom, L. P. Fried, P. Hogan, A. Kalache, & S. Jay Olshansky (Eds.), *Global population ageing: Peril or promise* (pp. 25–28). Geneva, Switzerland: World Economic Forum. Retrieved from http://demographic-challenge.com/files/downloads/6c59e8722eec82f7ffa0f1158d0f4e59/ageingbook_010612.pdf

Mollot, R. J., & Demissie, R. (2017). The identification of resident harm in nursing home deficiencies: Observations & insights. Retrieved from http://nursinghome411.org/identification-of-resident-harm-in-nursing-home-citations

O'Neil, M., & Haydon, A. (2015). *Aging, agency, and attribution of responsibility: Shifting public discourse about older adults.* Washington, DC: FrameWorks Institute.

Ornstein, C. (2015, December 21). Nursing home workers share explicit photos of residents on Snapchat. *ProPublica.* Retrieved from https://www.propublica.org/article/nursing-home-workers-share-explicit-photos-of-residents-on-snapchat

Ouchida, K. M., & Lachs, M. S. (2015, October 22). Not for doctors only: Ageism in healthcare [Blog post]. Retrieved from http://asaging.org/blog/not-doctors-only-ageism-healthcare

Palmer, K. (2017). 10 things you should know about age discrimination. *AARP.* Retrieved from https://www.aarp.org/work/on-the-job/info-2017/age-discrimination-facts.html

Palmore, E. B. (1999). *Ageism: Negative and positive* (2nd ed.). New York, NY: Springer Publishing.

Palmore, E. B., & Manton, K. (1973). Ageism compared to racism and sexism. *Journal of Gerontology, 28*(3), 363–369. doi:10.1093/geronj/28.3.363

Perri, F. S., & Brody, R. G. (2011). The dark triad: Organized crime, terror and fraud. *Journal of Money Laundering Control, 14*(1), 44–59. doi:10.1108/13685201111098879

Sanjek, R. (2009). *Gray Panthers.* Philadelphia: University of Pennsylvania Press.

Spencer, C. (2009). *Ageism and the law: Emerging concepts and practices in housing and health.* Toronto, ON, Canada: Law Commission of Ontario. Retrieved from https://www.lco-cdo.org/wp-content/uploads/2014/01/older-adults-commissioned-paper-spencer.pdf

Swartz, J. (2016, December 2). 90 age-discrimination complaints reflect growing issue for tech. *USA Today.* Retrieved from https://www.usatoday.com/story/tech/news/2016/11/22/90-age-discrimination-suits-reflect-growing-issue-tech/93110594

Sweetland, J., Volmert, A., & O'Neil, M. (2017). *Finding the frame: An empirical approach to reframing aging and ageism.* Washington, DC: FrameWorks Institute. Retrieved from http://frameworksinstitute.org/assets/files/aging_elder_abuse/aging_research_report_final_2017.pdf

Thomas, W. H. (2004). *What are old people for?: How elders will save the world.* Acton, MA: VanderWyk & Burnham.

Tompson, T., Benz, J., Agiesta, J., Junius, D., Nguyen, K., & Lowell, K. (2013). *Long term care: Perceptions, experiences, and attitudes among Americans 40 or older.* Chicago, IL: Associated Press–NORC Center for Public Affairs Research.

Walker, E. (2016, September 29). U.N. International Day of Older Persons [Blog post]. Retrieved from https://acl.gov/news-and-events/acl-blog/un-international-day-older-persons

Wallis, D. (2014, March 14). As living standards fall for seniors, some see signs of 'silver revolution.' *The New York Times.* Retrieved from https://www.nytimes.com/2014/03/15/your-money/as-living-standards-for-seniors-decline-some-see-signs-of-silver-revolution.html?_r=1

Workfront. (2015). State of enterprise work report. Retrieved from https://resources
.workfront.com/ebooks-whitepapers/the-state-of-enterprise-work

Yoffe, E. (2011, April 14). Please take the gold watch. Please! The abolition of mandatory
retirement, and how it changed America in unexpected ways. *Slate*. Retrieved from
http://www.slate.com/articles/life/silver_lining/2011/04/please_take_the_gold
_watch_please.html

4

"Health Justice Is Social Justice"[1]: A Public Health Perspective

Of all the forms of inequality, injustice in health is the most shocking and inhuman.
—Martin Luther King Jr., Associated Press, 1966

INTRODUCTION

Health policy in the United States has historically been based on a medical model that highlights the clinical diagnosis and treatment of diseases and institution-based care. The doctor–patient relationship is core. Under the model, keeping the public healthy requires making medical care and treatment available to as many people as possible, including physician and hospital care, prescription drugs, nursing homes, rehabilitation services, and medical clinics. Biomedical research, which is associated with the medical model, seeks to find the causes and cures for diseases. As Chapter 3 suggested, allegiance to the medical model has preempted consideration of approaches that may be better aligned with social justice. It has further exposed the healthcare system to the influence of powerful special interests.

Increasingly, service providers in the fields of aging and elder abuse prevention are embracing public health approaches as alternatives to, or to complement, medical approaches. They have focused on community interventions and enlisted new actors, including epidemiologists, social workers, navigators, and community health workers. They are collaborating with health justice advocates and community stakeholders to address threats to health and safety.

Despite this enthusiasm, neither the aging nor the elder abuse prevention networks have fully explored or capitalized on the public health model and

---

[1] Adewale Troutman, former president of the American Public Health Association.

© Springer Publishing Company DOI: 10.1891/9780826147578.0004

the approaches it offers for policy and practice. This chapter makes a case for doing so. It begins by offering a basic introduction to public health and how it has been applied in aging services and abuse prevention. It goes on to suggest ways to unleash its full power.

A BRIEF HISTORY OF PUBLIC HEALTH FOR ELDER JUSTICE ADVOCATES

The field of public health is said to have begun during a cholera outbreak in London during the 1850s. John Snow, a physician who was treating the sick, noticed that many of his patients got their water from the same well on Broad Street. Suspecting that something was wrong with the pump, Snow checked out his hunch by inquiring about the sick and asking where they had gotten their water from. He explored and compared their experiences, which led him to conclude that a relationship did, in fact, exist between the pump and the disease. He prevailed upon local authorities to remove the pump handle, thereby stopping the epidemic and launching a new field.

After hearing this account, students of public health are typically asked to consider why the simple act of removing the handle of a pump was such a big deal that made it worthy of discussion more than a century and a half later.

What distinguished Snow's actions from his normal practice as a physician was that rather than *treating* sick individuals, he *prevented* them from getting sick in the first place. In doing so, he eliminated immeasurable suffering and death. His simple act further protected the whole neighborhood—the beneficiaries included the rich and the poor.

Equally remarkable was that he had stopped the epidemic without knowing its cause. It was not until years later that the bacterium responsible for cholera was isolated and identified. Others at the time had speculated that the disease was the result of "foul air." His response was based on a simple observation and calculation: People who used the pump were more likely to get sick than those who did not.

These essential steps—observing who gets sick or dies, identifying commonalities among them, estimating the probability that others will suffer similar fates, and taking steps to prevent that from happening—remain core to public health.

Of course, things are much more complicated today. Snow's inquiries about the sick and dying have evolved into the systematic tracking of diseases known as "surveillance," and public health officials monitor disease and death rates (called "morbidity" and "mortality") to detect trends and patterns. While mobility and world travel pose new challenges to surveillance, innovations and accelerations in sensing devices, communications, and computing have permitted epidemiologists to explore countless diseases, disabling conditions, and other health threats. These developments also create new challenges for protecting individuals' rights to privacy, which are discussed in Chapter 7.

Snow's conclusions that a link existed between the pump, cholera, and the sick set the stage for epidemiology, the research methodology associated with public health. Epidemiologists examine *incidence*, or new cases of diseases as they are identified, and *prevalence*, the number of people in a community at any given point in time who are affected. When these rates are higher than expected, epidemiologists look for common characteristics among the affected, or "risk factors." Those with the characteristics are said to be "at risk."

Risk factors may be behavioral (drinking water from a well, smoking, or engaging in unprotected sex), environmental (living in a particular neighborhood or climate), occupational (working in certain jobs or settings), or genetic (gender, race, ethnicity). Another way of talking about risk factors is as "predictors" of disease or problems. Conversely, commonalities that are found to exist among those who do not get sick are referred to as *protective* factors.

Some risk factors are "modifiable." People can reduce or eliminate them by giving up smoking, changing jobs, or moving to other locations. Nonmodifiable risk factors include race, gender, age, and other factors beyond one's control. Women are at heightened risk for breast cancer, African Americans are at greater risk for sickle cell anemia, and the risk for Alzheimer's disease increases dramatically with age.

Public health employs a hierarchy of approaches to disease prevention. "Primary prevention" is identifying people at risk and taking steps to keep them from getting sick (or developing conditions, becoming the victim of violence, getting injured, etc.) in the first place. Examples include vaccines, adopting safer or healthier behaviors, adopting safety standards for cars and the workplace, or myriad other measures. Secondary prevention, which is second best, involves catching problems in their early stages, which is typically done through screenings, checkups, or surveys to discover people who are in the early stages of diseases, conditions, or problems, and encouraging them to begin treatment or take other steps to eliminate or reduce their risk. Tertiary prevention focuses on people who are already sick or experiencing problems, and taking steps to prevent relapses, alleviate symptoms, or reduce harm. Common harm reduction strategies for substance abuse, for example, focus on preventing overdoses, stopping the spread of substance abuse–related illnesses like viral hepatitis (e.g., through needle exchanges), and reducing other substance abuse–related consequences like isolation, malnutrition, unemployment, and involvement in the criminal justice system (Riley & O'Hare, 2000). Harm reduction strategies for Alzheimer's disease include modifying living environments to prevent those with the disease from getting lost, agitated, or hurt.

Although public health initially focused on infectious diseases, those in the field came to recognize that some of the greatest threats to public health and safety come from social problems like violence (ranging from intimate partner abuse to gang violence), accidents (ranging from automobile accidents to falls), environmental threats, and climate change.

Public health is credited with increasing the life spans of Americans by 25 years during the 20th century by controlling infectious diseases; reducing deaths from coronary heart disease and stroke; making food safer and healthier; implementing maternal and child health programs, advances in motor vehicle safety, and workplace safety measures; and reducing tobacco use (Centers for Disease Control and Prevention [CDC], 1999).

SOCIAL DETERMINANTS OF HEALTH

Since the late 1990s, epidemiologists have increasingly explored the relationship between wealth and health inequality and attempted to explain the markedly lower life expectancies and heightened rates of disease and disability among economically disadvantaged groups (National Academies of Sciences, Engineering, and Medicine, 2015). They have attributed these differences, called *health disparities,* to *social determinants of health*, which the CDC defines as "preventable differences in the burden of disease, injury, violence, or opportunities to achieve optimal health that are experienced by socially disadvantaged population groups, and communities" (2018, para. 1). Disparities are tied to disadvantages based on race, ethnicity, socioeconomic status, gender and gender orientation, age, residence, and other factors linked to discrimination, social exclusion, and stigmas (Wallace, 2015).

The goal in addressing disparities is to achieve *health equity*. This requires increasing the availability of resources to meet daily needs like safe housing and healthy food, and improving access to educational and economic opportunities, healthcare, transportation, and social support. It requires addressing discrimination, distrust of government, and exposure to crime, violence, and social disorder. It further requires improving socioeconomic conditions like poverty and its associated stresses; segregation; and language and literacy barriers. In recent years, it has increasingly required improving access to social media, cell phones, and the Internet.

Since the 1970s, the CDC has signaled its plans and priorities in 10-year plans called *Healthy People: The Surgeon General's Report on Disease Prevention and Health Promotion*. The plans also report on progress in achieving milestones and outcomes. Social determinants have become increasingly prominent in *Healthy People* reports over the past three decades. *Healthy People 2020* establishes *health equity* as a top priority, explaining:

> Our health is also determined in part by access to social and economic opportunities; the resources and supports available in our homes, neighborhoods, and communities; the quality of our schooling; the safety of our workplaces; the cleanliness of our water, food, and air; and the nature of our social interactions and relationships. The conditions in which we live explain in part why some Americans are healthier than others and why Americans more generally are not as healthy as they could be. (Office of Disease Prevention and Health Promotion, n.d.-b, "Overview")

Healthy People 2020 highlights five key social determinants:

1. Economic stability, including poverty, employment, food security, and housing stability
2. Education, including language and literacy
3. Social and community context, including social cohesion, civic participation, discrimination, and incarceration
4. Health and healthcare, including access to healthcare, access to primary care, and health literacy
5. Neighborhood and built environments, including access to healthy foods, quality of housing, crime and violence, and environmental conditions (ODPHP, n.d.-b, "Approach")

THE ECOLOGICAL MODEL OF PUBLIC HEALTH

The myriad threats to health and the equally numerous ways to combat them led to the adoption of the *ecological model* to help organize thinking and identify opportunities for prevention. Although the model is not unique to public health, it is firmly entrenched and widely applied. The CDC, the federal agency responsible for overseeing public health, defines it as a "model of health that emphasizes the linkages and relationships among multiple factors (or determinants) affecting health" (Gebbie, Rosenstock, & Hernandez, 2003, p. 5). It **both** provides an overarching framework **and** has been adopted for specific diseases, conditions, and problems.

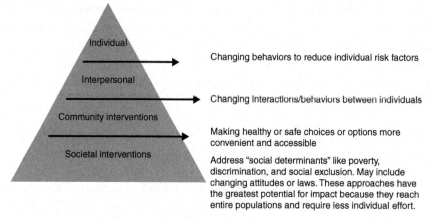

FIGURE 4.1   Levels of impact in public health interventions.

Source: Adapted from Frieden, T. R. (2010). A framework for public health action: The Health Impact Pyramid. *American Journal of Public Health, 100*(4), 590–595. doi:10.2105/AJPH.2009.185652

The ecological model considers the interplay of individual (also called intrapersonal), interpersonal, community, and societal factors that contribute to or mitigate risk. Individual factors include personal traits or characteristics, behaviors, or attitudes. Interpersonal factors include relationships among partners, acquaintances, and friends or family. Community factors relate to work settings, schools, and service systems. Institutional and societal factors include laws, regulations, and social attitudes and norms.

The CDC employs the Public Health Impact Pyramid to depict these four levels of focus, their relative importance, and potential interventions at each level (see Figure 4.1).

At its base are interventions that address *social determinants* such as poverty, discrimination, social exclusion, and where people live and work. It is the broadest band because interventions at this level have the greatest potential impact. Societal interventions include strategies for changing perceptions or attitudes (e.g., promoting the acceptance of "designated drivers" to prevent automobile fatalities) or laws. Public health laws include such far-ranging approaches as regulating the sale of unhealthy products, increasing access to healthcare, requiring employers to institute safety measures, changing zoning or land use laws (e.g., to authorize farmers markets), bans on smoking in public places, quarantining people with communicable diseases, and regulating the care of nursing home residents.

The next band up is community interventions, which includes making healthy or safe choices or options more convenient and accessible. Examples include community campaigns to bring farmers markets into urban "food deserts" or crime watch programs.

Public health threats related to relationships, reflected on the next band, can be addressed by changing interactions or behaviors between individuals. Examples include measures to prevent sexually transmitted diseases and interpersonal violence. Individual factors, at the top of the pyramid, focus on individual risk factors and measures that individuals can take to reduce their risk for disease, disability, or other health threats, such as exercising, getting vaccines and health screenings, or giving up smoking.

AGING AS A PUBLIC HEALTH ISSUE

Clearly, the goal of reducing health disparities is not new to the field of aging. As described in Chapter 2, advocates have sought to level the playing field through programs like Medicare, Medicaid, Older Americans Act programs, and the Patient Protection and Affordable Care Act. Those in the field of aging and elder abuse prevention have not, however, embraced public health as a primary vehicle for achieving health justice, focusing instead on the medical model and making medical care available to more people. This bias is understandable in light of the fact that much of the leadership in both fields has come from medical professionals, many of whom are affiliated with geriatrics programs in schools of medicine and nursing. Even those who come from the social sciences typically address the health challenges that older people face in ways that reflect medical perspectives and approaches.

Pam Teaster, Director of the Center for Gerontology at Virginia Tech, attributes this dominance of medicine over public health in part to an "us versus them" mentality between the fields. "The clinical people say 'you're taking resources away from treating patients' when we promote public health approaches" (P. Teaster, personal communication, May 7, 2018). She notes, however, that medical professionals with public health training are helping to break down the barriers between the two professions. "They get it; they understand that one component alone does not solve the problem, and that embracing public health gives you a wider berth for helping whole populations."

The acceptance of public health concepts in the field of aging can be seen in its embrace of age-friendly communities, the expanded use of screening, and the adoption by publicly funded health programs of incentives to keep beneficiaries healthy (see Chapters 2 and 9).

The public health field is also focusing greater attention on older people's health. Although it has always focused on diseases that affect older people, in recent years it has adopted a broader focus and holistic approaches. This is evident in the CDC's Healthy Aging initiative, which applies public health approaches to dementias, chronic conditions, caregiving, and injury prevention (including falls and elder abuse). It has further identified shingles, suicide, advance directives, hearing loss, oral health, and disaster preparedness as requiring more attention. Chronic conditions are addressed through programs that promote physical activity, strength training, self-care, and services for maintaining independence, and that focus on caregivers' needs. In recent years, the CDC has partnered with the Alzheimer's Association to develop a road map for meeting the needs of dementia patients and their caregivers with an emphasis on low-income families (Alzheimer's Association & Centers for Disease Control and Prevention, 2013).

Healthy People 2020 calls for the following approaches to meeting the needs of older Americans:

- Person-centered care planning that includes caregivers
- Quality measures of care and monitoring of health conditions
- Fair pay and compensation standards for formal and informal caregivers
- Minimum levels of geriatric training for health professionals
- Enhanced data on underserved elders (ODPHP, n.d.-a, "Emerging Issues")

In line with the field's expanded emphasis on social determinants, epidemiologists are exploring the impact of social determinants in advanced age. Recent studies, for example, suggest that being socially connected significantly reduces the risk for premature mortality (Holt-Lunstad, 2017) and that social isolation exceeds obesity, air pollution, smoking, and physical inactivity in impacting life expectancy. Social isolation is further linked to physical and mental health and functional status and its impact increases over time, leading to what has been referred to as "cumulative connectedness disadvantage." An entire issue of the journal *Public Policy & Aging Report* focuses on loneliness and its implications for society (Hudson, 2017).

The CDC has also initiated special initiatives to explore health disparities among elders (see the CDC's Healthy Aging Data portal at www.cdc.gov/aging/agingdata/index.html). Its *Healthy Aging* program supports research into how older African Americans, Hispanics, and Chinese Americans think about cognitive health and its association with lifestyle factors. CDC is also exploring the health and needs of American Indian and Alaska Native caregivers.

Despite these advances, progress has been slow. Few schools of public health offer specializations in aging, and age-related content remains rare in public health training curricula and texts. Few sessions on aging appear on the agendas of professional forums like American Public Health Association (APHA) conferences.

ELDER MISTREATMENT AS A PUBLIC HEALTH ISSUE

Jeffrey Hall, a behavioral scientist with the CDC, traces the emergence of elder mistreatment as a public health concern back to the early 1980s, when the CDC brought violence into the fold of public health, and included elder abuse along with domestic violence, sexual assault, and other forms of violence-related injuries and death (Hall, 2017). In 1993, it established the Division of Violence Prevention within the National Center of Injury Prevention and Control (NCIPC) to provide leadership.

The CDC proclaimed elder abuse to be a public health concern in its own right following the 2001 National Policy Summit on Elder Abuse, an event sponsored by the U.S. Department of Justice and the U.S. Department of Health and Human Services. Advocates believed that doing so would bring increased attention to the issue and attract new sources of funds.

The following year, the National Academy of Sciences convened a group of experts to discuss strategies for addressing elder abuse as a public health issue. The group adopted the ecological model and began formulating a blueprint to define the problem, identify risk and protective factors, and develop and test prevention strategies (Bonnie & Wallace, 2003).

Among the CDC's first efforts were to sponsor initiatives to explore abuse laws in hopes of accelerating policy-level interventions. Not surprisingly, it was not long before these efforts became mired in the definitional controversies that are endemic to the field (Nerenberg, 2008). The variability and inconsistencies in reporting laws made analyses and comparisons nearly impossible. State laws vary in the age used to define *elder*; the nature of relationships between abusers and victims (Did they have to be related or in relationships of trust or confidence?); intentionality (Did abuse have to be intentional?); and many other factors.

The problem of definitions also applied to research. Because standardized definitions are needed to estimate incidence, prevalence, and risk factors, the CDC attempted to produce a set of uniform definitions and core data elements. In 2016, it issued a report on definitions developed in collaboration with a group of elder abuse experts that defines elder abuse as an "intentional act or failure to act by a caregiver or another person in a relationship involving an expectation of trust that causes or creates a serious risk of harm to an older adult" (Hall, Karch, & Crosby, 2016, p. 28). Hall, who led the initiative, describes the importance of getting definitions right:

> Definitions shape our frames for seeing, thinking about, and interpreting behaviors that are abusive, neglectful, and exploitative and thus

must be created with care. They also determine how we view groups of persons in need of services and how we develop, implement, and evaluate strategies for action. In summary, definitions reflect a social construction process that undergirds the work researchers and practitioners do in elder abuse. (Siciliano, 2017, p. 12)

Hall further blames lack of data for the slow progress in preventing abuse. "One of the reasons for inaction is that every time there's a high-level discussion about elder abuse, people want to know how bad the problem is, what direction it's going, and where the trends lead. We haven't gotten to the place at a national or local level where we can answer in a purposeful way to target resources and drive interventions. There are people desperately trying to keep methodologies moving forward" (J. Hall, personal communication, May 7, 2018).

Epidemiologists have faced other problems in establishing the scope of the problem. Some, for example, have patterned elder abuse studies on those used to measure other forms of violence. These typically use injuries to estimate the number of people affected; that is, for each injury reported, it is assumed that there is one corresponding victim (Hall et al., 2016). But because multiple forms of elder abuse often occur together and are repetitive, the assumption does not hold. Common age-related conditions also often mask or mimic signs of abuse, making it difficult to distinguish inflicted from non-inflicted injuries or harm.

The fact that data on abuse is collected by multiple entities is also a barrier, leading some to explore ways to link data within and across different sources. In 2006, the American Bar Association's Commission on Law and Aging published a white paper describing data on abuse collected through the healthcare, long-term care, criminal justice, fiduciary, and legal services networks that could potentially be used by federal agencies and elder abuse professionals. Erica Wood, the investigator, called the project a "treasure hunt for relevant data that led to more blind alleys and dead ends than finds" (Wood, 2006, p. 21). However, the paper reveals an astonishing array of data ranging from crime reports collected by the Federal Bureau of Investigation (FBI), to reports of violent deaths made to the CDC, to reimbursement claims made to Medicare for abuse-related treatment, to nurse aide registries that contain information about aides banned from working because of abuse claims filed against them.

Each source was analyzed for its "potential for use or action." The recommendations that emerged range from adding abuse to the categories included in the International Classification of Diseases (ICD) to adding questions about elder abuse to the CDC's Chronic Disease Behavioral Risk Factor Surveillance System (BRFSS). Wood concludes, however, that "While each of the listed actions offers some potential to fill in the blanks in the national picture of elder abuse, taken together they are nonetheless insufficient and piecemeal" (Wood, 2006, p. 8).

The quest for data continues. Among the objectives contained in *Healthy People 2020* is increasing the number of states and tribes that collect and make publicly available information on the characteristics of victims, perpetrators, and cases of elder abuse, neglect, and exploitation (CDC National Center for Health Statistics, 2011).

Despite the setbacks and barriers, progress has been made in bringing public health methods and approaches to elder abuse, and there have been benefits for doing so. Acknowledging elder abuse as a public health issue has brought epidemiologists to the field who are applying their craft to discover new relationships and areas of exploration. Causal theories are being replaced by the identification of risk factors that predict who is likely to be mistreated, and that suggest preventive inventions. The research also reflects the CDC's focus on social determinants, with low social support and previous traumatic event exposure emerging as the strongest risk factors for abuse. Social support is now believed to be the strongest protective factor (Acierno et al., 2010; Acierno, Hernandez-Tejada, Anetzberger, Loew, & Muzzy, 2017; Holt-Lunstad, 2017).

Studies like these are pointing the way to promising interventions that address social determinants at the individual, interpersonal, community, and societal levels. Whereas elder abuse awareness campaigns, a prime example of primary prevention, have traditionally encouraged the public to report abuse, emphasized that abuse is a crime, or promoted respect and intergenerational exchange, campaigns are now beginning to focus on social determinants. For example, the National Center for Elder Abuse has undertaken efforts to reduce isolation and promote social engagement. However, most of these efforts have addressed isolation from solely the intra- or interpersonal perspectives (e.g., stemming from lack of family support or transportation) and not in a broader societal context, which might include social exclusion resulting from discrimination or poverty.

Secondary prevention in elder abuse has traditionally included screenings for abuse conducted by healthcare professionals in the course of taking medical histories as well as screenings designed to detect specific vulnerabilities such as problems understanding financial tasks and concepts, which are believed to be associated with susceptibility to financial abuse (Lichtenberg, 2017; Marson et al., 2009). Here again, a trend toward focusing on social determinants appears to be emerging. A health center in Venice, California, for example, has developed a protocol for assessing clients' health and risk for abuse that explores social determinants like housing, job security, and education. The protocol is also used by navigators to connect patients to behavioral health services, health insurance programs, or health education programs. Data gleaned from the protocol is entered into an electronic health record system and used to prioritize resources (McCarthy, 2017).

The effectiveness of some forms of elder abuse screening, however, has been questioned. In 2018, the U.S. Preventive Services Task Force (USPSTF), an independent, volunteer panel of national experts that makes recommendations on screening, announced that it was not recommending screening for abuse and neglect in older or vulnerable adults because there was insufficient evidence to warrant doing so.

Tertiary, or "after the fact," prevention in elder abuse includes the myriad interventions that are used today to stop abuse, treat its effects, and prevent reoccurrences, as described in Chapter 6. Although tertiary prevention is the least optimal option from a public health perspective, a substantial portion of resources go to emergency responses and interventions in the most egregious cases such as initiatives to increase prosecution rates and develop forensics expertise. They are also concentrated on the upper bands of the Public Health Impact Pyramid; that is, they address abuse on the individual or interpersonal levels.

An approach to tertiary prevention that deserves more attention is harm reduction, which might include, for example, interventions to prevent eviction, foreclosure, homelessness, institutionalization, poverty or financial insecurity, or other potential consequences of financial exploitation; restoring or establishing social support for victims; responding to abuse-related trauma; and addressing health problems and injuries resulting from abuse and neglect.

Some have voiced disappointment in the public health sector's overall response to elder abuse, claiming that the CDC has not focused enough scientific attention or funding on the problem (Connolly & Trilling, 2014). In their "Priorities for Consideration by the White House Conference on Aging," leading elder abuse researchers called for the CDC to do more (Pillemer, Connolly, Breckman, Spreng, & Lachs, 2015).

Not all of the blame rests with the field of public health. Many in the field of elder abuse prevention have been slow to adopt public health principles or practice. As is the case in the field of aging, many leaders in the elder abuse field also come from the medical professions and the medical model continues to dominate.

The disconnect between professionals in the fields of public health and elder abuse may stem in part from a lack of interdisciplinary exchange and training.

Few Adult Protective Services (APS) workers and other elder abuse prevention professionals have backgrounds in public health or receive on-the-job training in public health concepts and methods. There is little if any attention to elder abuse in public health training curricula or texts, or at professional forums for public health professionals. An exception is a book published by the APHA in 2006, which contained a collection of articles on the interface between elder abuse and public health (Summers & Hoffman, 2006). None of the articles, however, propose fundamental changes to how elder abuse is addressed, focusing instead on modifications and enhancements to current approaches. More is being done at the international level, with the World Health Organization collaborating with national and international nongovernmental organizations (NGOs) on abuse prevention initiatives that employ public health strategies in aging and elder abuse (World Health Organization, 2008).

PUBLIC HEALTH AND ELDER JUSTICE

Public health addresses health as a matter of justice. The application of public health theory and practice to age-related diseases and disabilities establishes the health and functionality of older Americans as matters of justice as well. Health justice must, therefore, be a core component of elder justice with public health playing a predominant role in achieving it.

There are multiple rationales and advantages for doing so. For decades, leaders in the field of aging have called for a new and unifying conceptual framework that better reflects social justice in healthcare and aging services, and many have advocated to reduce the medical bias in publicly funded programs that favor expensive technologies and institutional care. Public health's "health justice is social justice" ethos has broad public appeal.

Epidemiology further provides a clearer understanding of the differences between causation and correlation, opening the door to new areas of inquiry. It can lead to the revisiting of others and resolving long-standing disagreements. For example, calls for programs that relieve caregiver stress as a way to prevent elder abuse have been dismissed by those who argue that no causal link between stress and abuse has ever been conclusively established. But, as Dr. Snow so famously demonstrated, the discovery of positive correlations between factors may justify risk reduction interventions even as those relationships continue to be explored. Had Snow waited for a causal link to be established between a pump and cholera, many more people would have gotten sick or died. Similarly, public health programs to stop smoking and prevent the spread of AIDS were well under way before the causes of these deadly diseases were conclusively established.

Fully adopting a public health model can further expand the focus of aging and elder abuse policy and practice from micro- to macro-level interventions. This will include crafting systemic responses to systemic problems associated with illnesses, premature death, and disability. Clearly, systemic approaches are needed to effectively address such widespread problems as Alzheimer's disease and elder abuse.

Perhaps the most compelling reason for adopting public health outlooks and approaches to elder justice is that current approaches to healthcare are unsustainable. As proposals to ensure the solvency of programs like Medicare are discussed, it is critical that advocates identify and alert the public and policy makers to their consequences for justice and equity (see Chapter 11). Public health offers new ways to think about healthcare as a social justice issue and offers strategies for achieving health equity.

CONCLUSION

Public health theory and practice provide powerful tools for elder justice. Adopting public health principles and practices to elder justice will require (a) applying the ecological model beyond elder abuse and Alzheimer's disease to encompass a wider array of elder justice issues, (b) expanding on the use of epidemiological research to identify health disparities, (c) building upon and prioritizing prevention strategies, (d) forging new alliances and collaborations, and (e) achieving public support.

The elder justice paradigm suggested in Chapter 11 draws heavily from the ecological model of public health and incorporates variations of it that have already been adapted for elder abuse and other age-related conditions and health challenges. It is well suited to the multidimensional and multifaceted circumstances and needs of older people and can guide research, policy, and practice. It focuses on social determinants that impact health and quality of life in old age and emphasizes systemic approaches to addressing them.

Epidemiology can play an enormous role in achieving elder justice. By identifying social determinants and risk factors, it suggests how risks can be reduced, and identifies groups at greatest risk. Incidence and prevalence data can demonstrate the impact of interventions to improve health outcomes for older people and reduce disparities through primary, secondary, and tertiary interventions at the intra- and interpersonal, community, and societal levels. Public health's primary, secondary, and tertiary approaches to prevention can guide in the development of elder justice interventions and suggest balanced approaches to addressing individual, interpersonal, community, and societal risks.

Promoting health justice through public health approaches will require new partnerships and greater exchange and collaboration among those in the fields of public health, aging, and elder abuse prevention. It will further require raising awareness among policy makers, professionals, and the public about health injustices; if and how they are being addressed; and what the public can do to help.

Specific steps for applying public health concepts in elder justice are described in the Elder Justice Agenda in Chapter 12.

REFERENCES

Acierno, R., Hernandez, M. A., Amstadter, A. B., Resnick, H. S., Steve, K., Muzzy, W., & Kilpatrick, D. G. (2010). Prevalence and correlates of emotional, physical, sexual, and financial abuse and potential neglect in the United States: The National Elder Mistreatment Study. *American Journal of Public Health, 100*(2), 292–297. doi:10.2105/ ajph.2009.163089

Acierno, R., Hernandez-Tejada, M. A., Anetzberger, G. J., Loew, D., & Muzzy, W. (2017). The National Elder Mistreatment Study: An 8-year longitudinal study of outcomes. *Journal of Elder Abuse & Neglect, 29*(4), 254–269. doi:10.1080/08946566.2017.1365031

Alzheimer's Association and Centers for Disease Control and Prevention. (2013). *The Healthy Brain Initiative: The public health road map for state and national partnerships, 2013–2018.* Chicago, IL: Alzheimer's Association.

Associated Press. (1966, March 26). King berates medical care given Negroes. *Oshkosh Daily Northwestern*, p. 3.

Bonnie., R. J., & Wallace, R. B. (Eds.). (2003). *Elder mistreatment: Abuse, neglect, and exploitation in an aging America.* Washington, DC: National Academies Press.

Centers for Disease Control and Prevention. (1999). Ten great public health achievements— United States, 1900–1999. *Morbidity and Mortality Weekly Report, 48*(12), 241–243. Retrieved from https://www.cdc.gov/mmwr/preview/mmwrhtml/00056796.htm

Centers for Disease Control and Prevention. (2018). Health disparities. Retrieved from https://www.cdc.gov/healthyyouth/disparities/index.htm

Centers for Disease Control and Prevention, National Center for Health Statistics. (2011). *Healthy People 2020.* Retrieved from https://www.cdc.gov/nchs/healthy_people/ hp2020.htm

Connolly, M.-T., & Trilling, A. (2014). Seven policy priorities for an enhanced public health response to elder abuse. In Institute of Medicine & National Research Council (Eds.), *Elder abuse and its prevention: Workshop summary.* Washington, DC: National Academies Press. Retrieved from http://www.ncbi.nlm.nih.gov/books/NBK208578

Frieden, T. R. (2010). A framework for public health action: The Health Impact Pyramid. *American Journal of Public Health, 100*(4), 590–595. doi:10.2105/AJPH.2009.185652

Gebbie, K., Rosenstock, L., & Hernandez, L. M. (Eds.). (2003). *Who will keep the public healthy?: Educating public health professionals for the 21st century.* Washington, DC: National Academies Press. doi:10.17226/10542

Hall, J. (2017). Centers for Disease Control and Prevention: An overview of elder abuse prevention initiatives. In X.-Q. Dong (Ed.), *Elder abuse: Research, practice and policy* (pp. 653–669). Gewerbestrasse, Switzerland: Springer International.

Hall, J., Karch, D. L., & Crosby, A. (2016). *Elder abuse surveillance: Uniform definitions and recommended core data elements for use in elder abuse surveillance, Version 1.0.* Atlanta, GA: National Center for Injury Prevention and Control, Centers for Disease Control and Prevention. Retrieved from https://www.cdc.gov/violenceprevention/pdf/ EA_Book_Revised_2016.pdf

Holt-Lunstad, J. (2017). The potential public health relevance of social isolation and loneliness: Prevalence, epidemiology, and risk factors. *Public Policy & Aging Report, 27*(4), 127–130. doi:10.1093/ppar/prx030

Hudson, R. B. (2017). Lack of social connectedness and its consequences. *Public Policy & Aging Report, 27*(4), 121–123. doi:10.1093/ppar/prx035

Lichtenberg, P. A. (2017). New approaches to determining financial capacity and risk for exploitation. *Journal of Mental Health and Clinical Psychology, 1*(1), 1–3. Retrieved from http://www.mentalhealthjournal.org/articles/new-approaches-to-determining-financial-capacity-and-risk-for-exploitation.html

Marson, D. C., Martin, R. C., Wadley, V., Griffith, H. R., Snyder, S., Goode, P. S., . . . Harrell, L. E. (2009). Clinical interview assessment of financial capacity in older adults with mild cognitive impairment and Alzheimer's disease. *Journal of the American Geriatrics Society, 57*(5), 806–814. doi:10.1111/j.1532-5415.2009.02202.x

McCarthy, L. (2017, December 5). Los Angeles clinics seek new ways of combatting the social factors undermining health. Retrieved from https://www.centerforhealthjournalism.org/2017/12/03/los-angeles-clinics-seek-new-ways-combatting-social-factors-undermining-health

National Academies of Sciences, Engineering, and Medicine. (2015). *The growing gap in life expectancy by income: Implications for federal programs and policy responses.* Washington, DC: National Academies Press.

Nerenberg, L. (2008). *Elder abuse prevention: Emerging trends and promising strategies.* New York, NY: Springer Publishing.

Office of Disease Prevention and Health Promotion. (n.d.-a). HealthyPeople 2020 topics and objectives: Older adults. Retrieved from https://www.healthypeople.gov/2020/topics-objectives/topic/social-determinants-of-health

Office of Disease Prevention and Health Promotion. (n.d.-b). HealthyPeople 2020 topics and objectives: Social determinants of health. Retrieved from https://www.healthypeople.gov/2020/topics-objectives/topic/social-determinants-of-health

Pillemer, K., Connolly, M-T., Breckman, R., Spreng, N., & Lachs, M. S. (2015). Elder mistreatment: Priorities for consideration by the White House Conference on Aging. *The Gerontologist, 55*(2), 320–327. doi:10.1093/geront/gnu180

Riley, D., & O'Hare, P. (2000). Harm reduction: History, definition, and practice. In J. Inciardi & L. Harrison (Eds.), *Harm reduction: National and international perspectives* (pp. 1–26). Thousand Oaks, CA: Sage.

Siciliano, M. (2017). *Judith D. Tamkin International Symposium on Elder Abuse: Closing the research gaps: Moving the field forward.* Los Angeles: University of Southern California. Retrieved from http://eldermistreatment.usc.edu/wp-content/uploads/2017/02/Tamkin_whitepaper_digital.pdf?pdf=white-paper

Summers, R. W., & Hoffman, A. M. (Eds.). (2006). *Elder abuse: A public health perspective.* Washington, DC: American Public Health Association.

Wallace, S. P. (2015, February 17). Equity and social determinants of health among older adults [Blog post]. Retrieved from http://www.asaging.org/blog/equity-and-social-determinants-health-among-older-adults

Wood, E. (2006). The availability and utility of interdisciplinary data on elder abuse: A white paper for the National Center on Elder Abuse. Retrieved from https://ncea.acl.gov/resources/docs/archive/Availability-Utility-Interdisciplinary-Data-EA-White-Paper-NCEA-2006.pdf

World Health Organization. (2008). *A global response to elder abuse and neglect.* Retrieved from https://www.who.int/ageing/publications/ELDER_DocAugust08.pdf

5

Elder Justice on the Global Stage

INTRODUCTION

In the aftermath of World War II, world leaders came together to ensure that the atrocities the world had just witnessed would never occur again. They established the United Nations (UN) on October 24, 1945, under a charter calling for the "human rights and fundamental freedoms of all humans without distinction as to race, sex, language, or religion" (U.N. Charter art.1, para. 3).

Two years later, UN leaders established the Commission on Human Rights to develop plans for implementing the charter. First Lady Eleanor Roosevelt was appointed to chair the body, which included delegates from around the world. The group drafted and approved the Universal Declaration of Human Rights, which has uncanny relevance today, addressing such "contemporary" issues as asylum, immigration, torture, and access to healthcare.

Given the central role the United States played in shaping the postwar world order, it is not surprising that the declaration mirrors the U.S. Constitution and Bill of Rights in many respects. But the declaration is more expansive, and the United States never adopted many of its provisions, including those barring racial discrimination, since slavery was still legal in some states at the time. Interest by U.S. policy makers in the declaration, and UN activities in general, has ebbed and flowed over the decades, reflecting the ideologies of the individuals and political parties in power.

As early as 1948, the UN acknowledged the rights of old people. Understanding and appreciating these efforts requires a basic understanding of the UN's structure, processes, and the sprawling network of specialized agencies, programs, and collaborators that make up the "UN family." What follows is a brief description of key UN entities and their roles in elder rights and abuse prevention.

© Springer Publishing Company DOI: 10.1891/9780826147578.0005   **61**

UNITED NATIONS 101 FOR ELDER JUSTICE ADVOCATES

The UN's primary components (called "organs") are the General Assembly, the Security Council, the Economic and Social Council (ECOSOC), and the Secretariat. The General Assembly includes representatives from the 193 member states,[1] which are recommended for inclusion by the Security Council. The council is responsible for maintaining international peace and security and its members have to be approved by the other members.

The ECOSOC coordinates the World Bank, the United Nations Children's Fund (UNICEF), and the World Health Organization (WHO), all of which operate as specialized, autonomous organizations. The council also serves as a forum for discussing international economic and social issues and formulating policy recommendations.

The Secretariat includes the Secretary-General, who serves as the UN's chief administrative officer and spokesperson and makes annual reports to the General Assembly. The Secretariat also includes the UN Department of Economic and Social Affairs (UN DESA), which is responsible for follow-up to major UN summits and conferences, and the Sustainable Development Division, which helps countries implement development plans (see the following).

The UN also has "specialized agencies," committees, councils, and commissions that play significant roles in promoting elder justice. They include the WHO; the Educational, Scientific and Cultural Organization (UNESCO); the Human Rights Council; the Ageing[2] and Life Course Development Unit; and the Department of Public Information (DPI).

Five regional outposts in Europe, Asia and the Pacific, Latin America, Africa, and Western Asia operate under the aegis of Regional Commissions, which set regional goals and strategies.

Collaboration With Nongovernmental Organizations (NGOs)

Much of what has been accomplished in elevating elder rights and abuse prevention internationally has been accomplished by NGOs that work in

---

[1] The term "states" refers to sovereign states, which are defined in international law as having a permanent population, defined territory, a single government, and the capacity to enter into relations with other sovereign states.

[2] The UN uses the British spelling of the word, which is also the preferred spelling in many countries outside the United States and Canada. It is used in this chapter when referencing documents and entities that employ it.

collaboration with the UN, are supported by the UN, or that focus on influencing UN policy and programs. For NGOs to be recognized by UN entities, they have to be granted "consultative status." There are two types: general and special. "General consultative status," the higher of the two, is granted to organizations that address most of the activities of the divisions they interact with, make substantive and sustained contributions, broadly represent major segments of society in multiple countries, and have large memberships. Organizations with this status are entitled to make oral presentations during meetings. The International Federation on Ageing (IFA), AARP, and HelpAge International (HAI) are among the NGOs with general consultative status to UN entities, advising them on aging issues.

"Special consultative status" is granted to organizations that are concerned with some of the activities and issues addressed by the divisions they work with. The International Network for the Prevention of Elder Abuse (INPEA) has this status. UN entities also maintain rosters of additional organizations that are brought in occasionally to assist.

The Conference of NGOs in Consultative Relationship With the United Nations (CoNGO) is a network of NGOs with consultative status that promotes partnerships among its members on issues and advocates on behalf of members for access to UN meetings, conferences, and special events. CoNGO has a Committee on Ageing with subcommittees on elder abuse and older women, as well as a Committee on Social Development, which addresses some aging issues.

UN STRATEGIES

UN entities employ a wide range of strategies to address aging issues, which are summarized in the following and described later in greater detail.

- **International Assemblies** have been major drivers in shaping international and national policies on aging. There have been two major world assemblies on aging.
- **Sustainable Development Plans.** A top UN priority is strengthening democracy and promoting good governance, health, food security, human rights, and the environment in developing countries.[3]

---

[3] The term "developing countries" typically refers to the poorer countries of the world, including most of Africa and parts of Asia, Central America, and South America. There is disagreement, however, about what states are included, and the term itself has undergone changes. "Developing" has largely replaced the terms "industrialized," "third world," and "Western." The terms "global south" and "global north," which reflect the geographic alignment of poor and wealthy countries, are also increasingly being used.

It encourages countries to adopt plans that reflect agreed-upon principles. Although they are not legally bound to follow the principles or adhere to their plans, there are incentives for them to do so. To receive UN economic aid, for example, countries may be required to demonstrate how they will address income inequality, contribute to women's economic security, or address violence against women and children. Some advocates have pushed for using a similar approach for older people.

- **Treaties and Conventions** are formal international agreements. The landmark 1948 Universal Declaration of Human Rights, described earlier, was the UN's first agreement and was followed by two additional "covenants" (another term for treaty) that were adopted in 1966—the International Covenant on Civil and Political Rights and the International Covenant on Economic, Social and Cultural Rights. The Universal Declaration and covenants make up the International Bill of Human Rights.

Despite the "universal" scope of these agreements, advocates have continually fought to highlight the rights of specific groups. This has led to the passage of seven "conventions" that spell out the rights of specific groups. They are developed through painstaking processes informed by studies, forums, and debate. Member states are then encouraged to ratify and adopt them, and the UN requires regular monitoring and reporting. There are conventions for:

1. The Elimination of All Forms of Racial Discrimination (passed in 1965)
2. The Elimination of All Forms of Discrimination Against Women (1979)
3. Torture and Other Cruel, Inhuman, or Degrading Treatment or Punishment (1984)
4. The Rights of the Child (1989)
5. The Rights of All Migrant Workers and Members of Their Families (1990)
6. The Rights of Persons With Disabilities (2006)
7. The Protection of All Persons From Enforced Disappearance (2006)

Although these agreements are nonbinding and often criticized for their lack of teeth, signing them subjects countries to scrutiny and monitoring by "treaty bodies." There may be measures to promote compliance, such as questionnaires to track progress, and manuals and guides for policy makers. Another common criticism of conventions is that they are biased toward the values and goals of Western-oriented organizations despite efforts to solicit input from all affected countries.

- **Public Awareness Events and Observances** spotlight UN interests and new initiatives. In 1990, the General Assembly designated October 1 as the International Day of Older Persons and announces a new theme each year. The themes in recent years reflect the UN's evolving interests in aging: In 2011, the theme was "The growing opportunities and challenges of global aging," followed by: "Longevity: Shaping the future" (2012); "What older persons are saying" (2013); "Leaving no one behind: Promoting a society for all" (2014); "Sustainability and age inclusiveness in the urban environment" (2015); "Take a stand against ageism" (2016); "Stepping into the future: Tapping the talents, contributions and participation of older persons in society" (2017); and "Celebrating older human rights champions" (2018).
- **Special Procedures.** The Human Rights Council uses "Special Procedures" to study specific issues. Among the most common is the appointment of independent human rights experts, called "special rapporteurs" or "independent experts," who report and advise UN entities on specific aspects of human rights or country-specific perspectives. The experts work alone or with groups or committees. They are not UN employees, are not paid, serve in their individual capacity, and are not associated with governments or organizations.

THE UN'S ROLE IN PROMOTING THE RIGHTS OF OLD PEOPLE

Because the Universal Declaration of Human Rights applies to all people, it tacitly protects old people. The two covenants are also universal although clarifications were added later that single out specific groups. Of the seven conventions, four specifically mention older people. The Convention on the Rights of Persons with Disabilities (CRPD) calls on nations "to ensure access by persons with disabilities, in particular women and girls with disabilities *and older persons with disabilities,* to social protection programmes and poverty reduction programmes" (UN, n.d.-b, para. 4). It further ensures *age-appropriate* accommodations for accessing justice and *age-sensitive assistance* to ensure freedom from exploitation, violence, and abuse. Its protections for "those who have long-term physical, mental, intellectual or sensory impairments" (UN, n.d.-a, para. 2) also clearly apply to older people. It further calls for a shift from the traditional medical model toward rights-based approaches to disability which have clear implications for older people.

Critics, however, point out that the convention does not go far enough in spelling out the special needs of older people with disabilities (Fredvang & Biggs, 2012). For example, older people may lose the ability to make decisions late in life when they are enmeshed in legal or contractual arrangements or need to take legal actions, which sets them apart from people whose impairments are present earlier in life.

The Convention on the Elimination of All Forms of Discrimination Against Women (CEDAW) mentions age as a contributing factor to gender-based discrimination (Kanter, 2009). Of particular significance for older women are its protections for Social Security and paid family leave. However, the convention fails to address circumstances that are specific to older women. For example, older women in some African and Asian countries experience violence stemming from allegations of witchcraft, which is not addressed.

Similarly, the Convention on the Protection of the Rights of Migrant Workers and the Members of Their Families (ICMW) acknowledges that older migrant women and their families may need special protections but does not specify what they are. The Convention Against Torture and Other Cruel, Inhuman, or Degrading Treatment or Punishment also has implications for older people. Although historically the convention has been applied primarily to interrogations and punishment, it has been extended to apply to practices in healthcare settings, including involuntary medical interventions, the denial of pain treatment, and guardianship.

THE FIRST WORLD ASSEMBLY ON AGEING

Beginning in the 1970s, international NGOs formed to draw attention to older people and urge the UN to address aging. During a 1972 AARP-sponsored event in London, representatives from 13 countries called for an international organization to promote information exchange and met again a year later to launch the IFA. Among the IFA's first initiatives was to join with several other international organizations in calling on the UN to conduct a world assembly on aging.

The UN agreed and collaborated with the IFA and other NGOs to plan the event. The Secretariat, General Assembly, regional commissions, specialized agencies, and the ECOSOC initiated or facilitated events over 3 years, which included listening sessions around the world. These yielded ideas and recommendations that were incorporated into a draft of the International Plan of Action on Ageing. The First World Assembly on Ageing was held in Vienna from July 26 to August 6, 1982.

Although the event has been largely overshadowed by the Second World Assembly that was held 20 years later, the first assembly has particular resonance today in that it occurred against a backdrop of raging conflicts and deteriorating political, social, and economic international situations in many countries that were much on the minds of many delegates. Some argued that aging could not be addressed in isolation of those events, which in some cases impacted the old even more than the young. They called for the assembly to join the chorus of appeals by other international groups for peace and disarmament. Some delegates went even further, insisting that for governments to be able to devote sufficient resources to old people, they needed to divert resources from military and defense purposes. Some pointed out the effects of colonialism, racism, and foreign intervention, aggression, and occupation in the lives of old people and urged the assembly to call for "the elimination of these odious vestiges of the past."

Following the assembly, the draft plan was finalized and titled the Vienna International Plan on Ageing (United Nations, 1983). It was sweeping in scope, offering 116 recommendations that addressed health and nutrition, consumer protections, housing, the environment, family, social welfare, income security, employment, education, and more. The plan laid out basic principles and a framework that form the foundation of subsequent documents, reports, declarations, and initiatives.

Still, many were troubled by what was not included. The following year, organizations in Canada, Colombia, Kenya, India, and the United Kingdom formed HAI in response to concerns that the Vienna Plan failed to adequately address old people in the developing world. Today, HAI has general consultative status with both the ECOSOC and WHO and primarily focuses on countries going through rapid demographic transitions. It tracks UN entities' and members' progress in achieving goals contained in resolutions, plans, and declarations.

Throughout the 1980s and 1990s, UN entities issued proclamations based on the plan's recommendations. In 1991, the General Assembly issued *Principles for Older Persons* (General Assembly resolution 46/91) under the slogan, "To add life to the years that have been added to life." They highlighted five key themes:

1. *Independence,* including the right to adequate food, water, shelter, clothing, healthcare, income and support, the opportunity to work and retire, education and training, safe living environments, and the right to live at home for as long as possible
2. *Participation,* including opportunities for older people to participate actively in formulating and implementing policies that affect their well-being, sharing their knowledge and skills with younger generations, being able to serve their communities as volunteers or by forming movements or associations

3. *Care*, which includes family and community care; healthcare; social and legal services; institutional care that offers adequate protections, rehabilitation, and social and mental stimulation in a humane and secure environment; and fundamental rights and freedoms for those in shelters and care/treatment facilities
4. *Self-Fulfillment*, which holds that older people should be able to pursue opportunities to develop their full potentials through access to educational, cultural, spiritual, and recreational resources
5. *Dignity*, which holds that older people should be free of exploitation, physical or mental abuse, and be treated fairly regardless of age, gender, racial or ethnic background, disability, or other status

Another noteworthy event during this period occurred in 1992 when the General Assembly issued the Proclamation on Ageing, which heralded the "revolutionary change in the demographic structure of societies (that) requires a fundamental change in the way in which societies organize their affairs" (para. 4). It further acknowledged that aging was a lifelong process, preparation for which has to start in childhood. It urged the UN to highlight older people's needs, rights, and special circumstances into development plans with respect to other "mainstream" concerns like reducing poverty, promoting health and well-being, the advancement of women, crime prevention, and youth. This "mainstreaming" of age into all aspects of life became a prominent theme. Mainstreaming involves ensuring that age equity and the needs and perspectives of old people are reflected in policy development, research, advocacy/dialogue, legislation, resource allocation, and planning, implementation, and monitoring of programs and projects. "Affirmative action," which is sometimes referred to as positive discrimination in favor of older people through institutional preferences to compensate for past inequalities, was also prominent. The proclamation also called for partnerships among UN entities, NGOs, and the private sector and encouraged the media to promote UN awareness events and principles. It called for the observance of 1999 as the International Year of Older Persons.

SECOND WORLD ASSEMBLY AND ACTION PLAN

A Second World Assembly on Ageing was held in Madrid, Spain, on April 8–12, 2002 (United Nations, 2002). It was preceded by the drafting of the Madrid International Plan of Action (MIPAA). In a foreword to the plan, the then Secretary-General Kofi Annan observed that the world had "changed almost beyond recognition since the first World Assembly" and pointed out that aging had evolved from being mostly a concern of developed nations to one with enormous impact on the developing world, with major demographic shifts yet to come.

The plan, which was endorsed by 159 governments during the assembly and adopted by consensus later that year by the UN General Assembly, reiterated many of the Vienna Plan's commitments but introduced new elements and responded to criticism that the earlier plan had not focused enough on poverty and development. It featured three primary priorities: (a) older people and development, (b) advancing health and well-being into old age, and (c) ensuring that older people benefit from enabling and supportive environments. Specific themes included health and well-being across the life span, ensuring universal and equal access to healthcare, providing services for older persons with HIV or AIDS, training care providers and health professionals, meeting the mental health needs of older persons, providing appropriate services for older people with disabilities, and providing care and support for caregivers. The plan also emphasized the importance of aging in place.

MIPAA further linked aging to economic development and public health and promoted mainstreaming. It also reflected growing interest in elder abuse (oddly, the topic was categorized among "environmental issues") and called for using public health approaches to prevent neglect and violence against older people. The plan included a built-in process for reviewing progress and recommending new strategies every 5 years (referred to as MIPAA +5 [2007–2008], Madrid +10 [2011–2012], and Madrid +15 [2017–2018]).

HAI played a major role in the subsequent reviews (Till, 2011). In the lead up to Madrid +10, for example, it worked with the UN Population Fund (UNFPA) to produce progress reports that reflected input from over 20 UN entities and international organizations and reflected progress in 133 countries (United Nations Population Fund and HelpAge International, 2012). The reports covered a broad range of topics with all five UN regional economic commissions, the IFA, and the INPEA providing input.

The review demonstrated impressive results. Forty-eight countries had approved and published national policies on aging, 10 had enacted legislation, 64 had set up official bodies and institutions to respond to aging (including ministries), and 51 had produced research or surveys on aging.

It also pointed out gaps. Many countries were shown to lack accountability measures, funding, and binding legal mechanisms for implementation. Many failed to provide information on their budgets for implementing policies and programs. Many reported that they had not mainstreamed aging into policy related to emergencies, migration, HIV and AIDS, mental health, disabilities, or family violence. In response, HAI offered recommendations, which included calling for a special rapporteur or expert, and a convention on the rights of older people.

THREE APPROACHES TAKE SHAPE

In the post-Madrid era, three distinct approaches to older people and their rights coalesced: age as: (a) a human rights issue, (b) a public health concern, and (c) a matter of sustainable social and economic development.

Age as a Matter of Human Rights

Responsibility for ensuring human rights within the UN rests with the Office of the High Commissioner for Human Rights although other UN bodies review progress, hold events, and issue documents.

The *Report of the Expert Group Meeting "Rights of Older Persons"* stands out in particular for its granularity in addressing age as a human rights issue (United Nations Department of Economic and Social Affairs, 2009). It emerged from a 2009 meeting in Bonn, Germany, and highlights the complexity of older people's legal rights, pointing out that they fall within multiple areas of law and policy, including: (a) age discrimination; (b) guardianship; (c) Social Security, pensions, and superannuation; (d) wills and powers of attorney; (e) employment and retirement; (f) housing (including retirement villages and aged care homes); (g) elder abuse; (h) healthcare and long-term care (both institutional and community based); (i) consumer rights; (j) estate and financial planning; and (k) family law (including domestic violence, family care agreements, and custody of grandchildren).

The report also includes "report cards" of countries' progress. Its evaluation of the United States, for example, acknowledged that insurance coverage for older Americans was adequate for health and hospital care but noted serious shortcomings in long-term care; support for caregivers; income security; protections for the rights of older immigrants, minorities, and abuse victims; and the monitoring of nursing homes. Among the other common shortcomings noted in the report card were gaps between what countries were legally bound to do and what they were actually doing. In many countries, people who stood to benefit from programs did not know about them.

The report also pointed out fundamental social changes occurring in some developing countries, which provided opportunities to introduce innovations. For example, under the new legal system adopted in post-apartheid South Africa, the burden of proof in discrimination cases was shifted to alleged discriminators rather than those alleging discrimination.

The Expert Group offered 26 recommendations for national governments in five areas: (a) legal; (b) combatting discrimination; (c) policy-focused research; (d) changing attitudes; and (e) health and independence. Examples of noteworthy measures are listed by topic.

Legal

- Provide accessible and free identity documentation to older people to help them access their economic, social, political, and civil entitlements
- Provide support to older persons' associations to raise awareness about, monitor, or access entitlements
- Provide free paralegal support to defend elders' rights, help resolve disputes, and access judicial systems
- Provide support for strategic litigation to create legal precedents and change laws (e.g., on discrimination in Social Security provision or inheritance and property rights)
- Encourage alternative means of conflict resolution to promote mediation in the home, family, and society as early as possible
- Support legal mechanisms in late life planning, healthcare, wills, and powers of attorney, living wills, organ donations, and property
- Ensure legal capacity in late life with due process
- Develop elder-specific rules of ethics for legal services professionals

Combatting Discrimination

- Incorporate a gender perspective in all policy actions on aging
- Enact legislation to combat age- and gender-based discrimination with respect to Social Security, health, property and inheritance
- Ensure older people's participation in decisions that affect them

Policy-Focused Research

- Collect, analyze, and disseminate survey and census data disaggregated by age and sex
- Promote evidence-based studies on the empowerment of older persons, provision of healthcare, and long-term care on a systematic basis
- Request scholars include older persons' concerns in their research

Changing Attitudes

- Use media to create positive images of older persons
- Give visibility to older persons' rights among leading policy makers and educate them about the rights of older persons and the aging process

Health and Independence

- Provide affordable and appropriate healthcare, support, and social protection for older persons, including prevention and rehabilitation
- Encourage private investment in homes and hospitals designed for older persons
- Provide adequate protection and support of community-based senior centers
- Acknowledge basic rights, such as legal assistance, access to paid family leave, and tax incentives for formal care and relief for caregivers

Another milestone in addressing aging from a human rights perspective came in 2010 when the General Assembly appointed the Open-Ended Working Group on Ageing to consider the existing framework for elder rights and "holistic" approaches to ensuring them.

Heightened attention to elder abuse was also in evidence during the post–Second World Assembly period. A 2011 report by the Secretary-General highlighted violence against older people as one of four overarching themes, along with poverty, discrimination, and lack of measures and services. The report also noted that financial exploitation goes underreported and underdocumented.

First Independent Expert

In response to frequent calls for a special rapporteur or expert on the rights of older people, the Human Rights Council, in 2014, appointed Rosa Kornfeld-Matte as the first "Independent Expert on the Enjoyment of All Human Rights by Older Persons." Her charge was to review UN documents to identify key themes, trends, and best practices; participate in events around the world; and submit annual findings and recommendations.

Autonomy is an overarching theme in reports and statements issued by the Independent Expert between 2015 and 2017. She defined autonomy as the right to determine one's own rules and exercise choice; to live where and how one wants; to work, vote, and actively participate in all spheres of society; and to make decisions about one's own well-being without undue interference from family and others. In particular, she focused on autonomy with respect to dementia and long-term care.

Kornfeld-Matte points out that older people with dementias are increasingly being viewed as rights holders and that "autonomy-based" approaches to dementia have been adopted by national and international groups in Europe, the Americas, and Africa. These include providing older people with opportunities to make their wishes known in advance of disabling conditions through advance directives like powers of attorney and living wills. It includes ensuring access to "supported decision making" to help in explaining choices, simplifying them, or distilling them down to key points.

Kornfeld-Matte also notes a positive trend in setting standards for surrogate decision making, which includes measures like urging surrogates who do not know the preferences of those they are making decisions for to make an effort to identify past preferences. When that is not possible or practical, decision makers are directed to base decisions on "substitute decision making," which is their best interpretation of a person's will and preferences. The "best interest" standard, seen as the last resort, is making decisions based on what they think is best (see Chapter 10).

Ensuring autonomy for people with dementias also requires that protective measures like guardianships are free from conflicts of interest and undue influence; that they are proportional and tailored to people's circumstances; that they apply for the shortest time possible; and that they are subject to regular review by competent, independent, and impartial authorities or judicial bodies. Safeguards should also be based on the degree to which they affect peoples' rights and interests. Guardianships, for example, should require the highest levels of scrutiny and protection because of the significant extent to which they can restrict personal freedom and choice. Kornfeld-Matte reported that many nations were reforming their guardianship laws and addressing abuses by guardians.

In addressing autonomy in long-term care, she notes that countries have broadly defined "care" to include disease prevention; the provision of basic necessities like food, clothing, and shelter; and end-of-life care. Some have gone so far as to include ensuring an income in the event of unemployment, sickness, disability, or widowhood in old age as aspects of care, as well as care during disasters.

Kornfeld-Matte suggests that ensuring autonomy in healthcare requires acknowledging ageist attitudes among healthcare providers and moving away from needs-based, biomedical approaches that focus on disease and functional dependency, to a human rights–based approach in which older people's rights are an integral part of policies, planning, and service delivery. Autonomy further requires improving conditions in institutional settings and ensuring that staff are trained in geriatrics. Drawing from the Convention Against Torture and Other Cruel, Inhuman or Degrading Treatment or Punishment, Kornfeld-Matte makes the case that people have a right to palliative care and that denying them access to pain relief poses a threat to their rights to healthcare and to protection against cruel, inhuman, and degrading treatment.

Measures to enable and encourage families to provide home care and services are considered by some to be components of care. This may even include the provision of housing for caregivers. Some countries consider age-sensitive communities that allow older people with physical limitations to age in place, remain integrated and engaged in society, and to stay as active and independent as possible as components of care. Ensuring autonomy with respect to care further includes protecting older people's right to participate in health policy decisions.

Other issues that need to be addressed from an autonomy perspective, according to Kornfeld-Matte, are elder poverty and abuse. Poverty, she points out, deprives people of choices, basic necessities, and health. Measures to reduce it cover a broad range that include making prescription drugs and financial services (including loans, mortgages, or insurance) available.

Elder abuse is also a key theme, with particular attention paid to violence against older women and institutional practices that subject older people to intimidation, aggression, inappropriate behavior-control methods, negligence, and lack of care. Other concerns are raised about the plight of older refugees; elders facing conflicts, emergencies, or disasters; and those displaced by climate change. Kornfeld-Matte warns that austerity measures imposed by governments may pose particularly severe threats to older people's economic and financial autonomy and increase their risk of poverty, exclusion, and insecurity.

Applying autonomy to civil engagement requires that older people be included at all levels of society. Age cannot be used as a justification for exclusion from decision-making processes, active citizenship, holding office, and voting, which may require special arrangements for those in nursing homes and other institutional settings. And finally, the Independent Expert identified new potential threats to autonomy, which include assistive and robotics technology, artificial intelligence, and automation.

A Convention on the Rights of Older People

Calls for an international convention on the rights of older people have resounded since the Second World Assembly on Ageing. The measure, however, remains controversial. Proponents, which include most South American nations and NGOs, contend that when elders are not mentioned explicitly in human rights documents, they are ignored. Opponents, mostly groups and individuals in the United States, New Zealand, Canada, China, Switzerland, Norway, Russia, and European Union countries, counter that the universal civil rights protections contained in the International Bill of Human Rights and existing conventions obviate the need for a new convention. Some also worry that a convention opens the door for advocates for every subpopulation to demand special attention.

In "Strengthening Older People's Rights: Towards a UN Convention," nine prominent international organizations respond to critics' concerns, making the case for why a convention is needed and proposing what it should include (INPEA et al., 2011). It reiterates arguments offered in the past (e.g., that certain rights, like the right to Social Security, have more relevance in old age) and elaborates on its advantages. These include the claim that a convention would establish international standards for older people's rights and create a legal framework for obligating governments to ensure them. Other advantages are that a convention would permit human rights advocates to monitor situations in their countries and lobby governments to incorporate their international obligations into domestic law. It could potentially generate political will and public resources, promote awareness, educate the public (possibly leading to a shift in attitudes toward older people), and frame older persons' issues as an integral part of the broader international human rights agenda. It would offer specificity about human rights challenges faced by older people; articulate the duties of governments, the private sector, and individuals; and lead to better training for those involved in older persons' issues (e.g., healthcare personnel and the judiciary). It could further promote the view of older people as rights holders.

The report calls on advocates to discuss the human rights of older people at the local, regional, and international levels and ensure that older people have a central role. It directs them to educate the public about older people's rights and the shortcomings of the current system; to lobby their governments to support and advocate for a UN convention; and to work with WHO and other international organizations.

On June 15, 2015, member states of the Organization of American States (OAS) observed World Elder Abuse Awareness Day (WEAAD; described later) by signing the Inter-American Convention on Protecting the Human Rights of Older Persons. The document offers a model for an international convention that is very much in keeping with principles set forth in previous documents. Signatories to the Inter-American version include Argentina, Brazil, Chile, Costa Rica, and Uruguay.

Age as an International Public Health Issue

The UN also addresses aging from a public health perspective, an approach that predates the Second World Assembly on Ageing. In 2002, the year of the event, WHO released *Missing Voices: Views of Older Persons on Elder Abuse*, which applies a public health lens to abuse. WHO created the report in collaboration with INPEA. (UN initiatives in elder abuse are described later.)

Following the Second World Assembly, WHO stepped up its efforts in other age-related issues, using its resources and structures to establish international guidelines and standards, review policy needs, develop reports, and publish manuals, handbooks, and training materials for health workers. Working with partners, it has promoted aging in place and better access to health and public health services by older adults. It has continued to focus on eliminating discriminatory practices in health and public healthcare and on preventing or mitigating the impact of age-related health conditions. In recent years, WHO has turned its attention to Alzheimer's disease and other forms of dementia.

In 2010, WHO launched the Global Network of Age-Friendly Cities and Communities, partnering with communities around the world to "help people to remain independent for as long as possible, and provide care and protection when they are needed, respecting older people's autonomy and dignity" (WHO, 2015, p. 161).

Just as the field of public health in the United States has increasingly recognized that poverty, discrimination, immigration, race, and other social determinants are risk factors for disability and premature death (see Chapter 4), the same is true on the global stage. WHO and its partners have increasingly highlighted linkages between human rights and public health.

Age in the Context of Sustainable Social and Economic Development

In 2000, the UN hosted the historic Millennium Summit, the largest gathering of world leaders in history, to discuss the role of the UN at the turn of the century. There, leaders reaffirmed their commitment to UN ideals and agreed to work together to accomplish 17 Millennium Development Goals. The goals address poverty, hunger, health, education, climate change, gender equity, water, sanitation, energy, urbanization, environment, and social justice. A target date of 2015 was set to achieve the goals with follow-up progress reviews scheduled every 5 years.

Disappointed by the lack of attention to, and participation by, old people in the process, HAI enlisted others to form the Stakeholder Group on Ageing

(SGA) in 2013. The group has produced papers, helped older people participate in intergovernmental forums, and organized dialogues and events with member states and NGOs. It has also formed alliances with disability rights advocates and others.

As the 2015 deadline for the first stage of the Millennium Development Goals process approached, WHO released *Transforming Our World: The 2030 Agenda for Sustainable Development* to provide direction for ongoing work (United Nations Department of Economic and Social Affairs, 2015). Described as "a plan of action for people, planet, and prosperity," it was adopted by the General Assembly the same year. It laid out economic and social development goals under the slogan "leave no one behind." Member states are encouraged to conduct regular progress reviews and present their findings during sessions of the high-level political forum (HLPF), which meets under the auspices of the ECOSOC. The theme of the first review, which was conducted in 2017, focused on eradicating poverty. Of the 17 goals, 15 specifically mention older people.

To further ensure that old people would not be overlooked, WHO published the *Global Strategy and Action Plan on Ageing and Health* in 2017 (WHO, 2017). That same year, the Secretary-General also issued a plan for achieving agenda goals with respect to old people. In it, he points out the need for age-specific data to strengthen the international protection regime, eliminate financial exploitation and employment discrimination, establish adequate care facilities, and foster old people's participation in political life. The report also provides updates on developments in aging from regional commissions and offers recommendations to the General Assembly for ensuring that older people are not left behind in the implementation of the post-2015 development agenda (Stakeholder Group on Ageing, 2017).

NGOs have continued to take steps to ensure that older people's concerns are addressed in sustainable development plans. In its 2017 *Eradicating Poverty and Promoting Prosperity for Older Persons* position paper, SGA identified special considerations for old people in relation to six specific sustainable development goals (SDGs). With respect to Goal 1, for example, which is to eradicate extreme poverty and hunger, the SGA report described the causes of poverty in old age, emphasizing older women's vulnerability as a result of discrimination in pensions. It also describes the intergenerational impact of poverty and how increasing the wealth of old people can affect the well-being of younger generations. It notes, for example, that in South Africa, children in families that receive pensions are taller and have better nutritional status and that universal pensions in Georgia have yielded a 69%

reduction in child poverty rates. Similarly, with respect to Goal 3—to ensure healthy lives and promote well-being for everyone at all ages—SGA points out that HIV-AIDS and dementias are increasing among older people and calls for greater attention to older people's need for vaccinations.

ELDER ABUSE ON THE WORLD STAGE

As noted earlier, international interest in elder abuse began to grow during the post-Vienna Assembly period, with studies emerging from the United States, Australia, Canada, China, Norway, and Sweden in the 1980s. These were followed in the 1990s by studies from Argentina, Brazil, Chile, India, Israel, Japan, South Africa, the United Kingdom, and other European countries.

In 1997, members of the IFA formed the INPEA to stimulate research, raise awareness, promote education and training, and engage in advocacy (Krug, Dahlberg, Mercy, Zwi, & Lozano, 2002). INPEA is a membership organization with regional representatives in Africa, Asia, Europe, Latin America, North America, Oceania, the Middle East, and North Africa. It has special consultative status with ECOSOC and the DESA. It is also affiliated with the UN DPI and is a member of the Conference of NGOs (CoNGO).

Initiatives in elder abuse prevention by the UN fall into the same three categories described earlier—human rights, public health, and sustainable development—and are overseen by the same UN entities. They, too, are typically carried out in partnership with international NGOs.

WHO heads up the UN's public health efforts in elder abuse. These have included a collaboration with INPEA to produce the *Missing Voices: Views of Older Persons on Elder Abuse,* a groundbreaking exploration into how elder abuse is perceived by old people and caregivers around the world (WHO/ INPEA, 2002). Drawing from data collected through eight focus groups in developing countries (Argentina, Brazil, India, Kenya, and Lebanon) and developed ones (Austria, Canada, and Sweden), the report compares how old people are viewed. It also compares older people's perceptions about abuse with those of primary healthcare (PHC) workers.[4] The report defined abuse

---

[4] PHC workers are nonphysicians, ranging from medical assistants and nurse practitioners to village "mobilizers," "promotores," volunteers, or aides, who combine modern health practices with traditional healing to address basic health issues like nutrition and disease prevention. Most are women and are chosen by their communities for their leadership.

broadly as "a single or repeated act, or lack of appropriate action, occurring within any relationship where there is an expectation of trust which causes harm or distress to an older person" (WHO/INPEA, 2002, p. 3).

Focus group members identified three categories of abuse: (a) neglect (isolation, abandonment, and social exclusion); (b) the violation of human, legal, and medical rights; and (c) being deprived of choices, decisions, status, finances, and respect. Prominent themes that emerged included gender, socioeconomic status, social exclusion, poverty, traditional cultural roles, and human rights. An overarching theme was that women—particularly poor, childless, and widowed women—are affected most. Specific forms of abuse described by participants included:

- Abandonment in healthcare facilities. Participants from Kenya estimated that between 15% and 30% of older patients were abandoned in hospitals because they or their families could not pay for services.
- Placement in long-term care was considered by many to constitute abuse.
- Disrespect of elders was perceived to be among the most painful forms of abuse.
- Conflicts between daughters-in-law and mothers-in-laws were mentioned by respondents in India, Lebanon, and Austria. Participants noted that in India, a law intended to protect daughters-in-law from dowry-related abuse by in-laws, which requires police to make arrests based on the word of daughters-in-law alone, had led to instances in which daughters-in-law used the law as a form of abuse by making false police reports.

Group members also offered explanations for abuse. Some attributed it to changing social roles, including women entering the job market, which reduced the supply of family caregivers. Some blamed insufficient retirement income, highlighting the fact that only 30% of elders worldwide are covered by pensions. Inheritance laws were also mentioned; in some African countries, property is passed from male decedents to their oldest sons or back to their own families, leaving widows subject to abandonment and "property grabbing." Economic crises and downturns were also blamed, with participants from Argentina and Brazil noting that adult children often move back into parents' homes as a result of financial insecurity, sometimes forcing the elders to move out. Focus group members in Kenya complained that hospitals were rife with corruption and conflicts of interest.

Lack of access to healthcare and social services was another common theme. Decreasing rates of communicable diseases in the developing world over the past few decades have led to increased rates of long-term, disabling diseases and a heightened need for long-term care. Lack of public funding for services places financial pressures, stress, and burden on families and women in particular. Some focus group members saw healthcare workers as part of the problem, describing them as inadequately trained or not having enough time to listen. Some, however, viewed healthcare workers as victims too, citing their poor working conditions and low pay. Nurses at one hospital confessed that they "do not look kindly upon older patients who have trouble settling their bills" because their working conditions depended on patient revenue. Prejudice against geriatrics as a field was also mentioned, with focus group members observing that people who work with old people are viewed as less qualified by professionals and administrators and earn less.

Cultural traditions or beliefs were also brought up. In sub-Saharan Africa, acts of violence against elders in some countries stem from accusations of witchcraft or "mourning rites of passage" for widows that include cruel practices, sexual violence, forced marriages, and forced removal from homes.

On the other hand, cultural and religious values and traditions were described as important protective and mitigating factors. Religion, in particular, was seen as important by group members who cited examples of religious edicts to respect and care for older parents and religious institutions caring for destitute elders. Traditional healers play an important role in some countries by providing an alternative to healthcare systems that are underfunded, inaccessible to the poor, or seen as corrupt.

Focus group participants also suggested ways to stop elder abuse and neglect, which included raising awareness, encouraging positive contact between generations, empowering elders to advocate for themselves, and providing recreational facilities and opportunities to combat isolation. Solutions to "structural problems" included strong protective laws and improved healthcare.

The WHO/INPEA report further called for the development of a global elder abuse strategy and made recommendations for what to include. Several of the recommendations were subsequently implemented. For example, the report emphasized the need for the PHC and social services sectors to get more involved in identifying and responding to abuse. In response, WHO and the Center for Interdisciplinary Gerontology at the University of Geneva developed *A Global Response to Elder Abuse and Neglect: Building Primary Health Care Capacity to Deal With the Problem Worldwide*, an aging and life course (WHO, 2008). The report also identified the need for an instrument for PHC professionals in different geographical and cultural contexts to help them identify abuse, which led to the development of the Montreal Elder Abuse Suspicion Index (EASI; Yaffe, Wolfson, Lithwick, & Weiss, 2008).

Elder abuse is addressed as a social development matter in the *Global Strategy and Action Plan on Ageing and Health,* which calls for countries to build evidence on the scope and types of elder abuse in understudied areas (WHO, 2017). The plan also identifies the need for evidence-based guidance to countries in how to prevent elder abuse and strengthen their responses to it, information and support for abuse prevention efforts, and collaboration among international agencies and organizations.

National and international NGOs have also played a prominent role in elder abuse prevention. National organizations including Age Concern of New Zealand, the National Committee for the Prevention of Elder Abuse (United States), the Australia Prevention of Elder Abuse Task Force, the Canadian Network for the Prevention of Elder Abuse, the Japanese Center for the Prevention of Elder Abuse, and the Latin American Committee for the Prevention of Elder Abuse are examples. These groups play an important role as forums for professional exchange about policies and programs, including the feasibility and desirability of various approaches to prevention.

Black Blundell and Clare (2012) identified six intervention models of elder abuse prevention that countries have implemented or considered, pointing out the pros and cons of each.

1. The Adult Protective Services/Mandatory Reporting Model. While embraced in the United States (see Chapter 6) and explored by others, most countries have rejected the model in favor of rights-based advocacy approaches, citing concerns about infantilizing old people. Concerns about potential consequences have also been raised, including shaming and isolating victims and jeopardizing their housing. Some countries have adopted the model in limited ways, such as mandating abuse reporting in facilities.

2. The Domestic Violence Prevention Model. Originally developed to respond to spousal abuse, the model addresses power imbalances in relationships and focuses on empowering women, planning for safety, and promoting law enforcement interventions. Some countries have rejected the model out of concerns about the consequences of police involvement for victims, while others have adopted it in limited ways to address intimate partner abuse.

3. The Restorative Justice Model focuses on repairing family relationships and reducing risk by engaging victims, their families and social

networks, and offenders in mediation and family conferencing. Proponents contend that many victims want to stop abuse but also want to see abusive family members helped. They point out the model's preventive value and the benefits of involving communities in identifying solutions.

4. The Advocacy Model, which is used in Western and South Australia, focuses on supporting victims in speaking for themselves and making their own decisions with respect to rights and entitlements. Advocates may also represent victims' needs and concerns in court proceedings or other settings.

5. The Wellness/Active Service approach, which is widely used in Canada, focuses on decreasing old people's dependency and enhancing their quality of life, which are assumed to reduce the risk of abuse.

6. The Public Health Model (see Chapter 4) uses prevention strategies to avoid abuse and neglect, intervene during the early stages, mitigate its impact, and prevent recurrences.

INPEA has continued to explore emergent issues in elder rights and abuse prevention, including harmful cultural and traditional practices, violence against older widows, lack of social protection, extreme poverty, self-neglect, and dementia (S. Somers, personal communication, 2018). In 2006, it conducted an environmental scan that yielded responses from 362 respondents in 53 countries (Podnieks, Anetzberger, Wilson, Teaster, & Wangmo, 2010). Contributing factors to elder abuse that were identified included changing social and economic structures, victim isolation, inadequate knowledge of laws and services, intergenerational conflict, and poverty. The scan also revealed barriers that victims face in seeking resources, including cultural prohibitions, language and literacy issues, stigma, lack of mobility, lack of funding, and lack of Internet access. A second international scan was in progress in 2018.

Another major INPEA contribution to the field is WEAAD. Launched in 2006, the event highlights how elder abuse is viewed around the world and has prompted activities ranging from picnics, to policy hearings, to professional conferences. INPEA offers a tool kit to help nations conduct WEAAD events and, in 2017, tracked 167 events around the world.

U.S. INVOLVEMENT IN UN INITIATIVES ON AGING

U.S. involvement in UN-driven aging and elder abuse initiatives has been limited. This is not surprising given the fact that the United States has not ratified the CRPD or the Inter-American Convention on Protecting the Human Rights of Older Persons.

Some in government have supported greater U.S. involvement. Former U.S. Department of Health and Human Services (HHS) Assistant Secretary for Aging Kathy Greenlee sees value in UN initiatives like the CRPD. Although she sees as understandable the argument that conventions are not needed given that the Universal Declaration of Human Rights applies to everyone, she notes the gap between the Declaration's promise and reality and finds American officials' reluctance to get involved in UN initiatives as a missed opportunity to provide leadership (K. Greenlee, personal communication, April 16, 2018).

She did, however, make headway. In 2014, the U.S. Ambassador to the UN Human Rights Council, Keith Harper, hosted a special side event, Ending Elder Abuse: Breaking the Generational Cycle of Violence, during a council session in Geneva. Greenlee appealed to the council to address the needs of older women, pointing out that UN entities do not collect data on violence against women over the age of 49.

Charles Sabatino, director of the American Bar Association Commission on Law and Aging, sees U.S. reluctance to support UN conventions as stemming from both ideological and administrative concerns (C. Sabatino, personal communication, July 6, 2018). These include the government's aversion to obligations that fall outside its sovereignty and "treaty burden," or the demands of setting up costly new monitoring systems. Sabatino is among a handful of prominent leaders in the aging field in the United States who actively follow the work of the Open-Ended Working Group on Ageing, and provides updates on its work to the legal and aging services communities (Sabatino, 2017). He urges other NGOs to follow suit, pointing out that while UN conventions are nonbinding, they have had a remarkable influence on U.S. law, which usually starts in academic circles. He cites supported decision making (SDM) as an example. SDM, a process for providing guidance to people with limited or failing capacity that is highlighted in the CRPD, has clearly infiltrated thinking about guardianship and a growing number of states endorse its use in their guardianship laws. (For more on SDM, see Chapter 10.)

CONCLUSION

American advocates have much to gain from participating in the systematic, deliberative, and inclusive processes that the UN and international NGOs have applied to aging, elder rights, and elder abuse prevention. This includes the UN's tripartite approach to age as a matter of human rights, public health, and social development, each offering diverse strategies, resources, and opportunities. Dynamic and proactive strategies like mainstreaming and affirmative action can provide direction in confronting current, emergent, and yet to be revealed challenges. UN-produced, -supported, or -inspired research, reports, and treaties can further inform U.S. policy development and practice. International organizations also offer models and strategies for enlisting the public's participation in setting goals, tracking progress, marking milestones, and holding policy makers accountable for making good on promises.

Engaging in international initiatives further challenges American advocates to consider alternative approaches and recognize their own biases. It offers insights into contextual factors influencing older people's needs that can add richness and depth to a new elder justice paradigm. Perhaps even more importantly, it serves to remind advocates of the core values on which the UN was founded: "ensuring human rights and fundamental freedoms of all humans without distinction as to race, sex, language, or religion." Clearly, age is no exception.

REFERENCES

Black Blundell, B., & Clare, M. (2012). *Elder abuse in culturally and linguistically diverse communities: Developing best practice.* Perth, WA: Advocare.

Fredvang, M., & Biggs, S. (2012). *The rights of older persons: Protection and gaps under human rights law* (Social Policy Working Paper No. 16). Retrieved from https://social.un.org/ageing-working-group/documents/fourth/Rightsofolderpersons.pdf

International Network for the Prevention of Elder Abuse, International Federation on Ageing, Internet Learning Center-USA, International Association of Gerontology & Geriatrics, International Association of Homes and Services for the Ageing, HelpAge International, . . . AARP. (2011). *Strengthening older people's rights: Towards a UN convention.* Retrieved from https://social.un.org/ageing-working-group/documents/Coalition%20to%20Strengthen%20the%20Rights%20of%20Older%20People.pdf

Kanter, A. (2009). The United Nation Convention on the Rights of Persons with Disabilities and its implications for the rights of elderly people under international law. *Georgia State University Law Review, 25,* 527–572. Retrieved from https://readingroom.law.gsu.edu/cgi/viewcontent.cgi?article=2162&context=gsulr

Krug, E. G., Dahlberg, L. L., Mercy, J. A., Zwi, A. B., & Lozano, R. (Eds.). (2002). *World report on violence and health.* Geneva, Switzerland: World Health Organization.

Podnieks, E., Anetzberger, G. J., Wilson, S. J., Teaster, P. B., & Wangmo, T. (2010). WorldView environmental scan on elder abuse. *Journal of Elder Abuse & Neglect, 22*(1–2), 164–179. doi:10.1080/08946560903445974

Proclamation on Ageing, G.A. res. 47/5, 47 U.N. GAOR Supp. (No. 49) at 13, U.N. Doc. A/47/49 (1992).

Sabatino, C. (2017). Attention all non-profit groups in aging: Come to the United Nations. *Bifocal, 38*(4), 59–60. Retrieved from https://www.americanbar.org/groups/law_aging/publications/bifocal/vol_38/issue_4_april2017/attention-all-non-profit-groups-in-aging--come-to-the-united-nat

Stakeholder Group on Ageing. (2017). *Eradicating poverty and promoting prosperity for older persons* [Position paper]. Retrieved from https://sustainabledevelopment.un.org/content/documents/15726SGA.pdf

Till, C. (Ed.). (2011). The Madrid plan and you. *Ageways, 77.* Retrieved from http://www.helpage.org/silo/files/ageways-77-the-madrid-plan-and-you.pdf

United Nations. (n.d.-a). Article 1—Purpose. *Convention on the Rights of Persons with Disabilities.* Retrieved from https://www.un.org/development/desa/disabilities/convention-on-the-rights-of-persons-with-disabilities/article-1-purpose.html

United Nations. (n.d.-b). Article 28—Adequate standard of living and social protection. *Convention on the Rights of Persons with Disabilities.* Retrieved from https://www.un.org/development/desa/disabilities/convention-on-the-rights-of-persons-with-disabilities/article-28-adequate-standard-of-living-and-social-protection.html

United Nations. (1945). *Charter of the United Nations and Statute of the International Court of Justice.* New York, NY: United Nations, Office of Public Information.

United Nations. (1983). *Vienna international plan of action on aging.* New York, NY: Author. Retrieved from http://www.un.org/es/globalissues/ageing/docs/vipaa.pdf

United Nations. (2002). *Report on the Second World Assembly on Ageing.* Retrieved from http://undocs.org/A/CONF.197/9

United Nations Department of Economic and Social Affairs. (2009). *Report of the expert group meeting "rights of older persons."* Retrieved from https://www.un.org/esa/socdev/documents/ageing/reportofegm.pdf

United Nations Department of Economic and Social Affairs. (2015). *Transforming our world: The 2030 agenda for sustainable development.* Retrieved from https://sustainabledevelopment.un.org/content/documents/21252030%20Agenda%20for%20Sustainable%20Development%20web.pdf

United Nations Population Fund and HelpAge International. (2012). *Ageing in the twenty-first century: A celebration and a challenge.* Retrieved from http://www.unfpa.org/sites/default/files/pub-pdf/Ageing%20report.pdf

World Health Organization. (2008). *A global response to elder abuse and neglect: Building primary health care capacity to deal with the problem worldwide.* Retrieved from http://www.who.int/ageing/publications/ELDER_DocAugust08.pdf

World Health Organization. (2015). *World report on ageing and health.* Retrieved from http://apps.who.int/iris/bitstream/10665/186463/1/9789240694811_eng.pdf

World Health Organization. (2017). *Global strategy and action plan on ageing and health.* Retrieved from https://www.who.int/ageing/WHO-GSAP-2017.pdf?ua=1

World Health Organization & International Network for the Prevention of Elder Abuse. (2002). *Missing voices: Views of older persons on elder abuse.* Geneva, Switzerland: World Health Organization. Retrieved from http://apps.who.int/iris/bitstream/handle/10665/67371/WHO_NMH_VIP_02.1.pdf?sequence=1

Yaffe, M. J., Wolfson, C., Lithwick, M., & Weiss, D. (2008). Development and validation of a tool to improve physician identification of elder abuse: The Elder Abuse Suspicion Index (EASI)©. *Journal of Elder Abuse and Neglect, 20*(3), 276–300. doi:10.1080/08946560801973168

Elder Abuse as a Threat to Elder Justice

INTRODUCTION

The right to live free from abuse is seen today as a core component of elder justice. But *how* we prevent abuse is equally important. Do elder abuse policies pose threats to privacy, autonomy, choice, and dignity in the interests of safety and security? Are services available and accessible to everyone who needs them? Do policies and programs address discrimination and social determinants that heighten risk and impede solutions? This chapter applies an "elder justice lens" to the field of elder abuse prevention and suggests how it applies to policy, practice, and public consciousness.

THE CURRENT RESPONSE

Since elder abuse prevention laws and services were first enacted, researchers have attempted to measure the outcomes of specific services and interventions. Little attention, however, has gone to determining whether America's overall response to abuse is really solving the problem or simply offers piecemeal fixes.

Reporting laws and Adult Protective Services (APS) are central to the elder abuse response apparatus, a sign that communities have invested hope, if not resources, in the system's ability to protect and defend older adults. The aim of the system is to:

1. Identify cases that would not otherwise have come to light so help can be offered
2. Help victims recover from harm and trauma and reduce their future risk by providing, or making referrals for, services
3. Raise awareness by the public and professionals
4. Initiate action to constrain offenders and hold them accountable

© Springer Publishing Company DOI: 10.1891/9780826147578.0006

IDENTIFYING CASES

If identifying abuse that would not have come to light otherwise is a primary goal of mandatory reporting, it would follow that the success of reporting could be measured by increased reports. Yet first responders (mostly APS workers) are quick to point out that other factors besides the mandatory nature of reporting are at play. Some suggest, for example, that increases in reports have more to do with the publicity, training, and outreach that typically go along with reporting than with the mandates themselves.

APS personnel also point out the number of reports received and investigated reflects programs' resources (Nerenberg, 2016). When resources are scarce, outreach, publicity, and professional training are among the first functions to be eliminated and workers are forced to triage cases and prioritize the most urgent. The number of reports received by APS is also believed to be inversely proportional to communities' other health and social service resources—the fewer the resources, the greater the demand for APS. Others suggest that those who report would do so regardless of the mandate or penalties, as these measures are rarely enforced anyway (Backer, 2015).

Another way to look at the impact of reporting is to compare the number of reported cases to actual abuse prevalence. Researchers have suggested dramatic differences between the two. A 2010 elder abuse prevalence study reported that annually, only 1 in 23.5 cases comes to the attention of authorities; for financial abuse, that figure is 1 in 44; and for neglect, it has been estimated to be just 1 in 57 (Lifespan of Greater Rochester, Weill Cornell Medical Center of Cornell University, & New York City Department for the Aging, 2011).

Although comparing reported cases to actual abuse as a way to measure the impact of reporting may be sound conceptually, it is extremely difficult to put into practice. It would require accurate data on both reported cases and actual prevalence, neither of which is readily available. It is only recently that the federal government has begun to provide direction to states in collecting data on reports and the current capacity of states to do so varies widely.

Chapter 4 provided a brief summary of how epidemiological studies are used to establish prevalence and incidence and the challenges involved in applying the approach to elder abuse. Foremost among these are wide variations in how abuse is defined and lack of agreement by researchers, practitioners, and policy makers about what should be included. Variations of consequence include whether self-neglect is included as a category of abuse, whether abuse is limited to situations in which older people are vulnerable or dependent (as opposed to including able-bodied, older victims), and whether abuse refers exclusively to situations in which victims and abusers are family members, acquaintances, caregivers, or in "confidential relationships."

Without accurate information on reported cases and the actual extent of the problem, it is impossible at this point to evaluate the true impact of reporting laws in identifying cases. Since measuring the success of other systemic approaches such as public awareness campaigns and screening programs also require measuring changes in reports or incidence, their impact cannot be determined.

INTERVENTIONS AND SERVICES

Once APS workers receive reports, their task is to substantiate claims and see to it that victims get help. They do this by investigating what happened, assessing the risk of future abuse, and providing or making referrals for services that can prevent abuse and mitigate harm. Common interventions and services include the following:

- **Assessments.** An enormous amount of attention has gone to developing tools and techniques to assess whether abuse is occurring or is likely to, and the extent to which people are able to care for and protect themselves. There are many types:
  - Risk assessment tools alert investigators to signs and symptoms of abuse, factors that increase the likelihood that abuse may occur or recur, and the resources clients bring to bear (personal, financial, social networks, community resources) to protect themselves and recover (Gallione et al., 2017).
  - Cognitive assessments measure whether people are able to care for themselves and make decisions. In some abuse cases, purported victims' cognitive status is determinative of whether abuse has even occurred. Giving extravagant gifts is perfectly proper as long as donors understand what they are doing. If not, and gifts are made at the urging of others who stand to gain, the transfers may signal abuse. Cognitive assessments range from simple screening tools such as the Montreal Cognitive Assessment tool (Nasreddine et al., 2005) to the highly specialized Lichtenberg Financial Decision Rating Scale (LFDRS), which measures understanding of financial decisions as they relate to financial abuse and exploitation (Lichtenberg, Stoltman, Ficker, Iris, & Mast, 2015).

○ Functional assessments measure the extent to which people can perform everyday tasks that are key to survival, independence, health, or general well-being (e.g., walking, bathing, driving, shopping). They are used to determine whether people are able to manage on their own and the type of assistance, if any, they need to do so.

- **Crisis intervention** addresses the immediate effects of abuse and includes securing emergency funds, helping victims make police reports, petitioning for restraining orders, and blocking abusers' access to victims' assets. Crisis counseling addresses the trauma, anxiety, despair, fear, or hopelessness that victims may experience and can help them assess options and find services and resources.

- **Long-Term Care Ombudsman Programs (LTCOPs)** are charged to advocate on behalf of residents of nursing homes and residential care facilities. Volunteers routinely visit facilities, making themselves available to residents to accept complaints or respond to problems. When ombudsmen discover abuse or neglect, they typically report it to state regulatory and licensing agencies and inform victims and their families of available resources and remedies. Ombudsmen also assist in relocating residents when facilities are forced to close down. In a few states, including California, ombudsmen are charged with investigating reports of abuse and neglect by residents and witnesses under state mandatory reporting laws.

- **Guardians and public guardians** are court appointed representatives who manage the personal and/or financial affairs of vulnerable people who lack sufficient mental capacity to manage on their own (see Chapter 10). Professional guardians (family members and others may also be appointed to serve) may be proprietary or work for nonprofit agencies. Public guardians are publicly funded individuals or entities and are considered by many to be the "guardian of last resort" when other options are not available.

- **Emergency funds** may be needed for food, shelter, medical care, medications, emergency caregivers, mortgage payments, transportation, utilities, locks to secure victims' homes, court filing fees, repairs, and relocation costs.

- **Shelters** provide safe haven to avoid further victimization. Victims who have been evicted from their homes or abused or abandoned by caregivers may also need shelter while they secure new housing or care. Some need shelter because their homes are unsafe or unhealthy as a result of abuse, neglect, or self-neglect. A variety of shelter options exist, including accessible rooms in battered women's shelters, temporary stays in residential care facilities or apartments, and freestanding shelters designed specifically for elderly victims in dire need.[1]

- **Services for caregivers.** The risk of abuse or neglect by caregivers can potentially be reduced by skills training (e.g., managing difficult behaviors; information about disease progression) and services to reduce burden (e.g., respite care, support, and financial relief).

- **Counseling.** Group or individual counseling may address the immediate and long-term traumatic stress associated with abuse, codependency, depression, and diminished self-esteem. It may include emotional support while victims explore their options. Support groups or peer counselors can help victims break ties with abusers and establish social networks.

- **Daily money management,** which includes helping people pay bills or taxes, plan budgets, arrange for financial services, or apply for benefits, can serve as a safeguard against exploitation and neglect.

- **Legal assistance** includes helping victims secure orders of protection, annul fraudulent marriages and adoptions, sue for civil recoveries, create powers of attorney or revoke those that have been misused, contest guardianships, or recover losses. Lawyers and advocates also assist clients as they apply for or address problems with public benefits and resolve disputes with landlords, the Internal Revenue Service, and creditors.

- **Victim–witness assistance and advocacy** includes providing victims with information about the court process and the status of their cases; court accompaniment; and help securing compensation, restitution, and community services. Advocates also help victims exercise their rights to protection from abusers and to have a voice in sentencing or other decisions.

- **Support services** include meals, attendant care, adult day centers, friendly visitors, transportation, telephone reassurance, and other services that improve resilience, decrease vulnerability, and reduce dependency on others.

- **Case management** is an approach to "brokering" or coordinating services for individuals with multiple and changing needs. Case managers assess clients' physical and mental health and their ability to manage in their homes and communities using assessment tools like those described previously to develop care plans, often in consultation with professionals from multiple disciplines. They arrange for services, respond to problems or emergencies, and conduct routine reassessments to detect changes.

---

[1] Examples include Sacramento's Senior Safe House and the Weinberg Center at the Hebrew Home in Riverdale (New York). Another innovation model that is currently being planned by Elder Abuse Services, Inc., in Fresno, California, will offer a comprehensive array of restorative justice interventions.

- **Multidisciplinary Teams (MDTs).** The multidimensional and multifaceted nature of abuse has led to the dominance of MDTs in the field. MDTs bring together professionals from diverse disciplines and agencies to discuss difficult abuse cases; learn what services, approaches, and resources various disciplines and agencies bring to bear; share information and expertise; and identify and respond to systemic problems. Members typically include health and social service providers, law enforcement personnel, long-term care ombudsmen, mental health professionals, advocates, lawyers, and others. A variety of specialized teams have emerged in response to specific needs and challenges. These include Financial Abuse Specialist Teams (FASTs), which typically recruit members with expertise in banking practices, investments, trusts, estate planning, public benefits, and other financial matters. Other specialized MDTs include rapid response teams, fatality review teams, and teams operated by forensics centers (Navarro et al., 2016; Teaster, Nerenberg, & Stansbury, 2003).

Surprisingly little is known about the effectiveness of these services and interventions. After reviewing the literature on interventions from around the world and finding much of it lacking in scientific rigor, a team of leading elder abuse researchers concluded that just five demonstrated promise for preventing abuse: caregiving interventions, money management, helplines (to direct people to services), emergency shelters, and MDTs (Pillemer, Burnes, Riffin, & Lachs, 2016).

Like so many aspects of elder abuse, the lack of evidence about its prevention is largely a matter of resources. Few programs have the resources or capacity to track or measure the outcomes of specific interventions, particularly over the long term (Wangmo et al., 2014).

Another barrier to understanding the impact of services is that many service programs lack sufficient resources to do what they are supposed to. As noted earlier, if APS programs have not been fully implemented as envisioned for lack of funding, they may need to limit the number of reports they accept and investigate or the level of service they provide, thereby reducing their impact. Programs tend to prioritize clients in crisis or those with urgent needs as opposed to intervening when abuse is in its early stages when preventive measures could potentially reduce risk and prevent losses.

The same is true for other programs that provide the services listed earlier. If programs lack sufficient resources to operate the way they are supposed to, poor performance may reflect lack of support rather than flaws in the programs. Evaluations of programs and services are therefore needed that not only consider impact under optimal conditions, but that also consider whether the programs are working the way they are supposed to. Also needed are studies to determine the point at which underfunded programs become futile or counterproductive and to explore potential modifications and enhancements that can improve effectiveness and efficiency under nonoptimal conditions.

Evaluating the service response to elder abuse requires going beyond evaluating the effectiveness of individual services to assessing service delivery systems. This includes ensuring that needed services are available and well-coordinated.

Many communities lack the services listed earlier. Those that are in particularly short supply include public guardians, ombudsmen, legal assistance programs, law enforcement, courts, shelters, case management programs, and transportation. Even when services are available, they may not be accessible or acceptable to certain groups. Fairness and equity in access to services are discussed later.

Lack of coordination among service providers further exacerbates the problem. The failure of APS, law enforcement, public health, agencies responsible for licensing and overseeing professionals and businesses, and others to coordinate their efforts can result in inconsistencies in how cases are handled, and confusion about who has authority and responsibility.

Identifying and exposing abuse without providing services to treat it raises ethical and practical concerns. It endangers victims and conveys the message that abuse is intractable, that APS and other service providers are ineffective, or that abusive conduct will be tolerated.

Obviously, services are only effective if victims use them. Studies of service utilization have identified key factors in predicting whether or not victims seek out and use services. Factors that have been found to best predict whether those who need services do in fact access them include the type and severity of the abuse and whether or not those in need have sought out and used services in the past (Burnes, Rizzo, Gorroochurn, Pollack, & Lacks, 2016). Help-seeking is also correlated with gender, health, how victims perceive danger, their relationships with perpetrators, and whether they, themselves, sought help or others did so for them. Victims of financial abuse who are most likely to use services are females in poor health who perceive their danger as high and have sought help in the past. Hispanics and married individuals were found to be less likely to seek out and use services generally. John Dussich, Fresno State professor emeritus of criminology and a pioneer in the field of victimology, has observed the same to be true for members of other marginalized groups, including the Hmong, Punjabi, and Native American communities in California (J. Dussich, personal communication, July 25, 2018).

Georgia Anetzberger, a leading expert in APS and elder abuse, believes that clients' trust in the agencies that provide services is key to their getting the help they need (G. Anetzberger, personal communication, May 24, 2018). She suggests that in the case of APS, trust has been undermined by unrealistic expectations about programs. She attributes this to the fact that, over time, APS programs have been hollowed out and offer fewer of the direct services the programs were originally created to provide, which makes them appear weak.

Even less is known about why those who witness abuse choose to report or decide against doing so. An emerging body of research on "bystander interventions" is revealing the decision-making processes of professionals who are not covered under reporting laws. Researchers have noted, for example, that when professionals suspect financial abuse, uncertainty about victims' mental capacity is among the factors that discourage them from acting (Gilhooly et al., 2013).

Negative perceptions or distrust of the system discourage others. With respect to APS, researchers at the FrameWorks Institute, a communications research and consulting firm, found that the public does not understand the program or what will happen if they report (Volmert & Lindland, 2016). Because the elder abuse reporting system mimics the better understood child abuse reporting system, it seems likely that some mistakenly assume that victims will be treated like children, which could involve such drastic measures as removing them from their homes to protect them. Other would-be reporters may fear misconstruing what they witness and making matters worse or damaging their relationships with the parties involved.

Confidentiality restrictions that prevent APS and others from disclosing outcomes to those who report may also have a chilling effect. It can contribute to victims' and witnesses' anxieties about reporting or affirm suspicions that reporting is futile or counterproductive. Anecdotal evidence further suggests that some see reporting as coercive and believe that it infringes upon, rather than protects, victims' rights.

APS, POORLY DEFINED AND UNDERSTOOD

Confusion about APS is not just a matter of public perception. Rather, from the start, the field has struggled with a lack of clarity about its goals, roles, and methods. Much of the problem, according to Paula Mixson, another leading expert in the field, can be attributed to the merging of APS's original charge with its abuse reporting duties, creating what she calls "the decades-long, research-confounding, progress-impeding impasse among the elder abuse and adult protective community around reporting, age and disability eligibility criteria, and self-neglect" (Mixson, 2010, p. 26). As described in Chapter 2, APS was created to provide a safety net of social and legal services for adults who could not meet their own needs and lacked formal or informal supports to assist. The formal duty to respond to abuse reports came later.

APS leaders adopted the term "self-neglect" to refer to cases involving non-abused clients whom they were charged to serve and who comprised a large portion of their caseloads (Teaster, Dugar, Mendiondo, Abner, & Cecil., 2006). These included clients whose needs were not met for myriad reasons, including dementia, trauma, mental illness, substance abuse, and poverty. As Rosalie Wolf (2000) pointed out years later, advocates calculated that Congress's interest in elder abuse and APS's central role in responding to it would create a potential new stream of funding for APS. Attaching the "self-neglect" label to nonabused clients, they believed, would ensure that any new funds could be used to serve these clients as well. As was also noted in Chapter 2, the federal assistance to states that Congress had called for never materialized. Instead, APS was left with a definition that remains problematic.

The term "self-neglect" does little to shed light on commonalities among those who fall within the category. Some consider it stigmatizing, implying that these individuals lack the discipline or motivation to take care of themselves when in fact their conditions may be outside of their control. Removing self-neglect from the definition of elder abuse could potentially lend greater clarity to elder abuse as well as highlight the need for homelessness prevention interventions, behavioral health and substance abuse programs, affordable chronic care management, harm reduction, financial relief, treatment for trauma, and support for caregivers, all of which are critically needed.

Mixson suggests that the term also contributes to a blurring of the roles and responsibilities of various community agencies. In response, she offers a prescription for differentiating self-neglect from abuse by others:

- Acknowledge that "self-neglecting" individuals may need a wide range of social services, including financial assistance, mental healthcare, or long-term case management, that cannot be provided by APS alone. Meeting these needs over time should be a shared responsibility among community agencies.
- Divide neglect into categories:
  - "Societal neglect" resulting from ignorance about services, poverty, lack of resources, cultural and language barriers, and financial or logistical barriers to access services
  - Neglect resulting from capacity deficits in combination with other factors that prevent those in need from using services that are available

Mixson (2010) goes further. She calls for distinguishing clients who need traditional case management from those in need of protective services based on their ability to determine their own needs and consent to (or refuse) services. This would make it clear that only those who cannot protect themselves need protection from others. She also suggests using extent of vulnerability instead of age as an eligibility criteria for APS.

Anetzberger too suggests that over time APS programs have been saddled with reports that are better responded to by other systems (G. Anetzberger, personal communication, May 24, 2018). For example, she contends that sexual abuse against older women belongs with domestic violence programs and fraud belongs in the criminal justice system. She would also like to see APS programs focus more on abandonment and providing support to caregivers.

RAISING PUBLIC AWARENESS ABOUT ABUSE

Public awareness campaigns have generally focused on alerting those who are likely to observe abuse to its signs and symptoms, encouraging victims and witnesses to report, deterring abusers, instructing victims and families how to protect themselves, and changing attitudes about older people. Some seek to instill fear about the consequences of not reporting, while others attempt to foster trust in agencies that can help.

Little is known about what approaches work best. The few studies that have tracked the impact of awareness campaigns suggest that while they do increase reports, the change is temporary. Studies on the extent to which training increases reports by professionals have focused on specific groups. They suggest that while training has resulted in increased reporting by certain groups, little or no impact has been observed for others. Recent studies of emergency room personnel, who are likely to see the most egregious cases, have found that an overwhelming majority fail to identify abuse (Evans, Hunold, Rosen, & Platts-Mills, 2017; Rodríguez, Wallace, Woolf, & Mangione, 2006).

According to researchers at the FrameWorks Institute, "While elder abuse receives some media coverage and advocates work tirelessly to bring attention to the issue, policymakers and the public largely ignore the issue in favor of other concerns" (Volmert & Lindland, 2016, p. 1). They further observe that the public has a paternalistic view of abuse and what to do about it.

The issue of elder abuse triggers models of older people as deteriorating and dependent and prompts paternalistic thinking . . . that it is up to younger people to make decisions for older people. When this mode of thinking is active, the public understands older people as objects to be cared for and protected, rather than as actors with voices and minds of their own. (Volmert & Lindland, 2016, p. 4)

The FrameWorks Institute team also discovered glaring disparities between how abuse is viewed by the public and professionals. This bodes poorly for public awareness campaigns that are planned and executed by service providers, which most are.

CONSTRAINING PERPETRATORS AND HOLDING THEM ACCOUNTABLE

Little is known about what happens to perpetrators who are identified through reporting, including whether they are prosecuted, incarcerated, forced to pay restitution, served with restraining orders, barred from employment, court-ordered into treatment or educational programs (e.g., for substance abuse, mental health problems, anger management, or caregiver education), or forced to pay fines or penalties. Even less is known about the deterrent effect of these measures or their impact on recidivism. Common legal interventions that are used to hold perpetrators accountable are described in Chapter 7.

HOW WELL DOES THE ELDER ABUSE PREVENTION SYSTEM ACHIEVE SOCIAL JUSTICE GOALS?

Adopting an elder justice approach to elder abuse prevention requires ridding the system of ageism and adopting approaches that advance personal autonomy, independence, respect, and self-determination. It further requires that help be provided in ways that are fair and equitable, which requires addressing systemic as well as interpersonal risk factors and social determinants. The first step toward achieving these goals is to critically consider:

1. Is the system ageist or otherwise stigmatizing?
2. Does it conform to ethical and legal standards?
3. Does it address the "big picture" (systemic risks and solutions)?
4. Are there conflicts of interest?

I. Is the Current System Ageist or Stigmatizing?

The specter of ageism and paternalism that has hung over the elder abuse response system since its inception may well stem from its being patterned on child protective services. Older victims are infantilized by the program's inherent assumption they cannot or will not seek help for themselves as the result of physical, communication, or cognitive barriers or because they are under the control of abusers. As noted in Chapter 2, APS programs already existed when mandatory reporting laws were enacted and were originally created to serve dependent or vulnerable adults, which may account for these lingering biases.

It was these concerns that prompted early leaders in the field to formulate principles of good practice that highlight choice, least restrictive alternatives, personal autonomy, and due process. They also assert clients' right to refuse help under normal circumstances. Despite these efforts, the taint of ageism persists. A respondent to a New York survey of stakeholders puts it bluntly:

> For those older adults with the ability to make decisions regarding risks they confront, mandatory reporting represents an invasive and paternalistic approach to assistance. For example, in most states, when a person is 59 and a physician identifies that s/he is being abused, the physician can use a person-centered approach to care, determining with the patient the best response. But if the patient is 60 years old (or 65, depending on the state), that same doctor would be mandated to report. This triggers an investigation, which may or may not be welcomed by the older adult. If it is not welcome, it can rupture the trusted, sacred doctor-patient relationship, with negative consequences . . . not returning to the doctor for medical care. (Backer, 2015, "Limitations of Mandatory Reporting")

Whether APS programs deserve the ageist label is a difficult call since ageism has not been clearly defined or quantified. Some service providers rely on makeshift or shorthand tests. Whenever the question arose during meetings of a San Francisco MDT, members were asked to consider: "Would we be recommending this intervention if the client were thirty as opposed to eighty?"

Clearly, ageism is in the eye of the beholder, and beholders whose views matter are victims, service providers, policy makers, program developers, and the public. Victims and the vulnerable will not seek out or accept services they perceive as paternalistic or disrespectful, nor will witnesses report. Service providers will not employ methods they view as demeaning or offensive, and the public will not appeal to lawmakers to fund them.

Rooting out ageism will require reevaluating how abuse and its victims are defined. A primary consideration, for example, is whether reporting laws are inherently ageist by suggesting that all people over a certain age need protection. It will further require determining if investigations, response systems, and services are unjustifiably invasive or coercive. And finally, it will require assessing the need for new or expanded services that empower and enhance independence and autonomy.

2. Does the Elder Abuse Response System Conform to Ethical and Legal Standards?

Adopting a social justice approach to elder abuse requires living up to the principles of autonomy, least restrictive alternatives, and privacy defined by APS leaders and others. It requires that protective and preventive services be delivered in ways that are fair and inclusive. This includes removing barriers faced by disenfranchised groups, active outreach to underserved groups, and making services available to the nonaffluent.

Ensuring justice further requires determining whether elder abuse policy and practices infringe on constitutionally protected rights as some have suggested. Chapter 7, which focuses on legal concepts and the legal system, addresses these questions and, in particular, looks at mandatory reporting from a constitutional perspective.

Adopting a social justice approach may also warrant deciding if and when violations of individual rights should be considered to be elder abuse (e.g., and therefore subject to elder abuse remedies and actions) and conversely, when does elder abuse (or interventions to prevent it) violate individual rights? Answers to questions like these will undoubtedly have implications for practice that need to be explored. For example, would labeling the violation of a right (e.g., the right to contest guardianship) as abuse lead to it being taken more seriously and compel action? Other common violations of individual rights that are often not taken seriously include disregarding advance directives and age-based discrimination in the work setting, housing, and healthcare. Violations of older people's privacy are also common, and even such blatant abuse as posting humiliating photographs or videos of older people that are taken surreptitiously on the Internet are likely to go unpunished (Ornstein, 2015).

3. Addressing Systemic Abuses, Risks, and Barriers

Researchers estimate that one in nine older people are victims of abuse, neglect, and exploitation (Acierno et al., 2010). Worldwide, an estimated one in six older adults, or 141 million seniors, are victimized (Yon, Mikton, Gassoumis, & Wilber, 2017). Many experts agree that even these staggering figures are undercounts. Eradicating a problem of this magnitude cannot be accomplished on a case-by-case basis or by focusing exclusively on individual acts, risk factors, and interpersonal dynamics. This is particularly true in the case of large-scale or systemic abuses, such as neglect or corruption by nursing home chains that affect many residents or mass marketing fraud. Combatting abuses like these effectively will require new laws, regulations, and enforcement measures at the state, national, or international levels.

Significantly reducing abuse will also require addressing social determinants associated with it (see Chapter 4), which include low income and socioeconomic status, financial dependence, poor health, functional impairment, social isolation, ethnicity, and previous exposure to traumatic events (Acierno et al., 2010; Pillemer et al., 2016; Yon et al., 2017).

Some, including Robert Butler (1969), have speculated that abuse stems from societal attitudes toward older people and ageist social norms (see Chapter 3). This would seem to suggest that the public's perceptions and attitudes about abuse need to change to significantly eliminate the problem. To date, however, there is little empirical evidence to substantiate the assumption (Pillemer et al., 2016).

4. Conflicts of Interest

Just as members of different disciplines bring different skills, beliefs, and resources to abuse prevention, they also bring different perspectives on justice and rights, which may be in conflict.

APS workers, ombudsmen, legal assistance providers, and others operate in the advocacy mode, which means that their role is to vigorously defend their clients' rights. Although they may address the needs of victims' families or caregivers to some extent, when interests compete, clients' interests come first.

In contrast, law enforcement personnel operate under the principle that society sets standards of conduct, encoded in criminal laws, which everyone must abide by for the greater good of society. When criminals break the law, it is "the People" to whom they answer. Police and sheriffs are serving in the interests of the people when they investigate crimes and apprehend criminals. The same is true for prosecutors, judges, and juries. Although criminal justice professionals take victims' wishes into account, victims are considered to be witnesses to the crimes committed against them and have little control over what happens in criminal proceedings. They may even be compelled to give testimony and provide evidence against their will (see Chapter 7).

The fact that professionals from different disciplines view and pursue justice in different ways can lead to conflicting opinions about how cases should be handled. This is not a problem for those who recognize the importance of applying checks and balances to ensure that the rights and interests of all parties—victims, perpetrators, and society—are considered.

These differences may, however, become problematic, especially when professionals' roles are unclear. APS workers' roles as advocates may be compromised by reporting laws that require them to report abuse to law enforcement against clients' wishes or to assist law enforcement as they investigate, substantiate claims, and collect evidence. Doing so may damage their relationships with clients, particularly when prosecutors pressure them to testify or provide evidence. Some APS programs have acknowledged the conflict by assigning certain workers to investigate and others to provide services and advocacy.

In some cases, APS workers may be held responsible for ensuring due process for alleged perpetrators, creating another potential conflict of interest. This additional burden arises in the context of abuser registries. APS programs that collect and share information about alleged perpetrators must ensure that abusers are treated fairly, particularly if the information collected is used to build legal cases against them or bar them from employment. It also potentially exposes APS workers and programs to liability if they breach perpetrators' rights.

Advocates may also be faced with balancing rights against one another. An example is balancing the right to freedom against the right to safety when clients choose to remain in unsafe situations. The greater the risks to either freedom or safety, the more highly charged these conflicts become. When guardianship is being considered as an option, it is of particular concern as it essentially strips people of basic freedoms. For that reason, it is typically viewed as the option of last resort and is only contemplated in the face of substantial risks to the safety and security of clients and others.

Abuse prevention programs may face competing interests when setting priorities and allocating resources. They may need, for example, to balance resources for helping single victims (ensuring individuals' rights) with those needed to pursue societal goals (e.g., outreach aimed at improving access to services by underserved groups in the interest of fairness).

MOVING TOWARD SOLUTIONS

An elder justice approach to elder abuse prevention requires that individual rights and social justice principles are reflected in abuse prevention theory, practice, policy, and public understanding of the problem. Accomplishing this begins with adopting a conceptual model of elder abuse that reflects social justice goals and ideals and that suggests approaches to achieving them. It will require putting theory into practice through policy and service programs, tracking success, changing public perceptions, and building partnerships with other networks devoted to social justice.

An Elder Justice Framework for Elder Abuse Prevention

Adopting elder justice approaches to elder abuse starts by changing how we think about abuse. This begins by adopting a conceptual framework that reflects a social justice and individual rights perspective.

Conceptual models reveal the thinking behind approaches to problems. They reflect assumptions about causes and solutions that can guide research, policy, and practice. They also reveal biases. Critical theories, as the name implies, offer critiques for why problems exist, and "models of change" actively promote reform.

Research and practice in elder abuse has, for the most part, been based on conceptual models that focus on the personal characteristics of victims and perpetrators and the interpersonal dynamics between them. Personal characteristics of victims that have been explored include gender, age, dependency, cognitive status, financial literacy, social isolation, and risk-taking. Personal characteristics of abusers, which are considered to be more important, include mental health problems, substance abuse, emotional and financial dependency on victims, and unemployment (Acierno et al., 2010).

Models that have frequently been referenced to explain interpersonal dynamics between victims and abusers include social exchange theory, which focuses on imbalances between what victims and abusers contribute to relationships; domestic violence theory, which describes how perpetrators exercise power and control over intimate partners; and the caregiver stress theory, which describes the dynamics between care providers and those they care for. Other theories that have been explored include the intergenerational transmission of violence and family systems theories.

Some models used to explain interpersonal dynamics in elder abuse can also be applied to social relationships. For example, in addition to explaining the give-and-take between individuals, social exchange theory can explain elders' reciprocal relationships to their communities and society. For example, Harbison suggests that the belief by some that old people take more from society than they contribute with respect to entitlement programs might explain the lack of spending for critical protective services for older adults (Harbison et al., 2012).

Similarly, feminist theory, which describes the role of gender in shaping the lives of women and girls, has been applied to both explain how gender-based power and control dynamics give rise to individual acts of violence and at the systemic level to explain society's complicity and failure to combat the problem forcefully.

In declaring elder abuse to be a public health issue (see Chapter 4), the field adopted the ecological model, which has been applied to elder abuse in general as well as specific types of abuse (Richard et al., 2008; Schiamberg & Gans, 1999; Wangmo et al., 2014). Here again, the focus in applying the model has been on individual and interpersonal interpretations and interventions, although that appears to be changing. In recent years, the ecological model has been applied to "polyvictimization" in elder abuse, which refers to the multiple co-occurring types of abuse and their repetitive nature (Teaster, 2017). Researchers in polyvictimization have acknowledged that "macrosystems," which include ideological values, norms, and cultural and institutional patterns, contribute to abuse.

Of all the models that have been proposed to explain elder abuse, the ecological model seems best suited for incorporating elder justice principles. It has already been applied to specific forms of elder abuse and offers the breadth, scope, and flexibility to address an even wider range of concerns. It is also geared toward action. The model is therefore proposed in Chapter 12 as the overarching framework for elder justice writ large.

Expanding the Ecological Approach to Elder Abuse

The ecological model of elder abuse can be expanded upon to ensure that social justice principles are reflected in the four levels of abuse prevention (see Chapter 4). Approaches to abuse prevention at the individual and interpersonal levels need to be reviewed to detect ageism and threats to individual rights (e.g., threats to victims' privacy, autonomy or freedom, and to both victims' and perpetrators' rights to due process; see Chapter 7). Interventions are also needed that highlight independence, choice, and autonomy. This may, for example, include a greater focus on restorative measures such as mediation (Groh, 2013), supported decisionmaking (SDM), greater attention to guardianship reform and monitoring, and abuse prevention interventions that seek to achieve victims' goals.

Prevention at the community and societal levels needs to focus on the social determinants of elder abuse and point the way to structural and systemic reforms. It requires recognizing and responding to abusive institutional and systemic practices through public policy, robust enforcement of regulations, and punitive measures against those responsible. This includes interventions like class action lawsuits to hold corporate entities accountable and provide justice for multiple victims who lack the means to seek justice individually.

Whistleblower protections are needed to protect employees of long-term care facilities from retribution for reporting systemic abuse. Attorneys also need incentives to take cases that have broad social impact and provide options for the nonaffluent. Law enforcement officials also need encouragement and resources to pursue perpetrators of systemic abuses, particularly when they pose an ongoing threat to others.

The expanded ecological model of elder abuse described here will need to be incorporated into the broader elder justice agenda. This is done in Chapter 12, which further proposes specific strategies and actions.

Measuring Success

As noted earlier, little is known about the impact of abuse prevention interventions and services in preventing abuse, particularly with respect to systemic approaches and systemic problems. Still less is known about the negative or positive effects that services have on the rights of the parties involved; at present, criteria for defining those rights do not yet even exist. Measures are also needed to define what success would look like. A promising step in that direction is a study that used "goal attainment measures" to determine how well abuse prevention interventions reflect clients' individual needs and meet their goals, which might be construed as a rough measure of autonomy and self-determination (Burnes & Lachs, 2017).

Determining whether systemic solutions result in systemic change is even more challenging. As noted earlier, measuring the impact of systemic interventions like state laws is virtually impossible in the absence of prevalence measures. Lack of prevalence data also makes it impossible to measure the impact of long-term care policy, tax policy, entitlement programs, and immigration policy on elder abuse. Nor is it possible to measure the impact of interventions aimed at reducing economic and health disparities that are now known contributors to risk. Applying an elder justice lens to elder abuse will require greater attention to policies like these that address social determinants of elder abuse.

Honest appraisals of the elder abuse response system should include cost–benefit analyses and comparisons to alternative approaches to see if resources could be better spent.

As noted in Chapter 2, when Title XX funds were block-granted to states, a rationale for doing so was that it would permit states to serve as laboratories of innovation by giving them discretion in using federal protective service dollars. That did not happen, with only one state, New York, opting for voluntary, as opposed to mandatory, reporting. It is, therefore, the only state level alternative approach against which state mandatory reporting programs can be compared. Although formal comparisons have not been made, the survey of New York stakeholders mentioned earlier offers insights about its benefits and further suggests variations for consideration by New York and other states (Backer, 2015):

- **Mandatory training** to healthcare workers, social workers, and others as a requirement for state licensure
- **Permissive reporting** that includes procedures and protocols for voluntary reporting that ensure immunity from liability
- **Limited mandated reporting** that is narrowly focused to protect adults with cognitive impairments that impede their decision-making ability

Anetzberger notes that cities and counties have taken different approaches to abuse response systems that can serve in lieu of state-to-state comparisons (G. Anetzberger, personal communication, May 24, 2018). Her own state of Ohio serves as an example. Because the state did not provide funds or direction to counties for implementing programs, they developed their own models using Social Services Block Grant (SSBG) funds and local tax levies, which the state allows them to collect, for services. Franklin County's APS program, which is overseen by the county's Department of Job and Family Services, funds the county's Office on Aging to receive elder abuse reports and conduct investigations. As a recipient of senior levy funds as well, the Office on Aging provides direct services to prevent abuse. In Summit County, APS takes reports and conducts investigations but then, if indicated, refers cases to the county's Department of Public Health, which it funds for case management and linkage to other local agencies providing direct services. What is key to both programs' success is that they are integrated into broader systems of care and are well-funded.

Changing Perceptions

The FrameWorks Institute report on elder abuse suggests that the public will respond favorably to casting elder abuse as a human rights issue (Volmert & Lindland, 2016). Conveying the message that abuse is a violation of human rights and that APS and other responders are charged to defend those rights may, therefore, be more effective in prompting reports than casting abuse as a crime or victims as frail and vulnerable.

Framing those who report abuse as champions of elder rights may well encourage reporting. Similarly, rights-based outreach messages may serve to portray professionals who respond to reports more favorably and rid the field of paternalistic overtones. Outreach campaigns can help build trust in agencies and institutions by providing accurate information about what they do (and what they cannot) and creating realistic explanations.

Rights-based outreach campaigns can further prompt the public to get involved by explaining systemic failures associated with abuse (e.g., lax enforcement of nursing home regulations) and point out the need for heightened protections and criminal justice responses. They can direct the public to opportunities to get involved in reform efforts.

Building Partnerships

Elder abuse prevention advocates have long recognized the importance of collaboration and partnerships in serving victims. Adopting a social justice approach to elder abuse prevention will require them to go further to develop partnerships with the aging and social justice advocacy networks and work collaboratively to affect systemic change. It will require raising awareness about the central role of health and mental health services, nutrition programs, case management, in-home services, emergency shelters, transportation, and other safety net programs in preventing abuse. It will further require building political support and alliances.

CONCLUSION

If, as the Elder Justice Act and advocates assert, freedom from abuse and neglect is a fundamental right, changes are needed in how we think about the problem and respond to it. As a right, freedom from abuse must be viewed in relation to those rights afforded to people of all ages, races, genders, and beliefs. It needs to be incorporated into the broader paradigm of social justice and human rights.

Although those in the field of elder abuse prevention have shown little appetite or enthusiasm for making fundamental changes to the existing abuse prevention system, there are compelling reasons for doing so. The field has been revisiting the same controversies and barriers for decades. Pressures on the existing system are mounting with the burgeoning of the elderly population, the loosening of regulatory protections, and ongoing threats to safety net and entitlement programs. Challenges to the constitutionality of current practices may well be in the offing (see Chapter 7). For over four decades, advocates, researchers, and service providers have described the field of elder abuse as being in its infancy. It is finally time to come of age.

REFERENCES

Acierno, R., Hernandez, M. A., Amstadter, A. B., Resnick, H. S., Steve, K., Muzzy, W., & Kilpatrick, D. G. (2010). Prevalence and correlates of emotional, physical, sexual, and financial abuse and potential neglect in the United States: The National Elder Mistreatment Study. *American Journal of Public Health, 100*(2), 292–297. doi:10.2105/ajph.2009.163089

Backer, P. R. (2015, January 8). New York state doesn't have mandatory reporting: Good or something to change? [Blog post]. Retrieved from http://nyceac.com/elder-justice-dispatch-new-york-state-doesnt-have-mandatory-reporting-good-or-something-to-change

Burnes, D., & Lachs, M. S. (2017). The case for individualized goal attainment scaling measurement in elder abuse interventions. *Journal of Applied Gerontology, 36*(1), 116–122. doi:10.1177/0733464815581486

Burnes, D., Rizzo, V. M., Gorroochurn, P., Pollack, M., & Lachs, M. S. (2016). Understanding service utilization in cases of elder abuse to inform best practices. *Journal of Applied Gerontology, 35*, 1036–1057. doi:10.1177/0733464814563609

Butler, R. N. (1969). Age-ism: Another form of bigotry. *The Gerontologist, 9*(4), 243–246. doi:10.1093/geront/9.4_part_1.243

Evans, C. S., Hunold, K. M., Rosen, T., & Platts-Mills, T. F. (2017). Diagnosis of elder abuse in U.S. emergency departments. *Journal of the American Geriatrics Society, 65*(1), 91–97. doi:10.1111/jgs.14480

Gallione, C., Dal Molin, A., Cristina, F. V. B., Ferns, H., Mattioli, M., & Suardi, B. (2017). Screening tools for identification of elder abuse: A systematic review. *Journal of Clinical Nursing, 26*(15–16), 2154–2176. doi:10.1111/jocn.13721

Gilhooly, M. L., Cairns, D., Davies, M., Harries, P., Gilhooly, K. J., & Notley, E. (2013). Framing the detection of financial elder abuse as bystander intervention: Decision cues, pathways to detection and barriers to action. *The Journal of Adult Protection, 15*(2), 54–68. doi:10.1108/14668201311313578

Groh, A. (2013). A community responds to elder abuse. In J. P. J. Dussich & J. Schellenberg (Eds.), *The promise of restorative justice: New approaches for criminal justice and beyond* (pp. 37–53). Boulder, CO: Lynne Rienner.

Harbison, J., Coughlan, S., Beaulieu, M., Karabanow, J., VanderPlaat, M., Wildeman, S., & Wexler, E. (2012). Understanding "elder abuse and neglect": A critique of assumptions underpinning responses to the mistreatment and neglect of older people. *Journal of Elder Abuse & Neglect, 24*(2), 88–103. doi:10.1080/08946566.2011.644086

Lichtenberg, P. A., Stoltman, J., Ficker, L. J., Iris, M., & Mast, B. (2015). A person-centered approach to financial capacity assessment: Preliminary development of a new rating scale. *Clinical Gerontologist, 38*(1), 49–67. doi:10.1080/07317115.2014.970318

Lifespan of Greater Rochester, Weill Cornell Medical Center of Cornell University & New York City Department for the Aging. (2011). *Under the radar: New York State Elder Abuse Prevalence Study.* New York, NY: Author.

Mixson, P. M. (2010). Public policy, elder abuse, and adult protective services: The struggle for coherence. *Journal of Elder Abuse & Neglect, 22*(1–2), 16–36. doi:10.1080/08946560903436148

Nasreddine, Z. S., Phillips, N. A., Bédirian, V., Charbonneau, S., Whitehead, V., Collin, I., . . . Chertkow, H. (2005). The Montreal Cognitive Assessment, MoCA: A brief screening tool for mild cognitive impairment. *Journal of the American Geriatrics Society, 53*(4), 695–699. doi:10.1111/j.1532-5415.2005.53221.x

Navarro, A. E., Wysong, J., DeLiema, M., Schwartz, E. L., Nichol, M. B., & Wilber, K. H. (2016). Inside the black box: The case review process of an elder abuse forensic center. *The Gerontologist, 56*(4), 772–781. doi:10.1093/geront/gnv052

Nerenberg, L. (2016). From blueprint to benchmarks: Building a framework for elder justice. Los Angeles: California Elder Justice Coalition. Retrieved from https://www.ccoa.ca.gov/docs/Publications/CCoAPublications/CEJC_From_Blueprint_to_Benchmarks_2016.pdf

Ornstein, C. (2015, December 21). Nursing home workers share explicit photos of residents on Snapchat. *ProPublica.* Retrieved from https://www.propublica.org/article/nursing-home-workers-share-explicit-photos-of-residents-on-snapchat

Pillemer, K., Burnes, D., Riffin, C., & Lachs, M. S. (2016). Elder abuse: Global situation, risk factors, and prevention strategies. *The Gerontologist, 56*(Suppl. 2), S194–S205. doi:10.1093/geront/gnw004

Richard, L., Gauvin, L., Gosselin, C., Ducharme, F., Sapinski, J.-P., & Trudel, M. (2008). Integrating the ecological approach in health promotion for older adults: A survey of programs aimed at elder abuse prevention, falls prevention, and appropriate medication use. *International Journal of Public Health, 53*(1), 46–56. doi:10.1007/s00038-007-6099-5

Rodríguez, M. A., Wallace, S. P., Woolf, N. H., & Mangione, C. M. (2006). Mandatory reporting of elder abuse: Between a rock and a hard place. *Annals of Family Medicine, 4*(5), 403–409. doi:10.1370/afm.575

Schiamberg, L. B., & Gans, D. (1999). An ecological framework for contextual risk factors in elder abuse by adult children. *Journal of Elder Abuse & Neglect, 11*, 79–103. doi:10.1300/J084v11n01_05

Teaster, P. B. (2017). A framework for polyvictimization in later life. *Journal of Elder Abuse & Neglect, 29*(5), 289-298. doi:10.1080/08946566.2017.1375444

Teaster, P. B., Dugar, T. A., Mendiondo, M. S., Abner, E. L., & Cecil, K. A. (2006). *The 2004 survey of state adult protective services: Abuse of adults 60 years of age and older.* Washington, DC: National Center on Elder Abuse. Retrieved from http://www.napsa-now.org/wp-content/uploads/2012/09/2-14-06-FINAL-60+REPORT.pdf

Teaster, P. B., Nerenberg, L., & Stansbury, K. L. (2003). A national look at elder abuse multidisciplinary teams. In E. Podnieks, J. I. Kosberg, & A. Lowenstein (Eds.), *Elder abuse: Selected papers from The Prague World Congress on Family Violence* (pp. 91–107). Binghamton, NY: The Haworth Maltreatment & Trauma Press.

Volmert, A., & Lindland, E. (2016). *"You only pray that somebody would step in": Mapping the gaps between expert and public understandings of elder abuse in America.* Washington, DC: FrameWorks Institute. Retrieved from http://frameworksinstitute.org/assets/files/elder_abuse_mtg_report_formatted_final.pdf

Wangmo, T., Teaster, P. B., Grace, J., Wong, W., Mendiondo, M. S., Blandford, C., . . . Fardo, D. W. (2014). An ecological systems examination of elder abuse: A week in the life of adult protective services. *Journal of Elder Abuse & Neglect, 26*(5), 440–457. doi:10.1080/08946566.2013.800463

Wolf, R. S. (2000). Introduction: The nature and scope of elder abuse. *Generations, 24*, 6–12.

Yon, Y., Mikton, C. R., Gassoumis, Z. D., & Wilber, K. H. (2017). Elder abuse prevalence in community settings: A systematic review and meta-analysis. *Lancet Global Health, 5*(2), 147–156. doi:10.1016/S2214-109X(17)30006-2

7

Seeking Justice Through the Justice System

INTRODUCTION

When the U.S. Constitution, the "supreme law of the land," was adopted in 1791, it immediately raised fears that the government would trample individual rights in the interests of maintaining social order. The Bill of Rights, which comprises the first 10 amendments to the Constitution, responded to those fears, as did many of the subsequent amendments. The rights established by the amendments are protected through statutes, regulations, and court decisions. These constitutionally protected rights may be positive or negative. Positive rights entitle people to goods, services, or benefits. Negative rights protect people from having protected rights impinged upon through government interference.

Nonlawyers in the fields of aging and elder abuse frequently talk about rights (e.g., the right to self-determination, confidentiality, privacy, and the right to refuse help) as ethical principles or practice guidelines. This chapter describes basic legal concepts that pertain to individual rights and explains some of the criticisms that have been leveled against aging and elder abuse policy on legal grounds. It points out the role that courts play in interpreting rights, determining when they have been violated, and finding that statutes and executive actions are invalid. It focuses on a few examples that have attracted scrutiny, particularly with respect to elder abuse and neglect.

Among the constitutional amendments that are most relevant to elder justice are the Fifth, which limits the government's authority to infringe on life, liberty, and the pursuit of property without due process, and the Fourteenth, which provides equal protection under the law. The following sections describe some of the constitutional considerations raised by elder abuse laws and regulations with respect to these and other rights.

Liberty

Although liberty is deeply associated with American values, it is not a constitutionally protected right. As legal scholar Nina Kohn explains, "To the extent that it is constitutional, liberty is the right to be free from government interference. That is, it is a negative right not a positive one" (N. Kohn, personal communication, July 19, 2018). Although commonly viewed as the freedom to do what one pleases, the right to liberty was never meant to be absolute. As Rebecca Brown, an expert on constitutional theory, puts it, ". . . the courts came to understand liberty as a concept shaped by the needs of the community. Accordingly, the nature of reasons that a state offers for restraining liberty is a key component of the meaning of liberty itself" (Brown, 1991, p. 67). The legal concept of "liberty interest" refers to the right to protection against unjustified intrusions in people's lives. Which intrusions are justified and which are not are often disputed.

Due Process

Due process measures the fairness and reasonableness of restrictions on liberty and individuals' rights, from two perspectives:

- Substantive. The government has to have a good reason for depriving people of their rights. It has to demonstrate that the good of the state legitimately supersedes the rights of individuals. Rights having to do with choices that are considered "intimate," like marriage, privacy, bodily integrity, families, and children, are believed by many to have the greatest implications for autonomy.
- Procedural: The government has to follow fair and impartial legal proceedings before depriving people of their rights. It includes, in some instances, the right to an attorney or fair hearing. Laws further prevent those receiving public benefits like Social Security Disability from having them revoked unless the government follows procedures such as giving notice, explaining the reasons, and providing an opportunity to contest decisions.

Equal Protection

The "equal protection" provision contained in the Constitution prohibits states from denying people equal protection under the law. This means that they must treat individuals in the same manner as others in similar conditions and circumstances. It requires government to govern impartially and not make distinctions based on differences that are irrelevant to governmental objectives. This is crucial to protecting civil rights. Laws do, however, treat people differently when there are good reasons for doing so. Laws that allow for classifying people for differential treatment, however, must be narrowly tailored to meet state interests.

Least Restrictive Alternatives

Many in the fields of aging, Adult Protective Services (APS), and elder abuse prevention are familiar with this concept as a principle of good practice. Although it is not grounded in constitutional law, it is required under certain statutes and regulations that apply to particular contexts. It means that government actions and laws must be narrowly tailored to achieve their goals in the least restrictive and intrusive way. Mental health laws, for example, call for the least restrictive alternatives to treatment, and some state laws require courts to consider less restrictive options before granting adult guardianships. Less restrictive alternatives have to be equally effective. In applying the standard, courts ask: "Can the benefits be achieved equally well through less restrictive means?"

Privacy

The right to privacy refers to the concept that one's personal information is protected from public scrutiny. While not explicitly stated in the Constitution, some amendments provide protections in certain circumstances. For example, the First Amendment protects the privacy of beliefs, the Fourth Amendment protects privacy against unreasonable searches, and the Fifth Amendment protects against self-incrimination, or the privacy of personal information. The right to privacy is complicated and has been interpreted in several ways. It refers to confidentiality and is protected in statutes like the Health Information Portability and Accountability Act (HIPAA), which protects people's health information. It is also associated with personal autonomy or people's right to make personal decisions and choices, as well as what former Supreme Court justice Louis Brandeis famously called the "right to be left alone." The right is balanced against the state's compelling interests, such as public safety.

THE RIGHTS OF ELDER ABUSE VICTIMS

Most laws pertaining to elder abuse are state laws and vary widely across the country. They include mandatory abuse reporting laws and civil and criminal statutes that hold perpetrators accountable. Federal laws and regulations address abuses in federally funded health and long-term care facilities, some forms of fraud and financial exploitation, and others.

Although many in the field of aging and elder abuse prevention have alleged that aspects of elder abuse reporting laws are paternalistic, few have questioned their legality. Among those who have is Nina Kohn, who suggests that some reporting laws violate victims' civil rights on both procedural and substantive grounds (Kohn, 2009). Kohn makes the case by applying the "Westinghouse test," a method for evaluating informational privacy rights that was developed by the Third Circuit Court of Appeals in *United States v. Westinghouse Electric Corporation* (1980). It calls on courts to consider seven factors in determining whether an intrusion on privacy is constitutionally permissible.

1. The type of record requested
2. The information it does or might contain
3. The potential for harm in any subsequent nonconsensual disclosure
4. The injury from disclosure to the relationship in which the record was generated
5. The adequacy of safeguards to prevent unauthorized disclosure
6. The degree of need for access
7. Whether there is an express statutory mandate, articulated public policy, or other recognized public interest militating toward access

In applying factors 1 and 2, which pertain to the information collected in abuse reports, Kohn points out that mandatory reporting laws may conflict with protected communications between professionals and their clients, confidential relationships between spouses, and relationships between clergy and those who seek their spiritual guidance. The potentially harmful effects of reporting (factor 3) include discouraging victims or observers from seeking help, stigmatizing the parties involved, or damaging their reputations. It may result in victims being institutionalized, placed under guardianships, or losing their independence.

Reporting can also damage relationships between victims, reporters, professionals, or abusers (factor 4). With respect to factor 5, many agencies that accept reports fail to implement adequate safeguards against disclosing information about clients, and uncertainties even exist about what information can be shared by members of multidisciplinary teams and forensic centers.

The need for access to the requested information (factor 6) depends to a great extent on the type of abuse in question, according to Kohn. Government involvement is more justified when older people cannot protect themselves as a result of cognitive impairment but less so when it comes to self-neglect by people with capacity. Factor 6 also suggests that states' interest also depends on the effectiveness of reporting. As was pointed out in earlier chapters, there is little evidence to suggest that mandatory reporting is any more effective than voluntary reporting or educational campaigns in identifying cases or linking victims with services.

The laws are on safer ground when it comes to factor 7, which considers whether there is an express statutory mandate, articulated public policy, or other recognized public interest that applies.

Kohn observes that some state reporting laws are better than others with respect to privacy. Wisconsin, for example, makes exceptions to its reporting requirements when reporting is not in the best interest of the victim and when alleged victims: (a) are at imminent risk of serious harm, and (b) cannot "make an informed judgment about whether to report the risk."

CIVIL AND CRIMINAL LAWS FOR ELDER ABUSE

Elder abuse is addressed by both the civil and criminal justice systems, and many have compared and contrasted their goals, approaches, effectiveness, drawbacks, and advantages (Stiegel, 2017). Less has been written about their implications for individual rights and social justice. The following sections point out some of these concerns, beginning with brief descriptions of how they address abuse.

Civil Lawsuits

Civil courts determine if people or entities (defendants) are liable for injuries or losses against others and compel liable parties to compensate those they have harmed. Courts can also order defendants to pay for noneconomic damages such as pain and suffering and impose punitive damages.

The most common civil remedies for elder abuse are "tort" and "contract" claims and actions. Tort claims compensate parties who have been intentionally or negligently harmed, or who have suffered property loss or damage through omissions, malpractice, or defamation. Financial abuse also includes breaches of fiduciary duty by attorneys-in-fact, guardians, or others that result in financial injury or loss to the elders while benefitting those entrusted to protect them. Other tort actions are for conversion, which is the civil equivalent of theft. Fraud is the intentional misrepresentation of facts made to deceive. Nonfinancial tort actions include assault and battery, wrongful death, false imprisonment, and negligence. A variety of "causes of action"—claims or sets of facts that give people the right to sue—have been filed against long-term care facilities for inadequate care, failure to protect residents from harm, and failure to provide adequate training and supervision to staff. Civil actions for assault and battery can be filed when residents are assaulted by employees or other residents.

Lawsuits against nursing homes may be for unlawful, unfair, fraudulent, or deceptive acts or business practices, or misleading advertising. State attorneys general have also brought civil actions seeking penalties to the Medicaid program for failure to provide adequate care, treatment, and services. Courts may order facilities to improve care, treatment, services, and protections to residents.

"Contract actions" address breaches of duties between parties arising out of oral or written contracts. Contract actions in abuse cases can result from abusers who convince elders who lack decision-making capacity to enter into contractual relationships that unfairly favor them (the abusers). Typically, claims are brought following transfers that are alleged to be improper. Contract actions also include claims that defendants breached written, oral, or implied promises with respect to the transfer of money or property, the provision of services, rental agreements, terms of employment, marriage, and other matters.

Some states have enacted special elder financial exploitation civil causes of action that include provisions designed to encourage private attorneys to take cases that may not otherwise be financially viable. For example, in cases involving older people, some states permit courts to order defendants to pay double or triple the amount they would otherwise award and pay attorneys' fees and the costs of those who initiated lawsuits. Some states allow for the expedited handling of elder abuse cases and permit lawsuits to survive even after victims die.

Class Action Lawsuits

Class action lawsuits allow for many victims to seek justice as a group by combining multiple claims that share similar fact patterns. Class action lawsuits, for example, may be filed against nursing homes for wrongful intentional or negligent actions that harm multiple residents. They include failure to provide medical care, neglect, maltreatment, false imprisonment, financial abuse and fraud, failure to provide sanitary living conditions, bed rail accidents, restraints, and choking. Class actions for abuse have also been filed against banks, insurance carriers, "living trust mills," and assisted living facilities.

Other civil remedies in elder abuse cases include divorce, separation, and annulment when the alleged abuse is by spouses. "Constructive trusts" are involuntary trusts created by courts to benefit parties that have been wrongfully deprived of assets or property through fraud, duress, or the abuse of confidential relationships. For example, when elders sue defendants for convincing them to deed their homes to them without payment, courts can impose constructive trusts on the properties, which means that defendants no longer own them. Instead, the properties are held in trust by courts for the elders' benefit. Eviction may be needed when abusers, including family members, live in elders' homes and refuse to leave or pay rent.

Protective Proceedings

Civil courts also handle orders of protection (restraining orders) and guardianships.[1] Restraining orders restrict abusers' conduct in various ways, depending on the threat. For example, harassment orders protect individuals who are being stalked or threatened, and domestic violence orders offer protection against abusive intimate partners and other family members. Orders may prevent restrained parties from physically harming protected parties or destroying their personal property. Stay-away orders prevent them from coming within specified distances (e.g., 100 yards) from protected persons or their homes, jobs, workplaces, or vehicles. Residence exclusions, or "move-out" orders, require restrained people to move out of protected persons' residences. No-contact orders prohibit restrained persons from contacting victims. Additional provisions, like requiring restrained persons to surrender firearms, may also be ordered. Orders may be granted on an emergency or temporary basis.

Guardianship, which is described in greater detail in Chapter 10, is a process by which courts assign trustworthy (hopefully) individuals or institutions to act on behalf of people who have physical or mental impairments that render them incapable of protecting their own interests or providing for their basic needs. Guardians may be family members or friends. Those who lack family or friends who can serve may have professionals appointed for them. Professional guardians may be proprietary or work for nonprofit agencies. Public guardians are publicly funded individuals or agencies and are considered by many to be the "guardian of last resort" when other options are not available.

---

[1] In some states, guardianships for adults are called "conservatorships," while in others, the term "guardianship" is used for personal affairs, while "conservatorship" refers to finances.

Criminal Justice System

Elder abuse may also constitute criminal conduct, in which case it may be addressed by the criminal justice system. Cases may be charged as traditional crimes like homicide and murder, assault and battery, domestic violence, sexual assault, fraud, theft, and criminal neglect, and handled in the same way. Some states, however, have also created new elder abuse crimes or enhancements to existing crimes that involve older victims in recognition of the fact that older people may be targeted for certain types of crime, have different vulnerabilities, and may be impacted differently. Some states' criminal statutes apply to all people over a specified age, while others only pertain to older people with age-related physical or cognitive vulnerabilities (Uekert, Keilitz, & Saunders, 2012).

Criminal elder abuse occurring in long-term care facilities may be investigated by Medicaid Fraud Control Units, which are typically located in offices of state attorneys general. Federal law enforcement agencies investigate certain elder abuse matters that occur in more than one state, crimes that are committed on Indian reservations and military bases, and federal crimes. Federal regulatory agencies also have law enforcement branches that investigate crimes associated with their specific functions. For example, because many frauds and scams are committed through the mail, the U.S. Postal Service may investigate these cases. Depending on the jurisdictions, prosecutors (who represent "the people" in criminal cases) may be district attorneys, attorneys general, or U.S. attorneys.

SPECIALIZED AREAS OF LAW

Public Health Law

As described in Chapter 4, elder abuse, dementia, family violence, and other problems affecting older people have been designated as public health matters, opening the door for public health law and policy. Public health law is a category of law and legal issues that pertain to public health. It focuses on statutes, regulations, lawsuits, and legal practice involving the government's legal authorities and duties "to ensure the conditions for people to be healthy" and covers a wide array of issues with enormous impact on older people. For example, public health laws apply to nursing homes and assisted living facilities, the licensure of medical professionals, and responses to public health emergencies, including infectious disease outbreaks and natural disasters. Public health laws pertaining to long-term care facilities address such rights as the right to medical services, choice of physician, freedom to refuse psychotropic medications, the right to remain in the facility, and freedom from physical restraint or involuntary seclusion.

Elder Law

The relatively new field of elder law focuses on retirement planning, access to benefits, healthcare, housing, and other legal and financial matters affecting older or disabled people. Some lawyers who specialize in these areas refer to themselves as "elder law attorneys" while others do not. They help clients draft wills and estate plans, assess long-term care options, and appoint legal guardians, trustees, or agents under powers of attorney. They may help arrange for long-term care, advise clients in how to pay for it, assist clients in obtaining public benefits, explain nursing home residents' rights, and help file nursing home claims.

Elder law attorneys also assist elder abuse victims to exercise their rights by representing them in the types of lawsuits described earlier. Some advocate for older people's rights as landlords or tenants.

Crime Victim Law

Some civil attorneys specialize in representing crime victims and identify themselves as "crime victim attorneys" or "victim rights attorneys." They assist clients to pursue perpetrators' assets regardless of whether or not the abuse resulted in criminal convictions. These attorneys may also help victims sue business owners and property managers who had a role in allowing crimes to happen or failing to promote safety, creating a powerful incentive for landlords and businesses to enact safeguards. The National Crime Victim Bar Association, which is operated by the National Center for Victims of Crime (NCVC) and the National Alliance of Victims' Rights Attorneys and Advocates (NAVRA), provides technical assistance and support to attorneys representing crime victims in civil suits.

Civil Rights Law

Civil rights law guarantees the right of individuals to receive equal treatment and prohibits discrimination in education, employment, housing, lending, voting, and other arenas. Stanford and Rivas (2017) have identified emerging civil rights issues that will significantly affect older people in the coming years, including the impact of the digital divide on civic engagement by older people, the "emergence of transgender elders from the shadows," and society's role with respect to suicide.

Consumer Rights Law

Consumer protection laws hold providers of goods and services accountable for their products and provide remedies for consumers who have been harmed by dangerous or ineffective products, abusive business practices, and fraud. Consumer rights laws, which include both federal and state laws, are enforced by government agencies, offices of attorneys general, and through private individual and class action lawsuits filed by or on behalf of victims. Consumer rights are also protected by regulations that set standards for what providers have to do to protect customers from harm and provide them with bargaining power. In recent years, providers of long-term services and supports have labeled users of care as "consumers." Chapter 9 explores the implications of this designation in the context of consumer rights and protections. The chapter also describes threats to older consumers in the face of the rampant fraud and predatory practices targeted against them.

WHOSE RIGHTS ARE SERVED?

Ensuring justice requires balancing the rights and interests of three entities that are involved in legal proceedings: (a) society at large, (b) alleged and actual harm-doers, and (c) harmed parties. The rights and interests of these entities are addressed differently by the civil and criminal justice systems and may be in conflict with one another. The roles these entities play in legal proceedings and their stakes in the outcomes also differ.

The "People's" Rights

The criminal justice system operates on the principle that society sets standards of conduct that apply to everyone for the greater good. When people break the law, it is the "People" (the public, or society) they have to answer to, and not just to victims. The People are represented by law enforcement officials who investigate crimes; prosecutors, who make arguments and bring forward evidence of the guilt of those alleged to have commited crimes (defendants); and judges and juries, who weigh the evidence and determine guilt and penalties. The guilty are compelled to pay a debt to society through incarceration, probation, or restitution. The public's role in crime prevention is to discourage crime, abide by laws, report crimes, serve as jurors, participate in neighborhood crime watch programs and on police commissions, and exercise political clout by lobbying legislators on crime-related issues.

The civil justice system provides opportunities for individuals who have been harmed by the misconduct of others, including powerful entities, to hold wrongdoers accountable. Unlike criminal defendants, the parties in civil matters do not typically have a constitutional right to legal representation. Representatives of special interests and disadvantaged groups can influence court decisions by filing amicus curiae (friend of the court) briefs in cases. Courts can also protect the public against abuses of power by holding legislatures, judges, and other powerful entities accountable.

The Roles and Rights of Defendants and Incarcerated People

The Constitution protects the rights of people who are alleged to have committed crimes. These rights are familiar to most Americans, many of whom can recite examples verbatim, thanks, in large part, to popular television dramas ("You have the right to remain silent. Anything you say can and will be used against you. . ."). Defendants can hire private defense attorneys to represent their rights and interests or, if they cannot afford to, public defenders are appointed for them.

An important right of criminal defendants that has special significance in elder abuse cases is articulated in the "confrontation clause" in the Sixth Amendment. It gives defendants the right to "be confronted with the witnesses against them," which allows their attorneys to cross-examine (question) accusers in their presence. For this reason, accounts of what happened that are made outside of court without defendants present, called "hearsay," are not generally admissible in criminal proceedings. There are exceptions to the hearsay rule, however, including "excited utterances" or "spontaneous statements" made by victims or other witnesses during or shortly after crimes are committed. These statements are typically considered by courts to be credible, and may therefore be admissible. Common examples include recordings of 911 calls.

The confrontation clause is particularly important in cases involving older victims who are in poor health and unable to come to court to testify. Rather than abandon these cases, prosecutors have attempted to relax confrontation clause requirements to give them more flexibility in using hearsay evidence. In the past, videotaped testimony by victims could be admitted as evidence, which was particularly important since criminals often allegedly seek out victims in failing health to increase the likelihood that they will not be available to testify. Similarly, defense attorneys have been accused of dragging out cases by asking for continuances (postponements). Relaxing the hearsay rule was seen as a way to protect victims' rights to equal access under the law.

Advocates for defendants, however, have successfully argued that these measures may violate defendants' rights. In the landmark *Crawford v. Washington* decision, the court significantly limited the scope of hearsay testimony that was admissible (Uekert et al., 2012). There are situations, however, in which hearsay testimony may still be used. A guide published by the National Center for State Courts includes a list of admissible evidence and testimony, which includes spontaneous statements/excited utterances; statements for medical diagnosis, including discharge; chance remarks heard by law enforcement; statements to nongovernmental parties; "dying declarations"; and business records (Uekert et al., 2012).

The Constitution also protects the rights of those convicted of crimes. Under the Eighth Amendment, criminals are protected against inhumane treatment or "cruel and unusual" punishment (what constitutes cruel and unusual, however, has not been clearly defined). Prison and jail inmates are protected against racial segregation, disparate treatment based on ethnicity or religion, and sex crimes or sexual harassment by other inmates or prison personnel. Courts have held guards, administrators, and even government officials liable for allowing abuses.

Inmates also retain basic First Amendment rights (including free speech and religion) to the extent that they do not interfere with discipline, order, and security. They have the right to complain about conditions, and prison officials have been found liable for placing inmates in solitary confinement after complaining (American Civil Liberties Union [ACLU], n.d.). Inmates generally lose their right to privacy, however, and prison officials can open incoming mail, read emails, and screen outgoing messages. Inmates are also not protected from warrantless searches.

Inmates with disabilities are entitled to some reasonable accommodations under the Americans with Disabilities Act. Disabled prisoners are entitled to the same medical care and mental health treatment as other prisoners; this, however, is minimal as prisons are only required to provide "adequate" care. What this means, for example, is that inmates with life-threatening illnesses are typically only given minimum treatment to keep them reasonably comfortable, as opposed to treatment to extend their lives or combat their illnesses. The question of what constitutes adequate medical care has come up in relation to compassionate release programs, which are programs designed to release inmates who are in the end stages of life and no longer perceived to pose a threat to society.

As part of former Attorney General Eric Holder's "Smart on Crime" initiative to curb the prison population, "compassionate release" policies were expanded to make more inmates eligible. However, eligibility requirements imposed by the Bureau of Prisons, including the provision that inmates had to be at least age 65 to qualify, seriously reduced the number of inmates who have benefited. This is despite the fact that older inmates experience age-related conditions at earlier ages and are significantly less likely to reoffend.

Enforcement of prisoners' rights is inadequate, according to the ACLU, which points out that the United States is the only democracy in the world that has no independent authority to monitor prison conditions and enforce minimal standards of health and safety (ACLU, n.d.; see Chapter 8).

The Roles and Rights of Victims and Harmed Parties

Many are surprised to learn that while the Constitution explicitly lists the rights of suspects and those convicted of crimes, it does not specify what rights victims have. Outrage over this omission led to the emergence of the victims' rights movement in the 1970s and efforts to enact a victims' rights amendment. Although unsuccessful in securing an amendment, advocates were successful in prompting Congress to enact the Victims of Crime Act (VOCA) of 1984, which established a national structure for victims' rights and services, and the Crime Victims Fund, which is used for victim services and compensation for crime-related losses. Sources of the fund include fines, forfeited bail bonds, and court assessments owed by federally convicted criminal offenders. Most of the fund money is believed to come from fines collected from "white collar" offenders and businesses.

The Office for Victims of Crime (OVC) within the Department of Justice has responsibility for distributing VOCA funds to states and establishes regulations for how they can be used. At the local level, victims' rights advocates, typically housed within district attorneys' offices, are charged to advocate on behalf of victims in criminal cases. Although they interact with police and prosecutors, their responsibility is to victims even when victims choose not to cooperate with prosecutors or police. Advocates keep victims apprised of the status of their cases or perpetrators' whereabouts, assist them to secure restitution or compensation for crime-related expenses and services, help ensure their safety, and facilitate their participation in sentencing and parole decisions. OVC also funds demonstration projects, technical assistance, and professional education programs.

Having lost the battle to secure a victims' rights amendment to the U.S. Constitution, advocates turned their attention to enacting state victim rights amendments. To date, 33 states have adopted amendments to ensure (a) that crime victims' rights are protected; (b) that crime victims' rights are a permanent part of the criminal justice system; and (c) that courts have the power to enforce crime victims' rights if they are violated (National Center for Victims of Crime, n.d.).

The Violence Against Women Act (VAWA) of 1994 was championed by women's rights activists and includes the first federal criminal law against battering and protections to victims of domestic and intimate partner violence. VAWA is administered by the Office on Violence Against Women (OVW), also part of the Justice Department, and provides funds and technical assistance to communities for developing programs and policies aimed at ending domestic violence, dating violence, and sexual assault. It also provides support for education and training for victim advocates, health professionals, law enforcement, prosecutors, and judges.

Originally, neither VOCA nor VAWA acknowledged the special needs and vulnerabilities of older victims. Reforms that were later instituted are described in Chapter 8.

STANDARDS OF PROOF

The legal system sets "standards of proof," which are criteria used to establish the level of certainty required to prove the facts of cases to judges and juries. The standards fall along a continuum that reflects the seriousness of the consequences—the greater the threat to individuals' rights, the higher the bar. Because the criminal justice system has the power to incarcerate perpetrators and deny them the basic right to liberty, the standard used in the criminal justice system is "beyond a reasonable doubt," which is the highest level of certainty the law requires.

Because civil court findings of liability usually involve monetary punishment, which is not viewed as being as drastic as incarceration, the standards of proof are lower. In civil cases, liability must be proven by a "preponderance of evidence," which essentially means that the "winner's" side of the story is more likely to be true than not. "Clear and convincing" is another standard used in some civil lawsuits, which means that claimants must prove that their versions of the facts are highly likely to be true. This typically occurs when something more than money is at stake. Examples include restraining orders, dependency cases (loss of parental rights), wills, and guardianships.

HOW JUST IS THE JUSTICE SYSTEM (IN PROTECTING ELDER RIGHTS)?

Little is actually known about the effectiveness of the criminal and civil justice systems in serving older people, which is due in large part to a lack of information about how often legal services and interventions are even used, let alone their impact, outcomes, and costs. This dearth of data extends to prosecutions involving older people, individual and class action lawsuits, restraining orders, guardianships, restitution orders and recoveries, compensation claims filed, and powers of attorney. Even less is known about how well the legal systems protect the rights and interests of those they serve.

Both the criminal and civil justice systems have been criticized for failing to provide adequate protection to older people. The problem stems in part from the fact that many people do not know what rights older adults have. Many are unaware that elder abuse can be criminal or what type of conduct constitutes crime. Some are unaware that age-based discrimination in housing, long-term care, and employment is often against the law, or are not aware of options for recourse. Options may not exist or be effective. Many are uninformed about legal assistance programs for older people. In response, efforts have been made to raise awareness about elder abuse laws, legal rights, and legal services.

Barriers to criminal prosecutions in elder abuse cases are frequently reported. They include aversion by many victims to subjecting family abusers to harsh punishments; the tendency of law enforcement and others to view crimes that involve contracts, deeds, trusts, advance directives, or other legal documents as strictly civil matters; difficulties in proving cases, particularly when questions arise about victims' capacity to provide testimony; lack of training and resources for police and prosecutors; impediments to accessing critical evidence, particularly when evidence is in the possession of financial institutions and long-term care facilities; and lack of forensic research and expertise.

Certain groups are particularly likely to be underserved. Nonaffluent older people are likely to go unrepresented because they are not aware of legal resources, are ineligible for free or affordable legal services, or cannot afford to hire lawyers. In addition, binding arbitration agreements, which are described in Chapter 9, may prevent consumers from suing individuals and entities for unfair treatment.

The criminal justice system also favors individuals with larger assets in some instances. For example, some elder financial crimes have thresholds for financial losses that are used in determining whether cases are pursued and how defendants are charged. These thresholds fail to acknowledge that small losses may be even more devastating to nonaffluent older people on fixed incomes as larger losses are to the wealthy.

Nursing home residents are also underserved. Again, while there is little data to draw from, anecdotal evidence suggests that abuse against nursing home residents is much less likely to be reported, investigated, and prosecuted than abuse in the broader community. Abuse against residents by staff are often treated as licensing, administrative, or personnel matters and investigated internally. Even when claims are substantiated, perpetrators may just be warned, suspended, or fired. Nursing home residents are also likely to be required or pressured into signing binding arbitration agreements at the time of their admission that prevent them from exercising their right to sue for abuse or poor care. A related criticism is that legal actions often focus on abuse toward or by individuals, as opposed to pursuing cases that involve multiple parties that would potentially have greater social impact.

Other groups that are believed to be underserved by the justice systems include elders of color and those with cognitive impairments. The special needs of these groups and efforts to overcome obstacles in serving them are discussed in greater detail in Chapters 8, 9, and 10.

Beyond these shortcomings in providing equal protection, civil and criminal approaches to elder abuse prevention may pose additional threats to individual rights, according to Kohn (2009). These include, for example, laws that prohibit consensual sexual activity by virtue of someone's age as is the case with statutes that make it unlawful for elders to have sexual contact with caregivers and those that set higher standards of conduct for people in positions of trust toward elders, including those in "confidential relationships."

Policies that reduce prosecutors' reliance on victims' testimony, while increasing the likelihood that perpetrators are brought to justice, may also infringe on victims' rights. Examples that require further scrutiny include no-drop policies that prevent prosecutors from dropping cases even when victims urge them to do so or recant their stories. Some defend practices like these in the belief that victims' reluctance may stem from explicit and implicit threats or intimidation made against them or susceptibility to undue influence.

Kohn believes that such issues would be better addressed if lawyers assumed a more prominent role in elder rights and abuse prevention and urges them to do so. She further urges elder law attorneys to address civil rights, including age-based discrimination, in their practices and suggests that groups like the National Academy of Elder Law Attorneys (NAELA) could play a leading role in promoting rights-based policy and practice.

INNOVATIONS AND REFORMS

A wide array of statutory and procedural innovations have been created to improve the civil and criminal justice systems' responses to older people. Examples include the following.

Model and Uniform Laws

Academic institutions, nonprofit organizations, and others have drafted model laws to provide guidance to policy makers and legislatures. The National Conference of Commissioners on Uniform State Laws (commonly called the Uniform Law Commission), a nonprofit organization, has issued more than 200 uniform laws that are developed through rigorous research, public review and comment, and formal approval by the commissioners. The commission also monitors states' adoption of its uniform laws. Those of particular relevance to elder justice are the Uniform Guardianship, Conservatorship, and Other Protective Arrangements Act (UGCOPAA), which was approved by the Uniform Law Commission in 2017, and the Uniform Power of Attorney Act, which was approved by the Commission in 2006. Both pertain to the rights of people with diminished mental capacity and are are available on the Uniform Law Commission's website (https:// www.uniformlaws.org/home) along with updates on what states have adopted them.

Other examples of model legislation include the Model Civil Provisions on Elder Financial Exploitation (NCVC, 2017), which were developed by the NCVC and the Commission on Law and Aging of the American Bar Association to help states hold exploiters accountable (NCVC, 2017).

The Protection of the Elderly Model Law, which was developed by the Johns Hopkins University School of Advanced International Studies International Human Rights Clinic, addresses the rights to dignity; freedom from abuse, neglect, exploitation, and discrimination; adequate healthcare; material assistance; property; participatition in society; and work (Johns Hopkins University School of Advanced International Studies International Human Rights Clinic, 2012).

Elder Courts

A few jurisdictions have developed special courts to accommodate older people's needs. Among the adaptations they include are separate calendars for cases involving older people (typically in the late morning) and the appointment of a single judge to handle cases throughout the process. Some employ case managers to explain the court system to victims; arrange for services like transportation, court accompaniment, and videotaping testimony; help victims secure compensation and orders of protection; make referrals to community services; and provide follow-up. When elders are unable to appear in court, judges may set up telephone hearings from court chambers or issue orders of protection by telephone. Elder courts also typically provide training for their staff to sensitize them to older people's needs and work closely with community agencies. They may handle both civil and criminal matters.

Forensic Research and Expertise

As more cases of elder abuse are prosecuted, it has heightened the need for compelling evidence to present to courts. This has led to heightened interest in forensics, which is often described as the application of science to law. In the early 2000s, new forensic studies began to emerge that identified medical markers like bruises, injuries, and signs of neglect that are suggestive of abuse that can be used to distinguish them from injuries or harm caused by other factors (Dyer, Connolly, & McFeeley, 2003; Mosqueda, Burnight, & Liao, 2005).

New forms of forensic research quickly emerged. Researchers examined coroners' reports of nursing home deaths to identify markers for systemic abuses and poor care such as aggregate rates of malnutrition and injuries; inconsistencies in reports and documentation; and personnel issues (Lindbloom et al., 2005). Forensic accountants identified markers of financial exploitation and forensic neurologists assessed victims' and witnesses' cognitive status, since determinations of incapacity frequently mean the difference between whether actions like giving gifts or engaging in sexual relations are criminal or illegal. Some APS programs have hired or contracted with forensic nurses or accountants to assist with investigations.

These discoveries and developments led to the creation of forensic centers, which bring together experts and use state-of-the-art science and analytic tools to identify abuse, support law enforcement, conduct research, and provide training (Schneider, Mosqueda, Falk, & Huba, 2010). Forensic centers may employ, contract with, or partner with legal, medical, social service, or law enforcement professionals to conduct medical forensic examinations, neuro-psychological testing, victim interviews, education, consultation, and research.

Forensic centers have demonstrated success in increasing rates of prosecution and guardianship (Navarro, Gassoumis, & Wilber, 2013). Their successes in achieving or even pursuing other elder justice goals have not, however, been explored. A move in this direction might include enlisting the participation of professionals from the field of forensic social work, which focuses on correcting social injustices and promoting individual rights. Forensic social workers, for example, consider the individual rights of parties involved in disputes and fair treatment in the criminal or civil justice systems. They also make recommendations regarding capacity, involuntary commitment, and alternative sentencing and may get involved in policy or legislative development to promote social justice goals (Frankel, 1989). Members of the profession can potentially help explore how forensic approaches can be applied to elder justice.

CONCLUSION

The legal rights that pertain to liberty, due process, equal protection, least restrictive alternatives, and privacy must be considered in crafting and evaluating laws and legal protections for older adults. This includes older adults' fundamental rights as citizens as well as their rights as members of groups that are afforded special protections (e.g., as consumers, crime victims, and long-term care residents). Elder justice advocates need to understand these rights and be prepared to defend them against practices and policies that potentially undermine them.

Ensuring justice for older people in the justice system will require the coming together of lawyers, advocates, social workers, healthcare providers, criminal justice professionals, older adults, and other stakeholders to ensure that the justice system is accessible and responsive for the young and the old. It requires overcoming obstacles to courts and legal representation.

Ensuring justice further requires that laws, government actions, and legal services and interventions affecting older people do not violate their constitutional rights. It requires understanding what is working and what needs to be improved; identifying promising practices and testing out new ones; removing barriers to the civil and criminal justice systems for all older people; and ensuring that legal professionals understand older clients' needs.

And finally, ensuring elder justice will require balancing individuals' right to protection against unwanted intrusions in their lives, balancing the rights of individuals toward one another, balancing the rights of defendants against their accusers, and balancing individual rights against society's compelling interests. Specific measures for accomplishing these ambitious goals are suggested in Chapter 12 as part of the broader elder justice agenda.

REFERENCES

American Civil Liberties Union. (n.d.). Prisoners' rights. Retrieved from https://www .aclu.org/issues/prisoners-rights

Brown, R. L. (1991). The fragmented liberty clause. *William and Mary Law Review, 41*(1), 65–93. Retrieved from https://scholarship.law.wm.edu/wmlr/vol41/iss1/4

Disability Rights California, Investigations Unit. (2010). *Victimized twice: Abuse of nursing home residents, no criminal accountability for perpetrators.* Oakland, CA: Author. Retrieved from http://www.disabilityrightsca.org/pubs/548801.pdf

Dyer, C. B., Connolly, M.-T., & McFeeley, P. (2003). The clinical and medical forensics of elder abuse and neglect. In R. J. Bonnie & R. B. Wallace (Eds.), *Elder mistreatment: Abuse, neglect, and exploitation in an aging America* (pp. 339–381). Washington, DC: National Academies Press.

Frankel, M. (1989). Ethics and the forensic sciences: Professional autonomy in the criminal justice system. *Journal of Forensic Sciences, 34*(3), 763–771. doi:10.1520/JFS12703J

Johns Hopkins University School of Advanced International Studies International Human Rights Clinic. (2012). *The protection of the elderly model law.* Washington, DC: Author. Retrieved from https://social.un.org/ageing-working-group/documents/fourth/ JohnHopkinsUnivModelLaw.pdf

Kohn, N. A. (2009). Outliving civil rights. *Washington University Law Review, 86*(5), 1053–1115. Retrieved from http://openscholarship.wustl.edu/law_lawreview/vol86/iss5/1

Lindbloom, E., Brandt, J., Hawes, C., Phillips, C., Zimmerman, D., Robinson, J., . . . McFeeley, P. (2005). *The role of forensic science in identification of mistreatment deaths in long-term care facilities: Final report.* Retrieved from https://www.ncjrs.gov/pdffiles1/nij/ grants/209334.pdf

Mosqueda, L., Burnight, K., & Liao, S. (2005). The life cycle of bruises in older adults. *Journal of the American Geriatrics Society, 53*, 1339–1343. doi:10.1111/j.1532-5415.2005.53406.x

National Center for Victims of Crime. (n.d.). Issues: Constitutional amendments: State amendments. Retrieved from http://victimsofcrime.org/our-programs/public -policy/amendments

National Center for Victims of Crime. (2017). Model civil provisions on elder financial exploitation. Retrieved from http://victimsofcrime.org/docs/default-source/ financial-fraud/model-civil-provisions-on-elder-financial-exploitation.pdf?sfvrsn=2

Navarro, A. E., Gassoumis, Z. D., & Wilber, K. H. (2013). Holding abusers accountable: An elder abuse forensic center increases criminal prosecution of financial exploitation. *Gerontologist, 53*(2), 303–312. doi:10.1093/geront/gns075

Schneider, D. C., Mosqueda, L., Falk, E., & Huba, G. J. (2010). Elder abuse forensic centers. *Journal of Elder Abuse & Neglect, 22*(3–4), 255–274. doi:10.1080/08946566.2010.490137

Stanford, E. P., & Rivas, E. E. (2017). Where do older adults fit in the evolution of civil rights in America? *Aging Today, 38*(3), 1, 4. Retrieved from https://www.asaging.org/blog/ where-do-older-adults-fit-evolution-civil-rights-america

Stiegel, L. (2017). Elder abuse victims' access to justice: Roles of the civil, criminal, and judicial systems in preventing, detecting, and remedying elder abuse. In X.-Q. Dong (Ed.), *Elder abuse: Research, practice and policy* (pp. 343–362). Gewerbestrasse, Switzerland: Springer International.

Uekert, B. K., Keilitz, S., & Saunders, D. (2012). Prosecuting elder abuse cases: Basic tools and strategies. Williamsburg, VA: National Center for State Courts. Retrieved from http://www.eldersandcourts.org/~/media/Microsites/Files/cec/Prosecution%20 Guide.ashx

United States v. Westinghouse Electric Corporation, 638 F.2d 570, 578 (3d Cir. 1980).

... and Justice for All: Parity and Fairness

INTRODUCTION

Social justice requires fairness in how governments distribute resources, provide services and opportunities, and protect rights. This chapter considers fairness with respect to older people from two perspectives: (a) fairness vis-à-vis other segments of the population, or "intergenerational equity"; and (b) fairness among older adults.

INTERGENERATIONAL EQUITY

The controversy that surrounds debates about entitlements stems at least in part from concerns about "intergenerational equity," or fairness among generations. Whereas some accuse older people of demanding more than their fair share of public resources, others point out how resources for protective services and victim assistance for older victims are dwarfed by those devoted to the non-elderly. Those in the field of elder abuse prevention have been particularly vocal about disparities, frequently citing, for example, a 2011 Government Accountability Office (GAO) report showing that seven agencies within the U.S. Department of Health and Human Services (HHS) and the Department of Justice devoted just $11.9 million in grants for elder justice activities in 2009 compared to $649 million in funding for violence against women programs (GAO, 2011).

Public funding for protective services, which overwhelmingly favors children over adults, is another example. Competition for protective services between the two groups is baked into funding mechanisms that require state and local program administrators to divide scarce funds between them. And while federal laws dictate how states fund and deliver child protection, child welfare, and adoption programs and services, there are no comparable mandates for adult protective services. The Children's Bureau within the HHS

© Springer Publishing Company DOI: 10.1891/9780826147578.0008

issues policies and regulations and requires or encourages states to do so as well (Child Welfare Information Gateway, 2016). As a result, many states have adopted caseload standards and guidance recommended by professional associations and accreditors like the Child Welfare League of America, which recommends that child protective workers carry no more than 12 active cases a month. This is in sharp contrast to Adult Protective Services (APS) workers, who, according to the Administration for Community Living, carry average caseloads of 26 to 50 in 21 states and more than 100 cases in four states (Administration for Community Living, 2016). States and local communities may also be required to focus on children as a result of class action litigation (Farber & Munson, 2007). Provisions in settlement agreements and consent decrees often require jurisdictions to meet specific caseload standards for child protective services.

In contrast, APS programs have fewer requirements and standards, most of which are voluntary. Lacking standards, accreditation, sanctions, or scrutiny, APS programs are at a clear disadvantage in competing with children's programs for funds. Program administrators who oversee the programs understandably prioritize children's services to avoid violating regulations and risking sanctions. Similar disparities exist with respect to training. In many communities, training dollars devoted to APS are a fraction of those devoted to child protective services, and training and educational requirements are generally lower. APS workers typically receive lower pay than their counterparts who work with children, making it a less attractive career choice.

Similar disparities exist with respect to services for crime victims. The Office for Victims of Crime, which administers Victims of Crime Act (VOCA) funds for victim compensation and victim assistance, expended just 0.5% of its budget on older victims in 2009, resulting in older victims being significantly less likely to receive help than their younger counterparts (GAO, 2011). Victim compensation is provided directly to (or for) individual victims for counseling, medical bills, and other crime-related expenses, and victim assistance funds go to public and private agencies to provide counseling, shelter, legal assistance, and other direct services.

States determine how VOCA funds are allocated and what services and programs they can be used for in accordance with federal regulations. Few provide services that are among the most highly valued and commonly needed by older crime victims such as shelter and help recovering restitution. With rare exceptions, victims of financial exploitation are not eligible for victim compensation despite the fact that this form of abuse is among the most common.

These disparities may be attributed in part to lack of funding for research that could substantiate the need for programs and policy. Connolly and

Trilling (2014) point out the circular relationship between research, resources, and policy. "Policy helps determine where to send resources. Resources fund research and programs that inform policy" (p. 65).

FAIRNESS AMONG OLDER PEOPLE

Disparities among older people with respect to opportunities, resources, and rights largely reflect lifelong discrimination and disadvantage based on race, class, gender, religion, gender identity, education, ethnicity, functional ability, immigration status, nation of origin, and other factors.

Discrimination and disadvantages experienced over the life span may overlap and accumulate. The terms "double jeopardy" and "triple jeopardy" are sometimes used to refer to the overlap of two or three forms of discrimination or disadvantage, and "intersectionality" describes their combined impact, which can be profound. For example, the poverty rate for older Hispanic women who live alone is nearly 40%.

Disparities among older people are evident in variations in (a) life expectancy, (b) health and functional status, (c) wealth, (d) access to services, and (e) the quality of care received. They also affect the likelihood that older people will experience abuse, neglect, and exploitation.

LIFE EXPECTANCY

The average life expectancy in the United States in 2016 was 78.6 years (National Center for Health Statistics, 2017). The poor and members of some minority groups die earlier:

- The richest 1% of men live 14.6 years longer on average than the poorest 1%. For women, the difference is 10.1 years (Chetty et al., 2016).
- Black life expectancy at birth is about 3.5 years lower than that of Whites (National Center for Health Statistics, 2017).
- The average life expectancy of American Indian and Alaska Natives served by the Indian Health Service from 2007 to 2009 was 73.7 years, with wide regional variations. In Billings, Montana, for example, the average was 69.4 years and in Nashville, Tennessee, it was 82.3 (Tilly & Hudgins, 2017).

Variations like these do not just reflect extremes—the very wealthy live long lives and the very poor die young. Rather, the farther up on the wealth continuum people fall, the longer they can expect to live (Chetty et al., 2016).

The reasons for these disparities are not fully understood, and multiple risk factors are being explored. They range from on-the-job stress associated with low paid work to historical traumas associated with slavery, internment, forced migration, and Indian boarding schools.

HEALTH

Similar disparities exist with respect to health and disability:

- Nearly 44% of African American men and 48% of African American women have some form of cardiovascular disease that includes heart disease and stroke (Centers for Disease Control and Prevention, 2017).
- American Indian and Alaskan Natives are at heightened risk for diabetes, heart disease, cancer, obesity, cardiovascular disease, and metabolic syndrome (Tilly & Hudgins, 2017).
- African Americans are about twice as likely to have Alzheimer's or other dementias as older Whites, and Hispanics are about 1.5 times as likely (Alzheimer's Association, 2017).
- Nearly 50% of low-income adults (less than $15,000/year) and 40% of adults who did not graduate from high school have disabilities compared with 10.8% of adults with household incomes of more than $50,000/year and 11.8% of college graduates, respectively (Courtney-Long et al., 2015).
- Lesbian, gay, bisexual, and transgender (LGBT) older adults are at heightened risk for obesity, high blood pressure and cholesterol levels, arthritis, cataracts, asthma, cardiovascular disease, and diabetes. More than half experience depression and 39% have seriously thought of committing suicide (Fredriksen-Goldsen et al., 2011).

As is the case with life expectancies, risk factors for disease and disability are not well understood. In recent years, researchers have begun to explore why some racial and ethnic minorities are more likely to develop dementia (Alzheimer's Association, 2017). Heightened rates among African Americans have been attributed to stressful life experiences, with one study showing that a single major stressful event in early life is equal to 4 years of cognitive aging. The same study showed that African Americans, on average, are over 60% more likely to experience major stressful events than White Americans over their lifetimes (Alzheimer's Association, 2017). Other studies have found that poverty, substandard housing, low education rates, and underemployment are correlated with poor cognitive performance.

Members of some groups are also likely to experience disabling illnesses and conditions at an earlier age, which has led to the lowering of the chronological age at which people are considered old. Studies of homeless elders, for example, have included those as young as 50 in their samples (Kushel, 2018).

Disparities in the quality of healthcare received by disadvantaged groups are also frequently reported. Multiple studies have shown that poor nursing home residents receive worse care and treatment than the nonpoor (Campbell, Cai, Gao, & Li, 2016; Feng, Fennell, Tyler, Clark, & Mor, 2011; Fennell, Feng, Clark, & Mor, 2010). This can be attributed in part to the fact that a relatively small number of nursing homes carry a very high proportion of Medicaid patients and are disproportionately located in poor areas. Those facilities have lower staffing levels, receive more citations for deficiencies, and are more likely to be terminated from the Medicaid/Medicare program and forced to close (Mor, Zinn, Angelelli, Teno, & Miller, 2004).

Discrimination has also been reported in nursing homes. Some facilities reportedly deny access to LGBT residents' visitors, do not allow same-sex couples to share rooms, refuse to place transgender adults in facilities that match their gender identity, and prevent residents' partners from participating in decisions about medical care.

WEALTH

The poverty rate for older Americans in 2016 was 9.3% for people aged 65 and over and another 4.9% were "near-poor" (their incomes were between the poverty level and 125% above it; Semega, Fontenot, & Kollar, 2017). In 2016, 10.6% of older women lived in poverty compared to 7.6% of men, and older women were much more likely to be financially insecure. As noted in Chapter 2, these figures fail to reflect the high proportion of their incomes that older people pay in medical and other expenses. This led to the creation of the "Supplemental Poverty Measure" (SPM), which adjusts for these added expenses. Applying the SPM, the poverty rate for older Americans is 14.5% (Cubanski, Koma, Damico, & Neuman, 2018). The poverty rate among people aged 65 and older was found to increase with age and to be higher for women, Blacks and Hispanics, and people in relatively poor health.

To a great extent, disparities in poverty rates among older people reflect disparities that began earlier in life. The fact that women receive less in Social Security than men (approximately $4,500 less in 2014) results from lower lifetime earnings, time taken off for caregiving, and working in lower wage jobs (National Council on Aging, 2016).

ACCESS TO AND QUALITY OF CARE

The *National Healthcare Quality and Disparities Report*, which is mandated by Congress, tracks disparities in access to care experienced by different racial and socioeconomic groups and disparities in the quality of care they receive using 250 measures. Although the report only includes a few measures that uniquely pertain to older people, it can be assumed that the impact of poor care earlier in life persists into old age. According to the 2016 report (Agency for Healthcare Research and Quality, 2017):

- Poor people (at or below 100% of the Federal Poverty Level) experience worse access to care compared with high-income people for all access measures except one.
- Blacks experience worse access to care than Whites for 50% of measures. They have far worse experiences with getting care quickly, getting needed care, office staff helpfulness, and health plan customer services.
- Hispanics experience worse access to care than Whites for 75% of measures.

Examples of limited access to care and poor treatment are frequently reported, with some groups being particularly disadvantaged. Funding for the Indian Health Service, which provides healthcare to about 2.2 million enrolled members of federally recognized tribes, is so limited in some places that its programs only serve people at immediate risk of losing their lives or developing serious impairments (Artiga, Ubri, & Foutz, 2017).

RISK OF ELDER ABUSE

Elders of color and older immigrants are known to be at heightened risk for certain forms of abuse, neglect, and exploitation. Among the most frequently cited examples is the finding that African American older adults are three times more likely than Whites to experience financial abuse and twice as likely to experience psychological abuse (Beach, Schulz, Castle, & Rosen, 2010).

Significant attention has been paid toward explaining the reasons for these differences, with most analysts focusing on ethnic, racial, or cultural factors. These include the loosening of cultural expectations or lack of access to culturally specific or appropriate services that could potentially mitigate risks.

Recent studies, however, suggest that social determinants may play a larger role than culture, race, or ethnic origin. In reanalyzing the findings of the frequently cited 2008 National Elder Mistreatment Study, for example, researchers discovered that poverty, social support, and health had greater predictive value than race or ethnicity (Hernandez-Tejada, Amstadter, Muzzy, & Acierno, 2013). Some also suggest that poverty contributes to or is often mistaken for neglect and self-neglect.

After surveying the literature on underserved populations, Jervis and colleagues concluded that there was a need to "widen the net beyond cultural perceptions of abuse to examine other areas, such as low socio-economic status (SES), rurality, inadequate access to healthcare, and the burden of discrimination" (Jervis et al., 2016, p. 313). They further challenge researchers to explore the role of sexual identity in heightening risk.

Barriers to research and surveillance have also impeded understanding of abuse in underserved communities. DeLiema, Gassoumis, Homeier, and Wilber (2012) suggest that abuse against low-income Latino immigrants has been undercounted as a result of limited English proficiency, economic insecurity, neighborhood seclusion, a tradition of resolving conflicts within the family, and mistrust of authorities.

To overcome these barriers, DeLiema and colleagues (2012) recruited and trained "promotores," local Spanish-speaking Latinos, to interview a sample of elderly Latino adults living in low-income Los Angeles neighborhoods. The study revealed that a shocking 40.4% of the elders had experienced some form of abuse and/or neglect within the previous year. This included psychological abuse (experienced by nearly 25%), physical assault (10.7%), sexual abuse (9%), financial abuse (16.7%), and neglect by caregivers (11.7%).

Vulnerable groups and those with limited literacy are significantly less likely to seek out or receive services that can potentially prevent abuse, promote independence, and protect rights. Abuse prevention services are not universally available to underserved groups, and, as described in Chapter 7, disparities exist in victims' access to the criminal and civil justice systems.

IMMIGRATION STATUS

In 2015, about 15% of adults 60 and over in the United States were foreign-born. Older immigrants represent a much larger proportion of the elderly populations in certain cities like New York, where they comprise 46% of the city's older adult population (Farrell, 2016).

As noted earlier, older immigrants are more likely than nonimmigrants to be poor. They are also less likely to receive benefits and services, which may result from lack of information or fears about deportation or other consequences. Less than one third of older adults who are eligible for the Supplemental Nutrition Assistance Program (SNAP), for example, receive it (National Council on Aging, 2016). Other problems affecting immigrants are isolation, loneliness, and exploitation.

Exploitation of older immigrants comes in multiple forms. They include "affinity frauds" in which con artists are or claim to be from immigrants' countries of origin (Deem, Nerenberg, & Titus, 2013). Some older immigrants are brought to the United States expressly to babysit for grandchildren, which, in some cases, becomes exploitative, and instances of human trafficking of older laborers have also been reported (Human Rights First, 2016).

INCARCERATED ELDERS

Little attention has been paid to the treatment of older inmates in America's prisons and jails despite the fact that inmates aged 50 and older are the fastest growing segment of the inmate population; this increase is occurring at the same time that the overall prison population is decreasing (Federal Bureau of Prisons, 2018). In February 2018, older inmates comprised 19% of the prison population nationally. In New York, older inmates made up nearly 20% of the prison population in 2016, which represents a 46% increase from 2007. In California, the share of prisoners 50 or older grew from 4% to 23% between 1990 and 2016 (Public Policy Institute of California, n.d.).

The overwhelming preponderance of people of color in America's prisons and jails holds true for older inmates. Black males age 65 and older are 4.4 times more likely to be imprisoned than older Whites (Bureau of Justice Statistics, 2018).

As described in Chapter 7, inmates retain some constitutional rights while incarcerated and after release (Maschi, 2013). These include the right to reasonable accommodations under the Americans with Disabilities Act (ADA), the right to free speech in some situations, adequate medical care, and protection against discrimination, violence, abuse, and cruel and unusual punishment. These rights are often violated, however, and the impact of violations are believed to be more acute on older inmates. The needs of older inmates also frequently go unmet. These include:

- Lack of physical modifications and accommodations. Older inmates may require handicapped-accessible cells or lower bunks, which overcrowding prevents prisons from providing. Those with limited mobility may have trouble navigating facilities with narrow sidewalks, uneven terrain, or stairs. The Bureau of Prisons (BOP), which has responsibility for overseeing prisons, has not conducted a nationwide review of the accessibility of its institutions since 1996 (Office of the Inspector General, 2016).

- Lack of assistance with activities of daily living. Few older inmates get help with personal care, including bathing, dressing, transferring, or navigating.
- Delays in medical care. Lacking their own resources for meeting older inmates' needs, prisons rely on outside institutions, which often results in long delays. A BOP report indicated that the average wait time for inmates, including older inmates, to be seen by outside medical specialists for cardiology, neurosurgery, pulmonology, and urology was 114 days in one facility.
- Lack of release planning. Older inmates are likely to have served long sentences, which makes reentry more complex. Many, for example, have untreated medical conditions and lack medical care (P. Vanderhorst, personal communication, April 18, 2018).
- Lack of staff who understand the needs of older inmates. According to the Inspector General report, BOP institutions lack appropriate staffing levels to address the needs of aging inmates and provide limited training for this purpose (Office of the Inspector General, 2016).
- Lack of programs. BOP programs typically focus on education and job skills, which may not be needed by aging inmates. Few facilities, even those with high percentages of aging inmates, have programs specifically for aging inmates.

Older inmates also face obstacles when they reenter their communities. Because prisons are only obligated to provide "adequate" care, many older inmates leave facilities in need of medical care (P. Vanderhorst, personal communication, April 18, 2018). Those who have been convicted of felony crimes are not entitled to public benefits, which may not only pose problems to themselves but to their families and communities as well.

WHAT ACCOUNTS FOR DISPARITIES

As noted earlier, disparities among older people can be attributed in large measure to discrimination that begins earlier in life. This includes discrimination in employment, housing, and access to healthcare, social services, and the justice system. The consequences may accumulate or compound through the forces of intersectionality. As people age, they may also lose the social and economic resources they once relied on to ease or mitigate the impact of discrimination. Their social and financial security may be compromised by the loss of employment, partners, and alliances. Physical and financial challenges may render them less resilient.

The social and advocacy networks and services that older members of disadvantaged groups aligned with earlier in life may no longer meet their needs or take pains to accommodate them. Civil rights groups, women's rights groups, disability rights groups, LGBT rights groups, and others have not typically embraced or recruited older members. Many fail to recognize older members' unique circumstances or needs.

Public policies may further exacerbate disparities, disadvantaging the disadvantaged still further. Lack of research on underserved groups and the obstacles they face, as well as lack of data to demonstrate disparities, also stand in the way of reform.

POLICIES THAT EXACERBATE DISPARITIES

Public policies may further disadvantage the already disadvantaged. Common examples include regressive taxes and age-based thresholds for resources and opportunities.

Adam Smith (1776), who is credited with creating modern free-market economics, wrote:

> The subjects of every state ought to contribute toward the support of the government, as nearly as possible, in proportion to their respective abilities; that is, in proportion to the revenue which they respectively enjoy under the protection of the state. (p. 861)

Smith was calling for proportional taxes, which is one of three basic types that are defined by the Internal Revenue Service as:

- Progressive tax—a tax that takes a larger percentage of income from high-income groups than from low-income groups
- Proportional tax—a tax that takes the same percentage of income from all income groups
- Regressive tax—a tax that takes a larger percentage of income from low-income groups than from high-income groups

The implications of these variations is clear. Sales taxes are a prime example of a regressive tax, and it is obvious that the impact of a $1,000 sales tax on a car places a greater burden on someone with an income of $30,000 a year than it does on someone whose annual income is $300,000 or three million. Opponents of the Patient Protection and Affordable Care Act (ACA), and even many of its supporters, criticized the program's mandate that required those without insurance to pay a fixed penalty because it essentially amounted to a regressive tax.

Income taxes are said to be progressive because higher earners pay a greater proportion of their incomes than lower earners. Many, however, claim that income taxes are not truly progressive and do not, in fact, place a greater burden on the wealthy (Tax Policy Center, 2017). With proportional taxes, everyone pays the same proportion of their incomes.

Payroll taxes, those taxes that are taken out of workers' paychecks to cover Social Security and Medicare, are a combination. They are progressive up to $128,400 (the "cap" in 2018). The more workers earn up to the cap, the more they pay. However, anyone earning more than the cap pays the same amount, which makes it regressive. It is why advocates for income equity call for "lifting the cap."

Another way that public policies contribute to disparities is the use of chronological thresholds for public entitlement programs. People with lower than average life expectancies are further disadvantaged by programs like Medicare and Social Security whose eligibility is determined by age. A person whose life expectancy is 70, for example, receives less proportionally than someone whose life expectancy is 80 or 90. In other words, raising the age of eligibility threatens to disadvantage the disadvantaged even more.

LACK OF RESEARCH ON UNDERSERVED GROUPS AND DISPARITIES

Responding to disparities requires recognizing that they exist in the first place and understanding the risk factors and patterns associated with them. For that to happen, all segments of the population need to be accurately represented in government surveillance, epidemiological studies, and needs assessments. These include, for example, the National Survey of Older Americans Act Participants, which is used by the HHS to decide how to allocate federal funding to agencies and organizations that serve older adults.

Advocates for American Indian/Alaska Natives have alleged that members of the groups they represent are left out of research studies altogether. Panelists at the 2017 Discrimination in America: Native American Experiences forum sponsored by the Harvard T.H. Chan School of Public Health highlighted the issue, calling the omission a modern form of discrimination (Discrimination in America: Native American Experiences, 2017).

Also critical is data that reveals disparities in specific groups' risk for premature death, illness, chronic conditions, access to services and benefits, poverty and economic security, elder abuse and exploitation, crime in general, isolation, and discrimination. Examples include the National Health Interview Survey (NHIS), which is used to monitor health; the Crime Victimization survey, which tracks people's experience with crime; and the U.S. Census, which not only determines how many seats states have in Congress but how the government allocates funds for services and resources.

THE GENERATIONAL DIVIDE

The "generational divide" narrative assumes that different generations are rivals for resources and, therefore, in conflict. Essentially, these narratives posit that the baby boom generation, people born between the mid-1940s and the early 1960s, is in conflict with Millennials, who were born between 1982 and 2004. With over 83 million members, the Millennials are the largest living cohort.

The narrative further portrays older people as a special interest group, with some suggesting that the perspective has been promoted for political advantage. Polivka (2015), for example, blames neoconservatives for creating an "us versus them" mentality based on the notion that government support for older people takes away from programs for other age groups. The narrative further suggests that old people are to blame for the current healthcare crisis because they have not saved enough or taken care of their health. Some allege that by crafting policies to drastically reduce benefits that do not take effect for 10 years or longer, politicians are assuming that older voters will support the measures because they are not concerned about younger generations. Conversely, the narrative assumes that younger generations will not stand up for Medicare because they see the program as only affecting old people, whose welfare is not their concern.

There is also a cultural dimension to the intergenerational divide. Approximately 44% of Millennials belong to racial or ethnic minority groups compared to 21.7% of Baby Boomers (U.S. Census Bureau, 2015), accounting for what is referred to by some as the "racial generation gap" (Pastor, Ito, & Carter, 2015).

Accius and Yeh (2016) point out that understanding demographic trends like these is essential to achieving intergenerational parity and that the "destinies of racially and ethnically diverse younger and older generations are intertwined." As the country's White Baby Boomers age and retire, and racial minorities account for increases in the labor force, the older generation's well-being increasingly depends on the prosperity and security of younger minorities. Conversely, social policies that affect the well-being of Millennials depend on the support of older Whites, who make up a significant voting bloc and will remain one for several election cycles.

EMERGING THREATS

Threats to equity and fairness abound today. They range from cuts to programs that level the playing field for disadvantaged groups like the ACA, Medicaid, Social Security, Supplemental Security Income, and nutrition programs, to anti-immigrant rhetoric, which discourages older immigrants from accessing services and benefits they are entitled to. The hollowing out of civil rights units within government agencies has reduced access to recourse when civil rights violations occur and resulted in the relaxing of enforcement.

Threatened cuts to research aimed at exposing disparities are also of concern. For example, in 2014, questions about sexual orientation and gender identity were added to the National Survey of Older Americans Act Participants to better understand the vulnerabilities and needs of older LGBT Americans. The new questions about gender identity and sexual orientation were eliminated without warning in a draft of the 2017 survey. After a public outcry, the questions were reinstated.

Mounting fears about the solvency of Social Security and Medicare have prompted calls to raise the age at which beneficiaries are eligible. Proponents point to increases in average life expectancies since the programs were created and the improved health status of elders today to justify the measure. But as described earlier, raising the age would unfairly disadvantage people with shorter life expectancies, including the poor and people of color, who receive benefits for fewer years. Because these groups are also likely to experience age-related chronic diseases and disabilities at a younger age, they would be less likely to receive the benefits when they need them.

The poor also depend on benefits more. Although Social Security was created as a supplement to retirement savings, for approximately a third (32%) of White beneficiaries, it accounts for 90% or more of their incomes. That percentage for African Americans is 45% and 52% for Latinos. Narrowing eligibility for the programs will increase the number of non-Whites living in poverty to a much greater extent than for Whites (Center on Budget and Policy Priorities, 2018).

Threats to equity like these can be expected to escalate as the older population continues to grow and calls for "entitlement reform" are proposed to offset the growing budget deficit.

PROGRESS AND INNOVATIONS

In the face of looming threats, it is critical to recognize where progress has been made, what works, and where gains are achievable. The ACA decreased the number of uninsured women aged 19 to 64 by nearly half, from 20%

(19 million) in 2010 to 11% (11 million) in 2016. Among low-income women, the uninsured rate fell from 34% to 18% (Griffith, Evans, & Bor, 2017).

Similar gains were made by Blacks and Hispanics. During the first 2 years of the ACA's coverage expansions, the uninsured rate dropped 9% for Black adults aged 19 to 64 and 12% for Hispanic adults. The uninsured rate for White adults, which was already much lower, declined by 5%. These declines mean an estimated two million more Black adults, 3.5 million more Hispanic adults, and 6.7 million more White adults had health insurance in 2015 compared to 2013 (Griffith, Evans, & Bor, 2017). These successes affect people of all ages and will follow young beneficiaries into advanced age.

Like other federal healthcare programs, the ACA also prohibits discrimination by participating programs. It requires hospitals receiving Medicare or Medicaid funds to respect the rights of LGBT patients to choose who visits them and to make medical decisions on their behalf.

Key provisions of the ACA have been retracted and continued threats loom. But these setbacks have served to significantly elevate the issue and generate support for expanding healthcare coverage. In 2017, when Senator Bernie Sanders unveiled "Medicare for all," a plan for universal healthcare, 16 senators and 60% of House democrats supported the measure. Momentum for this plan continues to build. Several states are moving ahead on their own to extend coverage.

Groups around the country are also developing programs, policies, and services aimed at achieving income and health equity, improving access to health and social services by underserved groups, protecting the rights of the disenfranchised, and combatting abuse, discrimination, and exploitation. The following examples provide a sampling.

- The Alzheimer's Association has launched a major initiative to address disparities in rates of dementia and access to dementia care among African Americans.
- Wisdom Warriors, a 6-week program in Washington State, teaches tribal elders with chronic illnesses ways to manage them more effectively. The program incorporates traditional activities and values.
- The Community Ambassador Program for Seniors (CAPS) in Fremont, California, is a collaboration among public agencies and ethnic, faith, and community organizations that trains older volunteers to help immigrant elders navigate bureaucratic systems like government benefits and nonprofit services.
- All of Us or None addresses the needs of older women who are reentering their communities following incarceration. A primary concern is the

high rates of serious disease and disability associated with prolonged untreated health problems (P. Vanderhorst, personal communication, April 18, 2018).

CONCLUSION

Achieving equity and fairness for older people is core to elder justice. It will require recognizing and mitigating health disparities across the life span and addressing their repercussions in old age. Ongoing surveillance and research will be needed to identify risk factors, trends, and underserved groups. Intergenerational equity will require combatting age-based discrimination in jobs, healthcare, housing, and lending, and ensuring fairness in access to services, protections, and opportunities. It will further require countering discrimination based on race, religion, ethnicity, gender identity, disability, and other factors.

Multifaceted approaches to policy and practice are needed. Proposed changes to the tax system, entitlement programs, and services need to be reviewed to identify winners and losers and to take steps to achieve fairer outcomes. Improved access to services by underserved groups will require culturally specific outreach and the use of community health workers, navigators, advocates, and interpreters.

Achieving intergenerational parity also requires rejecting "generations at war" narratives and efforts that pursue fairness for older people at the expense of others. It requires "across the life span" approaches such as the development of funding formulas for services that take into account the needs of children, adults with disabilities, and older adults. It requires that advocates for people of all ages support each other's efforts. Public awareness and engagement initiatives to promote intergenerational equity must be two-directional, countering ageism while conveying that the prosperity of the young, especially younger minorities, is vital to the old.

REFERENCES

Accius, J., & Yeh, J. C. (2016). America must invest in its next generations. *Generations,* *40*(4), 101–107.

Administration for Community Living. (2016). *Final national voluntary consensus guidelines for state adult protective services systems.* Washington, DC: U.S. Department of Health and Human Services. Retrieved from https://www.acl.gov/sites/default/files/programs/2017-03/APS-Guidelines-Document-2017.pdf

Agency for Healthcare Research and Quality. (2017). *2016 national healthcare quality and disparities report.* Retrieved from http://www.ahrq.gov/research/findings/nhqrdr/nhqdr16/index.html

Alzheimer's Association. (2017). Stressful life experiences age the brain by four years, African Americans most at risk. Retrieved from https://alz.org/aaic/releases_2017/AAIC17-Sun-briefing-racial-disparities.asp

Artiga, S., Ubri, P., & Foutz, J. (2017, September 7). Medicaid and American Indians and Alaska Natives. Retrieved from https://www.kff.org/medicaid/issue-brief/medicaid-and-american-indians-and-alaska-natives

Beach, S. R., Schulz, R., Castle, N. G., & Rosen, J. (2010). Financial exploitation and psychological mistreatment among older adults: Differences between African Americans and non-African Americans in a population-based survey. *The Gerontologist, 50*(6), 744–757. doi:10.1093/geront/gnq053

Bureau of Justice Statistics. (2018). *Prisoners in 2016* (NCJ 251149). Retrieved from https://www.bjs.gov/content/pub/pdf/p16.pdf

Campbell, L. J., Cai, X., Gao, S., & Li, Y. (2016). Racial/ethnic disparities in nursing home quality of life deficiencies, 2001 to 2011. *Gerontology and Geriatric Medicine.* doi:10.1177/2333721416653561

Center on Budget and Policy Priorities. (2018). Policy basics: Top ten facts about Social Security. Retrieved from https://www.cbpp.org/research/social-security/policy-basics-top-ten-facts-about-social-security

Centers for Disease Control and Prevention. (2017). Health disparities. Retrieved from https://www.cdc.gov/aging/disparities

Chetty, R., Stepner, M., Abraham, S., Lin, S., Scuderi, B., Turner, N., . . . Cutler, D. (2016). The association between income and life expectancy in the United States, 2001–2014. *Journal of the American Medical Association, 315*(16), 1750–1766. doi:10.1001/jama.2016.4226

Child Welfare Information Gateway. (2016). *Major federal legislation concerned with child protection, child welfare, and adoption.* Washington, DC: U.S. Department of Health and Human Services, Children's Bureau. Retrieved from https://www.childwelfare.gov/pubpdfs/majorfedlegis.pdf

Connolly, M.-T., & Trilling, A. (2014). Seven policy priorities for an enhanced public health response to elder abuse. In Institute of Medicine & National Research Council (Eds.), *Elder abuse and its prevention: Workshop summary* (pp. 59–67). Washington, DC: National Academies Press. Retrieved from http://www.ncbi.nlm.nih.gov/books/NBK208578

Courtney-Long, E. A., Carroll, D. D., Zhang, Q. C., Stevens, A. C., Griffin-Blake, S., Armour, B. S., & Campbell, V. A. (2015). Prevalence of disability and disability type among adults—United States, 2013. *Morbidity and Mortality Weekly Report, 64*, 777–783. doi:10.15585/mmwr.MM6429a2

Cubanski, J., Koma, W., Damico, A., & Neuman, T. (2018). How many seniors live in poverty? Retrieved from https://www.kff.org/medicare/issue-brief/how-many-seniors-are-living-in-poverty-national-and-state-estimates-under-the-official-and-supplemental-poverty-measures-in-2016

Deem, D., Nerenberg, L., & Titus, R. (2013). Victims of financial crime. In R. C. Davis, A. J. Lurigio, & S. Herman (Eds.), *Victims of crime* (4th ed., pp. 185–210). Thousand Oaks, CA: Sage.

DeLiema, M., Gassoumis, Z. D., Homeier, D. C., & Wilber, K. H. (2012). Determining prevalence and correlates of elder abuse using *promotores*: Low-income immigrant Latinos report high rates of abuse and neglect. *Journal of the American Geriatrics Society, 60*(7), 1333–1339. doi:10.1111/j.1532-5415.2012.04025.x

Discrimination in America: Native American Experiences. (2017). Forum sponsored by the Harvard T.H. Chan School of Public Health. Retrieved from https://theforum.sph .harvard.edu/events/discrimination-in-america-2

Farber, J., & Munson, S. (2007). Improving the child welfare workforce. Retrieved from http://youthlaw.org/ publication/improving-the-child-welfare-workforce

Farrell, C. (2016, December 12). The painful struggles of America's older immigrants. *Forbes.* Retrieved from https://www.forbes.com/sites/nextavenue/2016/12/12/the-pain ful-struggles-of-americas-older-immigrants/#5bef277f39d9

Federal Bureau of Prisons. (2018). Inmate age. Retrieved from https://www.bop.gov/ about/statistics/statistics_inmate_age.jsp

Feng, Z., Fennell, M., Tyler, D., Clark, M., & Mor, V. (2011). Growth of racial and ethnic minorities in US nursing homes driven by demographics and possible disparities in options. *Health Affairs, 30*(7), 1358–1365. doi:10.1377/hlthaff.2011.0126

Fennell, M. L., Feng, Z., Clark, M. A., & Mor, V. (2010). Elderly Hispanics more likely to reside in poor-quality nursing homes. *Health Affairs, 29*(1), 65–73. doi:10.1377/ hlthaff.2009.0003

Fredriksen-Goldsen, K. I., Kim, H.-J., Emlet, C. A., Muraco, A., Erosheva, E. A., Hoy-Ellis, C. P., . . . Petry, H. (2011). *The aging and health report: Disparities and resilience among lesbian, gay, bisexual, and transgender older adults.* Seattle, WA: Institute for Multigenerational Health. Retrieved from http://www.familleslgbt.org/1463149763/Fredriksen -Goldsen%202011.pdf

Government Accountability Office. (2011). Elder justice: Stronger federal leadership could enhance national response to elder abuse. Retrieved from https://www.gao.gov/ products/GAO-11-208

Griffith, K., Evans, L., & Bor, J. (2017). The Affordable Care Act reduced socioeconomic disparities in health care access. *Health Affairs, 36*(8), 1503–1510. doi:10.1377/hlthaff.2017.0083

Hernandez-Tejada, M. A., Amstadter, A., Muzzy, W., & Acierno, R. (2013). The National Elder Mistreatment Study: Race and ethnicity findings. *Journal of Elder Abuse & Neglect, 25*(4), 281–293. doi:10.1080/08946566.2013.770305

Human Rights First. (2016, August 2). Domestic servitude, an especially hidden form of labor trafficking [Blog post]. Retrieved from https://www.humanrightsfirst.org/ blog/domestic-servitude-especially-hidden-form-labor-trafficking

Jervis, L. L., Hamby, S., Beach, S. R., Williams, M. L., Maholmes, V., & Castille, D. M. (2016). Elder mistreatment in underserved populations: Opportunities and challenges to developing a contemporary program of research. *Journal of Elder Abuse & Neglect, 28*(4–5), 301–319. doi:10.1080/08946566.2016.1245644

Kushel, M. (2018). Hepatitis A outbreak in California—addressing the root cause. *New England Journal of Medicine, 378*(3), 211–213. doi:10.1056/NEJMp1714134

Maschi, T. (2013, December 2). Extending elder justice and human rights to incarcerated older adults, Part II: Promising programs and solutions [Blog post]. Retrieved from http://www.asaging.org/blog/extending-elder-justice-and-human-rights -incarcerated-older-adults-part-ii-promising-programs-a

Mor, V., Zinn, J., Angelelli, J., Teno, J. M., & Miller, S. C. (2004). Driven to tiers: Socioeconomic and racial disparities in the quality of nursing home care. *The Milbank Quarterly, 82*(2), 227–256. doi:10.1111/j.0887-378X.2004.00309.x

National Center for Health Statistics. (2017). *Health, United States, 2016: With chartbook on long-term trends in health.* Hyattsville, MD: Author. Retrieved from https://www.cdc .gov/nchs/data/hus/hus16.pdf#015

National Council on Aging. (2016). Economic security for seniors facts. Retrieved from https://www.ncoa.org/news/resources-for-reporters/get-the-facts/economic -security-facts/

Office of the Inspector General. (2016). *The impact of an aging inmate population on the Federal Bureau of Prisons*. Retrieved from https://oig.justice.gov/reports/2015/e1505 .pdf

Pastor, M., Ito, J., & Carter, V. (2015). *Talkin' 'bout our generations: Data, deliberation, and destiny in a changing America*. Los Angeles, CA: USC Program for Environmental and Regional Equity.

Polivka, L. J. (2015, October 22). The legacy of Claude Pepper and the future of aging advocacy [Blog post]. Retrieved from https://www.asaging.org/blog/legacy-claude -pepper-and-future-aging-advocacy

Public Policy Institute of California. (n.d.). California's changing prison population. Retrieved from http://www.ppic.org/blog/tag/proposition-47

Semega, J. L., Fontenot, K. R., & Kollar, M. A. (2017). *Income and poverty in the United States: 2016*. Washington, DC: U.S. Government Printing Office. Retrieved from https:// www.census.gov/content/dam/Census/library/publications/2017/demo/ P60-259.pdf

Smith, A. (1776). *An inquiry into the nature and causes of the wealth of nations*. London, UK: Strahan & Cadell.

Tax Policy Center. (2017). *Briefing book: A citizen's guide to the fascinating (though often complex) elements of the federal tax system*. Retrieved from http://www.taxpolicy center.org/briefing-book/are-federal-taxes-progressive

Tilly, J., & Hudgins, K. (2017, October 23). *Community living for American Indian, Alaskan Native, and Native Hawaiian elders*. Washington, DC: Administration for Community Living. Center for Policy and Evaluation. Retrieved from https://ltcombudsman .org/uploads/files/issues/native-communities-issue-brief.pdf

U.S. Census Bureau. (2015). Millennials outnumber Baby Boomers and are far more diverse, Census Bureau reports. Retrieved from https://www.census.gov/news room/press-releases/2015/cb15-113.html

9

Consumer Choice: The Power and Perils

INTRODUCTION

A dramatic shift has occurred in the field of long-term care in recent decades in how providers talk about those they serve. Today, patients, clients, and residents of long-term care facilities are increasingly being referred to as "consumers," a change that is intended to elevate their role from passive recipients of care, whose preferences and complaints are likely to be overlooked or discounted, to active participants in their care. The term further suggests that care users are entitled to the same consumer rights afforded to consumers of other goods and services, including "consumer choice," or the assurance that they have choices to choose from and opportunities to choose.

But what does the change actually mean? Despite widespread support for the concept of consumer choice, little attention has been paid toward understanding what it means; that is, what rights consumers have with respect to care, and the power and perils that come with it.

This chapter explores challenges that older consumers face, some as a result of functional limitations and others resulting from problems inherent in the long-term care market itself. It acknowledges the special rights of users of medical care, nursing homes, assisted living facilities (ALFs), and health plans as articulated in patients' rights and residents' rights declarations and agreements. And finally, the chapter makes the case that consumers' rights should be a component of elder justice and that elder justice advocates and the public need to understand how to exercise and protect them. It suggests ways of doing so.

WHAT ARE CONSUMER RIGHTS?

Consumer advocates generally agree that consumers of goods and services are entitled to:

© Springer Publishing Company DOI: 10.1891/9780826147578.0009

1. Multiple goods and services that are reasonably safe and that vary in price and quality
2. Information enabling them to weigh alternatives and identify false and misleading claims in advertising and labeling
3. Protections by government and accountability by providers through regulation and channels of recourse
4. Privacy with respect to sensitive personal information they provide in everyday consumer transactions

The following sections focus on consumer rights in health and long-term care, as it is within these arenas that the concept of consumer choice has arisen. Challenges faced by older consumers do, however, extend to other markets and several examples are provided.

I. Access to Multiple Goods and Services That Vary in Price and Quality

For markets to operate the way they are supposed to, consumers need a variety of options to choose from to accommodate their tastes, preferences, and financial means. Producers and providers of services need to be able to compete fairly. When these conditions are met, the forces of competition kick in to drive prices down, which ensures that consumers are satisfied.

Baby boomers have never failed to inspire innovation in product design and new products—their sheer numbers move markets. They are courted and catered to by providers and have inspired a vast array of "age-friendly" products that offer variety and convenience. High-tech products like telemonitoring and robots that may be a boon for older people who want to remain independent are financially out of reach now but will likely become affordable as competition for the senior market increases. Entrepreneurs and investors are banking on it.

It is widely recognized that healthcare does not respond to market forces the same way that other goods and services do. The prices of medical care, nursing homes, drugs, and other products and services have skyrocketed in the absence of the forces that animate other markets. These can be attributed to a great extent to the way health services are financed and provided. Efforts to address these problems through public policy have created an industry in flux, posing new challenges to consumers, providers, and advocates.

Further contributing to uncertainty surrounding healthcare is the fact that many healthcare services that were traditionally provided by charitable and nonprofit entities are now offered by large, for-profit entities. The impact of the change on the quality and affordability of services and the need for regulation has not been adequately explored.

Controlling Costs

Much has been written about why the cost of healthcare in the United States continually goes up and vastly exceeds that of other developed countries that offer better coverage and outcomes. Many factors are responsible. Markets can be manipulated and governments impose laws or regulations that work against the "natural" market forces. The greatest disruptor of market forces in healthcare is arguably the prominence of third-party payers that serve as intermediaries between consumers and providers of healthcare and fee-for-service payment plans. In real free-market exchanges, no patient would pay 25 dollars for an aspirin, yet inflated prices are the norm when healthcare is paid for by third-party payers, including private health insurance plans and public programs like Medicare and Medicaid. Under fee-for-service health plans, third-party payers reimburse hospitals, clinics, physicians, and pharmacies each time patients use them. Since consumers pay little or none of the costs directly, they have little incentive to find the cheapest providers. If providers are reimbursed each time they provide care or services, they too have little incentive to hold back or conserve resources.

It therefore falls to third-party payers to keep costs down, which they have done by reducing services, raising premiums and copayments, denying coverage to those with preexisting conditions, imposing caps on what they pay, and dropping patients who use too much care. In the case of private health plans, these practices are often concealed, which makes choosing plans particularly fraught. As the largest single third-party payer of healthcare (accounting for more than a quarter of spending), the government, through Medicare and Medicaid, has an enormous stake in keeping prices low. As steward of the public good, it also bears responsibility for ensuring quality care and patients' rights. Politics, however, often gets in the way. For example, rather than using its enormous purchasing power to negotiate costs for drugs, Congress prohibits Medicare from doing so. The system's bias toward institutional, as opposed to home-based, care further drives prices up (see Chapter 2).

Much of the reform in health and long-term care that has taken place in recent decades has focused on changing these incentive structures by creating positive incentives for providers to keep prices down while simultaneously keeping quality high (or at least not harming consumers). As described earlier, the Olmsted Supreme Court decision also led to some rebalancing of Medicaid spending from institutional to community-based care.

The Patient Protection and Affordable Care Act (ACA) banned the most egregious practices of health insurance plans such as turning away patients with preexisting conditions and dropping them when they cost too much (see Chapter 2). It addressed spiraling costs by rewarding providers for keeping costs down while maintaining quality and punishing those who fail to do so. Examples include the Hospital Readmission Reduction Program (HRRP), which attempts to stop hospitals from discharging patients prematurely or with insufficient care plans by charging them penalties for readmitting patients within 30 days of discharge (Damberg et al., 2014).

The ACA also tackled the incentive problem by supporting models like accountable care organizations (ACOs), which are healthcare organizations made up of doctors, hospitals, and other providers.[1] ACOs are paid negotiated fixed rates, giving them an incentive to keep patients healthy since they achieve savings if patients do not get sick and assume the costs of treating those who do. This is accomplished through healthy lifestyle programs, health education, vaccines, interventions to reduce risks, and screening to detect and treat problems during their early stages. Another approach is "bundled payments," where providers are paid by Medicare based on the expected costs of treating specific conditions. For example, experts recommend a treatment plan for hip replacement surgery, the costs of which are estimated and adjusted to reflect regional differences and other variables. The price is then used in determining Medicare's reimbursement rate for the procedure. Quality performance measures are also established for each treatment. In 2016, an estimated 30% of traditional Medicare payments went through alternative payment models like bundled payments and ACOs (U.S. Department of Health and Human Services [HHS], 2016).

Little is known about whether programs like these are in fact leading to greater consumer choice and satisfaction, particularly in light of the hurdles some are facing. For example, when California implemented the California Coordinated Care Act, which moves beneficiaries of both Medicare and Medicaid (called "dual eligibles") into managed care plans, most eligible consumers and providers opted out, making it difficult to demonstrate that the change could save costs as well as improve patient health (C. Sewell, personal communication, August 11, 2018).

The Rise of Large, for-Profit Healthcare Providers

Another major change in the health and long-term care environment that affects consumers is the rise of large, for-profit hospitals, nursing homes, ALFs, and home-based services. Research on the impact of this trend is still

---

[1] ACOs are a variation on health maintenance organizations (HMOs) that operate on the same principle but which are often disparaged for lack of accountability.

in its infancy but some studies have shown that it has had a negative impact on quality, suggesting the need for greater attention to consumer protections, regulations, and remedies.

Today, one in five of the country's 6,210 hospitals are private and investor owned (American Hospital Association, 2019). Most quality comparisons between nonprofits and for-profits find that nonprofits provide superior quality care more often than for-profits and, surprisingly, do as well or better with respect to cost and efficiency. One study showed, for example, that for-profits had higher mortality rates, employed fewer trained professionals, and were more expensive than nonprofits and government-run facilities (Devereaux et al., 2004). Critics also charge that the growth of for-profits has decreased the availability of healthcare for "unprofitable" patients and provide fewer "unprofitable services" like mental healthcare (Horwitz, 2005). Other studies comparing performance have yielded mixed results, perhaps due to the difficulty in measuring patient outcomes (Rosenau & Linder, 2003).

The shift from nonprofit, charitable, to large, for-profit chains is also occurring in nursing home care. The sheer size of the population and the bias in Medicare and Medicaid toward institutional care has led to dramatic increases in the number of large, for-profit homes. This can be expected to increase as the ranks of the elderly population continue to rise—older people account for 85% of nursing home residents (Centers for Disease Control and Prevention, 2016). Today, of the country's approximately 15,500 nursing homes that are certified to offer care to Medicaid and Medicare beneficiaries, 70% are for-profit (Centers for Medicare and Medicaid Services [CMS], 2015). Until the late 1970s, most for-profit homes were small independent facilities, but by 1985, approximately 70% of the for-profit homes had become part of large nursing home chains (Almgren, 2017).

As is the case with hospital care, studies have shown that large, for-profit nursing home chains provide poorer care than smaller, for-profits, and that proprietary homes in general provide poorer care. A 2009 U.S. Government Accountability Office (GAO) report found that about 55% of the most poorly performing nursing homes were for-profit and chain affiliated (GAO, 2009). Another showed that the 10 largest for-profit nursing home chains employed 37% fewer registered nurses than nonprofit and government-run facilities between 2003 and 2008 and received 59% more inspection deficiency reports (Harrington, Olney, Carrillo, & Kang, 2011). A recent study comparing homes for quality using Medicare's five-star rating system (where one is the poorest care and five is the highest) found that 42% of the for-profit homes received one- to two-star ratings, which is about twice as many as the nonprofits. The smaller homes did better, with

39% of those with fewer than 60 beds receiving five stars (Boccuti, Casillas, & Neuaman, 2015).

The rise of large, for-profit nursing home chains has strengthened incentives for private attorneys to get involved in elder abuse cases, with homes facing soaring numbers of lawsuits in the past two decades. It is what *Wall Street Journal* reporter Jennifer Smith calls "a litigation boom aimed at for-profit nursing home operators" (Smith, 2014). They are holding the homes liable for pressure sores, falls, dehydration, improper or excessive restraints, wrongful death, sexual assault, improper medication or treatment, battery, infliction of emotional distress, and false imprisonment. Defending homes against claims is also a booming business.

The commercialization of long-term care also extends to care provided in the community, including the Program of All-Inclusive Care for the Elderly (PACE), which was designed as an alternative to nursing home care for those who want to live at home. PACE accomplishes this by providing both medical care and social support to frail people in their homes. Social support includes personal care attendants, home-delivered meals, adult day programs, home healthcare, case management, and other home- and community-based services.

Originally PACE programs could only be run by nonprofits, but when they, and programs like them, failed to catch on, the government allowed for-profit companies to try (Varney, 2016). The programs turned out to be even more lucrative than nursing homes, with profit margins averaging as high as 15%, compared to 2% for homes (Varney, 2016), This, along with Medicare enrollment expected to grow by 30 million people in the next two decades, has attracted the attention of private equity firms, venture capitalists, and entrepreneurs. New programs increasingly rely on technologies like video calls instead of in-person doctor visits and voice technologies like the Amazon Echo to keep costs down and profits high. The impact of these changes has yet to be determined.

2. Information Enabling Consumers to Weigh Alternatives and Identify False and Misleading Claims in Advertising and Labeling

Older consumers use a variety of highly complex goods and services, ranging from medical technologies to health and long-term care insurance plans. Consumers of health and long-term care often lack the information they need to make informed and appropriate choices. Products may be too complicated for the average consumer to evaluate, credible information may not be available, or information about them may be too complex. Product information may be intentionally vague or misleading, or it may only be available online, creating barriers for those who do not have access to computers or are not computer savvy. As noted earlier, providers of private insurance plans often reduce costs by cutting services, setting ceilings on what they provide, and taking other measures that are often concealed, which makes choosing among plans particularly fraught. Although the ACA reduced or eliminated some of these traps, changes to the act have weakened these protections and their future remains uncertain.

Providers of long-term services and supports (LTSS) often use cryptic, misleading, shorthand, or anachronistic terminology to describe services. Terms like "Medicaid waiver programs"[2] or "dual eligibles," which are frequently used by professionals, often find their way into outreach materials or are used by outreach workers or marketers despite the fact that they are unfamiliar to most consumers.

Cognitive and communication barriers, which are described later, pose additional challenges. Other barriers to understanding products and services include limited literacy. In addition to difficulties in reading or understanding English, consumers may have limited financial capacity (see Chapter 10) or financial literacy, or the information they are given may fail to reflect cultural variations or needs with respect to understanding.

Consumers are particularly unlikely to have adequate information about the personal care providers they hire. Selecting personal care workers and caregivers is among the most significant choices that many consumers make given the intimate nature of their contact with helpers, the long periods of time they spend alone together, and the largely unfettered access caregivers may have to their homes, assets, and personal information. Consumers often lack critical information about workers' backgrounds, including histories of criminality or substance abuse, credit problems, or immigration status, that could pose risks. The lack of access to this information stems from lack of abuser registries, the inability of consumers to access prior personnel records that could indicate past problems, and lack of coordination among agencies that collect information on caregivers. The difficulties consumers face in hiring workers is exacerbated by an acute shortage of qualified workers, which can largely be attributed to the low pay that workers earn and the lack of

---

[2] The term is sometimes used to describe programs created as an alternative to nursing homes. It refers to the fact that nursing homes were the only type of long-term care that Medicaid originally paid for. The waivers were granted to states to allow them to offer community, home-based services instead.

benefits and occupational safety standards. As a result, consumers may have a limited supply of workers to choose among, which makes their choices more challenging.

3. Government Protections and Provider Accountability

Consumer rights and protection laws set standards for what providers of goods and services can, must, and cannot do. They include statutes related to commerce, health and safety, public health, housing, lending, and other areas, which are too numerous to enumerate here (so too are the entities responsible for setting standards and regulations, monitoring, and enforcement). These entities may ban unsafe or unhealthy products, impose rules or obligations on providers, sanction violators, ensure that consumers have information on which to base choices, and empower consumers to fight back against unfair or fraudulent business practices.

Consumer protections and the parties that are empowered to implement and enforce them are determined by such factors as whether the government provides or pays for the services and goods, the type of services, and the settings in which they are provided. Sanctions for misconduct by providers and the entities charged to enforce them also vary.

Patients' and residents' rights in hospitals and nursing homes that are certified and paid for by Medicare and Medicaid, for example, are covered under the 1990 Patient Self-Determination Act (PSDA), and the CMS is the government entity responsible for promoting and enforcing those rights. Under the act, residents have a right to be protected against abuse, to be informed, to make their own decisions (this includes refusing treatment), and to have personal information kept private. The PSDA also requires nursing homes to provide information on advance directives at the time of admission. Federal law also prohibits nursing homes from discharging or evicting residents unless they cannot meet residents' needs and requires them to ensure that discharges are safe and orderly.

The most comprehensive federal law for protecting residents' rights in Medicare- and/or Medicaid-certified nursing homes is the Nursing Home Reform Act of 1987, which contains guidelines for nursing homes and grants residents the rights to adequate nutrition, personal hygiene, mental and emotional support, and social involvement. The act further entitles them to personalized written care plans—prepared by residents' families, a registered nurse, and a physician—that outline their nursing, medical, and psychosocial needs and how facilities intend to meet them. The plans also assess residents' functional capacity. Other services that residents are entitled to include:

- Medically related social services
- Proper healthcare, such as primary and dental care
- Accurate dispensing, receipt, and administration of medicines and drugs
- Dietary services that meet the daily nutritional needs of each patient
- Special services for residents with intellectual disabilities
- Personal, material, and financial privacy when requested
- Treatment that does not violate the resident's dignity or respect

CMS uses a system of regulation and penalties to ensure these rights. As pointed out in Chapter 3, the system has had limited impact. A 2014 study by the HHS Inspector General found that 22% of Medicare patients who stayed in nursing facilities for 35 days or less experienced harm as a result of their medical care, with an additional 11% suffering temporary injury. The report further estimated that Medicare spent $2.8 billion on hospital treatment in 2011 because of harm (Office of the Inspector General, 2014).

In 2015, CMS enacted new regulations that ensured additional rights and protections for residents. They include protections against physical or chemical restraints imposed for discipline or convenience and mandate training to staff in abuse prevention and dementia care. They further require homes to ensure that staffing decisions are based on residents' needs to ensure that their employees have the skills they need. They require homes to adopt "patient-centered" care planning that reflects residents' goals and preferences. There are provisions for improving discharge planning, giving residents more choices and flexibility in meals, improving infection control, and limiting the use of psychotropic medications.

A particularly significant reform from a consumer standpoint was a ban against facilities' use of arbitration agreements, which residents are typically asked to sign at admission. Many residents feel compelled to sign the agreements, fearing that they will be denied care if they refuse. In signing, they are essentially waiving the right to seek legal relief if they have disputes or experience abuse or neglect, regardless of how serious they are. Under the agreements, if disputes occur, residents' only recourse is arbitration proceedings, which often may be secretive. They are also waiving their right to participate in class action suits, which may be the only form of justice available to some low-income victims. Regulations that passed under the Obama Administration that prohibited the use of mandatory arbitration agreements in residential care contracts have been rescinded under the current administration.

Critics contend that these safeguards are vastly inadequate and that it is unreasonable to assume that residents, their families, and advocates understand their rights and are capable of defending them. This is particularly true in light of the frequent changes made to regulations.

As noted in earlier chapters, the Long-Term Care Ombudsman Program (LTCOP) was created under the Older Americans Act to advocate on behalf of nursing home residents. Ombudsmen investigate residents' complaints, support resident and family councils, advocate on behalf of residents facing illegal discharges, help residents file Medicaid applications and fair hearing requests, assist with Medicare and Medicaid appeals, and help residents retain legal counsel and make police reports for abuse (see Chapter 2). They can also draft letters revoking powers of attorney that are being used improperly and advocate for systemic reforms.

Among the most common violations of residents' rights received by ombudsmen are for illegal evictions, which is attributed to the fact that Medicare only covers nursing home care for a short time after patients are released from hospitals. After that, they or third-party payers have to pick up the costs, which are typically exorbitant; few patients have private insurance that covers them. As a result, many Medicare beneficiaries end up on Medicaid, which pays homes a fixed rate that is significantly lower than what Medicare, other third-party payers, or private payers pay. Homes therefore have an incentive to evict residents once their Medicare or other coverage ends to free up bed space for higher paying patients.

Ombudsman programs are increasingly reporting illegal discharges and evictions. A 2017 *Kaiser Health News* study cites the Illinois Ombudsman as estimating that reports have more than doubled in her state since 2011, and other states report similar increases (Wiener, 2017). The same study describes the enormous risks that some discharged and evicted residents face, detailing instances in which poor and disabled residents were discharged onto the street or into hotels or homeless shelters.

States have defined additional far-ranging rights for nursing home residents, including the right to exercise, be suitably dressed, smoke and consume alcohol, practice religion, and choose roommates (University of Minnesota School of Public Health, n.d.). Some have added the right to air conditioning, foods that comply with religious dietary rules and restrictions, and access to phones and mail.

It was not until 2014 that CMS set standards for other community-based services and required states to find ways of delivering care to Medicaid enrollees in home and community-based settings. States were given until 2019 to carry out plans but the deadline was extended by CMS in 2017 to give states an extra 3 years.

Consumer protection laws for ALFs have not kept pace with the industry, leading critics to brand them as an unfulfilled promise to consumers. ALFs were created to provide care to people who do not require skilled nursing level care but, rather, help with daily activities. In reality, many are unable to provide the level of care they promise and insist that residents who require higher levels arrange for it on their own. They are not regulated by the federal government, although some states require homes to be licensed (often failing to enforce the laws or respond to violations). As is the case with nursing homes, illegal evictions are common. Eric Carlson, lead attorney for the advocacy organization Justice and Aging, warns that "these newer assisted-living facilities still have a huge amount of discretion to push residents out as they wish. And people don't see an obvious way to challenge the evictions so they just pick up and move" (Serres, 2017).

States have defined additional far-ranging rights including the right of nursing home residents to exercise, be suitably dressed, smoke and consume alcohol, practice religion, and choose roommates (University of Minnesota School of Public Health, n.d.). Some assert the right to air conditioning, foods that comply with religious dietary rules and restrictions, and access to phones and mail.

The government's role in protecting long-term care consumers' rights and controlling the market is controversial, with conflicting attitudes in full view today as consumer protections are routinely challenged. The same is true with respect to other goods and services commonly used by older people. Areas of particular concern include financial products and services.

4. Privacy

Consumer privacy involves the handling and protection of sensitive personal information that individuals disclose to providers of goods and services. The Health Insurance Portability and Accountability Act (HIPAA) of 1996, which promotes affordability in and access to health insurance, is an example. It provides for stringent requirements on providers for protecting patient confidentiality and prohibits them from disclosing patients' health information to others for nonmedical reasons (e.g., providing health information to lenders that can be used as the rationale for denying them home mortgages or credit cards). HIPAA further holds providers accountable, through civil and criminal penalties, for violating patients' privacy rights.

Other concerns related to privacy protections that providers of goods and services are required to abide by have been described in other chapters, particularly as they relate to elder abuse. Examples include controversies surrounding nursing homes' surveillance of residents without their consent and the release of personal information about consumers by healthcare providers and financial institutions in the course of abuse investigations or care planning. These concerns suggest the need for further discussion about the challenges of balancing consumer privacy with concerns about their safety and security in the consumer context.

CONSUMER PERILS

As noted earlier, older consumers may face additional challenges including cognitive impairments, age-based discrimination, and consumer fraud. They may face the same or similar challenges with respect to other goods and services they commonly use, such as financial products and services.

"Capacity to Consume": Cognitive Impairments and Consumer Choice

Older consumers' ability to fully exercise their rights may be compromised by cognitive impairments that reduce their ability to compare options, negotiate costs, select and monitor service providers, or seek help when problems arise. Chapter 10 points out that different types and degrees of capacity are needed for different mental tasks and decisions. It further notes that lawyers and ethicists are in general agreement about how to determine whether people have the capacity that is needed for specific decisions or choices. For example, medical ethicists agree that to make treatment choices, patients need to be able to weigh the risks and benefits of proposed treatments. Lawyers are also in agreement about how to determine whether people are capable of executing wills and signing contracts. The more consequential the repercussions, the more certainty about decision makers' capacity is required.

Consumers' purchasing decisions also run the gamut in complexity and consequence, from selecting colors and flavors to choosing between complex health plans and home loans or determining whether professionals can be trusted. Surprisingly little attention has gone toward exploring consumers' ability to make choices—in other words, their "capacity to consume." This is particularly worrisome with respect to LTSS, as increasingly frail consumers are making decisions about their care. For example, publicly funded health programs are permitting LTSS consumers to "opt in" or "opt out" of health plans. Although the decision may seem relatively simple, it can have significant consequences such as forcing consumers to give up trusted family doctors. Other consequential decisions that older consumers are likely to be asked to make are whether to accept the terms of admission agreements for nursing homes and ALFs, and contracts for goods and services. These decisions may reduce consumers' options for recourse in the event that products are faulty or the conduct of service providers is abusive or negligent.

Understanding capacity in relation to LTSS and other consumer products is critical to determining when consumers need help, the type of help they need, and if surrogates are needed. Responsible providers also need to recognize when potential customers lack capacity so they do not inadvertently act improperly.

As noted earlier, consumers of home-based LTSS face a wide range of challenges, among the thorniest of which is exercising choice in hiring, supervising, and monitoring personal care attendants. As noted earlier, hiring decisions are particularly consequential given the nature of helpers' relationships to consumers. They are also extremely complex and little attention has been paid toward defining or assessing the decision-making capacity that is needed. The capacity needed to screen employees, negotiate agreements, supervise workers, terminate them if needed, and respond in emergencies (e.g., if a personal care worker does not show up to work or engages in misconduct) is not well understood and resources and safeguards to help consumers are vastly inadequate.

Age Discrimination and Fraud Against Older Consumers

Age discrimination in the consumer context includes impeding or prohibiting access to services, goods, or opportunities available to younger consumers. It also refers to providing worse care or lower quality goods to older people, failing to accommodate their needs, or treating them disrespectfully or dismissively.

Older consumers are frequent targets of age-based discrimination and illegal evictions by providers of housing. This is particularly true in communities with rent controls that prevent landlords from raising rents above specified amounts. Concerns about the rights of mobile home owners (also called trailers and manufactured homes) are increasingly being raised as more older people choose the option.

As per Robert Butler (1975), discrimination is also apparent in the disregard for older people's rights in nursing homes, and the failure of society to aggressively enforce patient and resident protection laws stems from ageism, a potent form of discrimination. As noted in Chapter 8, lesbian, gay, bisexual, transgender, and queer (LGBTQ) couples experience discrimination in nursing homes, and elders of color experience poorer care. The same is true for senior housing and retirement communities, and consumer rights organizations have gotten involved in cases regarding the targeting of elders of color by predatory lenders and mortgage companies (National Consumer Law Center, 2008).

The singling out and aggressive targeting of older people for scams and exploitation has also been described as a form of discrimination. Similarly, older immigrants are frequently targeted for "affinity fraud." An AARP-sponsored study described how corrupt or predatory businesses and con artists target older people and apply extreme pressure and deceptive tactics (Pratkanis & Shadel, 2005).

CONSUMER CHALLENGES
IN OTHER ARENAS

Older consumers face perils with respect to other products and services, including financial products like investments, insurance policies, and loans, many of which are highly complex, raising concerns about some older consumers' ability to weigh their benefits and risks, exercise informed consent, and withstand high pressure or coercion by salespersons.

A particularly disturbing example is the rise in foreclosures against older Americans with reverse mortgages, a product that is only available to people aged 62 or older. The mortgages allow homeowners to tap into the equity in their homes, often to purchase other goods or services. Lenders pay the homeowners a monthly advance while they continue to live in their homes. A 2017 report based on Freedom of Information Act (FOIA) disclosures showed a 646% increase in foreclosures in the past year against older people with federally insured reverse mortgages as compared to the previous 7 years (California Reinvestment Coalition, 2017).

Reverse mortgages are being aggressively marketed to older consumers, often by celebrities. Many consumers are unaware of how the loans work or that they can lose their homes if they default. Some, for example, fail to take into account the fact that interest is added to the loan's principal each month so that the amount owed increases as the interest compounds. They may not realize that if they fail to stay current with taxes or insurance, they can go into default and the mortgage company can foreclose. Consumers also complain that lenders refuse to refinance loans because there is insufficient remaining equity in their homes and that they do not keep adequate records.

There has also been an increase in widows being foreclosed on. Typically, loans become due at the death of the last borrower even if a surviving spouse who is not listed as a borrower is living in the home. Although the Department of Housing and Urban Development (HUD) has programs aimed at preventing this from happening, critics claim they are not doing enough to let survivors know about their options and are calling for HUD to do more.

Problems related to home loans in general include fraudulent or unscrupulous lenders deceiving senior borrowers through phony charges or inflated monthly payment amounts and vague service fees. Some withhold loan proceeds while forcing homeowners to make payments for the entire loan amount, foreclose on borrowers who are in compliance with loan terms, and fail to release liens on titles to borrowers' homes after loans are paid in full. Older homeowners who are at risk of foreclosure are also the frequent target of scammers offering to help.

Protections against practices like these include the Truth in Lending Act (TILA), which requires lenders to disclose important details regarding the cost and terms of home loans and allows homeowners to cancel up to 3 days after transactions and challenge predatory loans. The Real Estate Settlement and Procedures Act (RESPA) prohibits lender kickbacks to mortgage brokers for making referrals, and allows for triple damages and attorney fees for violations. States' unfair and deceptive practice laws also prohibit abusive practices such as the repeated and unnecessary refinancing ("flipping") of loans, making unaffordable loans to consumers, or misrepresenting terms of loans. States can also challenge excessive fees and costs, and other terms that are unfair to borrowers.

The rapid introduction of new products that target older consumers also poses potential perils. A notable example is the emerging market of "Internet of Things" products, which Jacob Morgan, a contributor to *Forbes*, describes as follows:

> basically connecting any device with an on and off switch to the Internet (and/or to each other). This includes everything from cellphones, coffee makers, washing machines . . . wearable devices and almost anything else you can think of. (2014, para. 4)

Internet of Things products are revolutionizing medical and long-term care, creating countless opportunities for both consumers and those who seek to profit from them. Reenita Das, also writing for *Forbes*, lists 10 "Internet of medical care" product categories that target older consumers and their caregivers (Das, 2017). They include voice-interactive digital assistants like Amazon Echo, portable diagnostics devices, personal emergency response systems, Bluetooth connectivity to smartphones, and even "smart implants," such as sensors embedded in orthopedic implants to monitor patients' recovery after surgery and glucose sensors that communicate diabetics' glucose levels to smartphones. Remote monitoring tools can alert family members to departures from their loved ones' routines that may signal problems.

While these products offer enormous new opportunities to older people, they may also pose challenges and threats. Challenges include educating consumers about the benefits and risks of myriad products, how to use them safely, and how to seek help when problems arise. Some, like the emerging market of alarmingly intrusive IoT products, pose serious threats to privacy.

MOVING FORWARD

As older consumers achieve greater prominence, their rights need to as well. These rights need to figure prominently in the Elder Justice Agenda, with special attention paid to:

- **Ensuring an adequate supply of goods and services.** Ensuring that the products and services available to older consumers are what they really want and need will require greater input by older people in their design. It will also require changes to Medicare, Medicaid, and other third-party payers to reduce or eliminate their bias for institutional care and cover goods and services that older consumers need to age in place. It will also require ensuring that products and services are affordable, which requires eliminating impediments to market forces such as government constraints on negotiating drug prices.
- **Ensuring the right to informed consent.** Special efforts are needed to ensure and protect the rights of older consumers by eliminating barriers to informed consent that result from diminished cognitive and decision-making capacity, undue influence, and literacy issues. This will require defining the capacity needed for weighing the benefits and risks of products and services, and providing access to supported and surrogate decision-making options when needed.
- **Ensuring the right to information about goods and services.** Information about products and services needs to be comprehensible and reflect the needs of diverse consumer groups with respect to language, literacy, and communication styles and abilities. Consumers need access to information about service providers to help them evaluate their trustworthiness and suitability.
- **Engagement and collaboration by advocates.** Neither aging advocates nor consumer advocates are adequately addressing the full range of threats and challenges that older consumers face. Doing so will require collaboration between the two groups to better understand older consumers' needs and respond to gaps and shortcomings. It will further require raising awareness among producers and marketers of goods and services about older consumers' special needs.
- **Ensuring recourse and accountability.** Special efforts are needed to strengthen protections for older consumers. This may require revising protections enacted or proposed under past administrations that have been overturned, weakened, or postponed in recent years, including bans on unfair practices by health insurers (e.g., dropping policy holders when they become seriously ill) and restrictions against unreasonable

binding arbitration agreements. Special attention is needed regarding products and services that are particularly prone to abuse such as home loans and financial products. Responses to consumer fraud and scams also need strengthening.

- **The right to privacy.** Special measures are needed to protect older consumers' privacy with respect to providers' access to information about older consumers' health and finances. Special attention is also needed regarding the privacy of consumers in long-term care and housing and threats to privacy engendered by computer-enabled products and services.

CONCLUSION

Acknowledging the rights of older people as consumers is key to elder justice. Consumer rights include the generally agreed upon rights to be free from exploitation, neglect, and abuse by providers of goods and services and the right to be free from discriminatory practices. But consumer rights go even further.

People express their autonomy, personal preferences, loyalties, and values in the choices they make about the services they use, the people they hire to help them, where and how they decide to live, and their medical care. They can demonstrate where they stand on issues as diverse as climate change and workers' rights through the products they buy and investments they make. Older people can further wield influence over what is produced and what services are provided through their collective purchasing power and the competition it generates among those who vie for their business.

Although this chapter has focused on consumer rights in health and long-term care, the rights it describes apply to the vast array of products and services that are currently available and those yet to come. Examples and specific steps that are needed to protect and defend older consumers' rights are contained in the Elder Justice Agenda in Chapter 12.

REFERENCES

Almgren, G. (2017). *Health care politics, policy, and services: A social justice analysis* (3rd ed.). New York, NY: Springer Publishing.

American Hospital Association. (2019). Fast facts on U.S. hospitals: 2019. Retrieved from https://www.aha.org/statistics/fast-facts-us-hospitals

Boccuti, C., Casillas, G., & Neuaman, T. (2015, May 14). Reading the stars: Nursing home quality star ratings, nationally and by state. Retrieved from https://www.kff.org/medicare/issue-brief/reading-the-stars-nursing-home-quality-star-ratings-nationally-and-by-state

Butler, R. N. (1975). *Why survive? Being old in America*. New York, NY: Harper & Row.

California Reinvestment Coalition. (2017, November 15). New FOIA response from HUD reveals 646 percent increase in foreclosures against seniors in 2016 [Press Release]. Retrieved from http://calreinvest.org/press-release/new-foia-response -from-hud-reveals-646-percent-increase-in-foreclosures-against-seniors-in-2016

Centers for Disease Control and Prevention. (2016). Table 92: Nursing homes, beds, residents, and occupancy rates, by state: United States, selected years 1995–2015. Retrieved from http://www.cdc.gov/nchs/hus/contents2016.htm#092

Centers for Medicare and Medicaid Services. (2015). Nursing home data compendium 2015 edition. Retrieved from https://www.cms.gov/Medicare/Provider-Enroll ment-and-Certification/CertificationandComplianc/Downloads/nursinghomedata compendium_508-2015.pdf

Damberg, C. L., Sorbero, M. E., Lovejoy, S. L., Martsolf, G. R., Raaen, L., & Mandel, D. (2014). Measuring success in health care value-based purchasing programs: Findings from an environmental scan, literature review, and expert panel discussions. *Rand Health Quarterly, 4*(3), 9. Retrieved from https://www.rand.org/content/dam/rand/ pubs/research_reports/RR300/RR306/RAND_RR306.pdf

Das, R. (2017, May 22). 10 ways the Internet of medical things is revolutionizing senior care. *Forbes.* Retrieved from https://www.forbes.com/sites/reenitadas /2017/05/22/10-ways-internet-of-medical-things-is-revolutionizing-senior-care /#5a91afa85c8f

Devereaux, P. J., Heels-Ansdell, D., Lacchetti, C., Haines, T., Burns, K. E. A., Cook, D. J., . . . Guyatt, G. H. (2004). Payments for care at private for-profit and private not-for-profit hospitals: A systematic review and meta-analysis. *Canadian Medical Association Journal, 170*(12), 1817–1824. doi:10.1503/cmaj.1040722

Harrington, C., Olney, B., Carrillo, H., & Kang, T. (2011). Nurse staffing and deficiencies in the largest for-profit nursing home chains and chains owned by private equity companies. *Health Services Research, 47,* 106–128. doi:10.1111/j.1475-6773.2011.01311.x

Horwitz, J. R. (2005). Making profits and providing care: Comparing nonprofit, for-profit, and government hospitals. *Health Affairs, 24*(3), 790–801. doi:10.1377/hlthaff.24.3.790

Morgan, J. (2014, May 13). A simple explanation of 'the Internet of things.' *Forbes.* Retrieved from https://www.forbes.com/sites/jacobmorgan/2014/05/13/simple-explanation -internet-things-that-anyone-can-understand/#892da401d091

National Consumer Law Center. (2008). Helping elderly homeowners victimized by predatory mortgage loans. *Consumer Concerns.* Retrieved from https://www.nclc .org/images/pdf/older_consumers/consumer_concerns/cc_elderly_victimized _predatory_mortgage.pdf

Office of the Inspector General. (2014). *Adverse events in skilled nursing facilities: National incidence among Medicare beneficiaries.* Retrieved from https://oig.hhs.gov/oei/ reports/oei-06-11-00370.pdf

Pratkanis, A. R., & Shadel, D. (2005). *Weapons of fraud: A source book for fraud fighters.* Seattle, WA: AARP Washington.

Rosenau, P. V., & Linder, S. H. (2003). Two decades of research comparing for-profit and nonprofit health provider performance in the United States. *Social Science Quarterly, 84*(2), 219–241. doi:10.1111/1540-6237.8402001

Serres, C. (2017, November 15). Speak up, and risk eviction. *StarTribune.* Retrieved from http://www.startribune.com/senior-home-residents-risk-eviction-when-they -speak-up/450626083

Smith, J. (2014, October 3). Lawsuits rattle nursing-home chains: Allegations of harmful treatment win big jury awards, spurring operators to flee certain states. *Wall Street Journal.* Retrieved from https://www.wsj.com/articles/lawsuits-rattle-nursing -home-chains-1412368400

U.S. Department of Health and Human Services. (2016, March 3). HHS reaches goal of tying 30 percent of Medicare payments to quality ahead of schedule [News release]. Retrieved from https://wayback.archive-it.org/3926/20170127191335/https:// www.hhs.gov/about/news/2016/03/03/hhs-reaches-goal-tying-30-percent -medicare-payments-quality-ahead-schedule.html

U.S. Government Accountability Office. (2009). Nursing homes: CMS's special focus facility methodology should better target the most poorly performing homes, which tended to be chain affiliated and for-profit. Retrieved from https://www.gao.gov/ new.items/d09689.pdf

University of Minnesota School of Public Health. (n.d.). NH regulations plus. Retrieved from http://www.hpm.umn.edu/NHRegsPlus/NH%20Regs%20by%20Topic/ Topic%20Resident%20Rights.html

Varney, S. (2016, August 20). Private equity pursues profits in keeping the elderly at home. *New York Times.* Retrieved from https://www.nytimes.com/2016/08/21/business/ as-the-for-profit-world-moves-into-an-elder-care-program-some-worry.html

Wiener, J. (2017, December 20). When nursing homes push out poor and disabled patients. *Kaiser Health News.* Retrieved from https://khn.org/news/when-nursing-homes -push-out-poor-and-disabled-patients

10

Elder Justice in Illness, Death, and Beyond

INTRODUCTION

Perhaps nowhere are the challenges to preserve individual rights and justice greatest than in the face of illness, disability, and death. From the family member struggling to decide when it is no longer reasonable to abide by the wishes of a loved one with advanced dementia, to the lawyer who questions whether a client is acting freely when making out-of-character changes to a trust or will, to the doctor whose patient refuses life-sustaining treatment, these individuals' ability to differentiate decisions that reflect personal values and beliefs from those based on distorted perceptions or pressure from others is critical.

Defending autonomy requires understanding *capacity*. Autonomy is, in fact, defined by some as the capacity to make informed, uncoerced decisions. It refers to people's truest, most authentic selves, reflecting their personal values, beliefs, and morality. To act autonomously, people must have the ability—the capacity—to exercise choice and resist external control and influence.

As people reach advanced old age and approach death, it becomes increasingly likely that their decision-making capacity will become impaired. They may become more susceptible to others' influence. Concerns about autonomy and individual rights in the face of *incapacity* will undoubtedly grow as the estimated 5.5 million Americans today living with Alzheimer's disease and related illnesses reach nearly 14 million by 2050 (Alzheimer's Association, 2018).

WHAT IS CAPACITY?

Functional capacity refers to the collection of skills needed to perform daily tasks, ranging from the ability to feed or bathe oneself to preparing meals, shopping, and balancing a checkbook. Those in the field of aging have developed assessment tools to measure and document daily living skills over time and to identify changes. The process is straightforward and relies on observation.

Measuring cognitive capacity, the skills needed to perform mental tasks, is more complicated. Although some skills, like the ability to remember names or count change, can be readily observed, assessing capacity to exercise choice and make decisions requires measuring such intangibles as judgment, interpretation, and abstract or critical thinking.

Different choices and decisions require different mental skills. Determining whether people are capable of exercising choice, or "have capacity" to do so, depends on the nature of the choices or decisions in question. Deficits affect cognitive capacity in different ways. Four components that are typically considered in determining whether people have capacity from a legal perspective are (American Bar Association [ABA], American Psychological Association [APA], & National College of Probate Judges, 2006):

1. **Understanding.** Those making decisions need to understand the meaning and implications of the choices or decisions in question. For example, patients faced with choices about medical care need to understand their diagnoses, treatment options, prognoses, and the pros and cons of alternatives.
2. **Communicating choices.** Decision makers need to be able to communicate choices unambiguously and consistently.
3. **Appreciation.** Although there is less agreement on its meaning, appreciation is generally interpreted to mean that decision makers are able to apply choices to their own situations and understand the benefits and risks to themselves.
4. **Reasoning.** This is the ability to give rational explanations or process information in a logically or rationally consistent manner.

The fields of psychology and law recognize that cognitive impairments vary in terms of their consequences in everyday life and the challenges they pose to individual rights and autonomy. Impairments that are particularly germane are mild cognitive impairment (MCI), capacity to provide self-care, executive function, and financial capacity.

MCI is a subtle decline in cognitive skills that includes losses in memory and thinking. It is of special interest to elder rights advocates because it impairs judgment and financial abilities, heightening the risk of financial abuse and exploitation. Furthering that risk is the fact that MCI is unlikely to be detected using traditional screening tools (Denburg et al., 2007; Marson et al., 2009).

People's ability to provide self-care, including daily activities that are needed to maintain health and well-being, is a primary consideration in determining if people can manage safely and independently in their homes and communities. Judgments about the ability to provide self care are used in determining whether people need help and the kind of help needed. They may be used in determining the need for nursing home care or guardianship, or to trigger powers of attorney (POAs). Conversely, demonstrating that someone has the ability to provide self care is key to countering the need for unwanted help or supervision.

Executive function refers to higher level cognitive skills such as the ability to plan for the future or switch between cognitive tasks. Like MCI, it plays a key role in financial decision making and making choices that require people to anticipate the outcomes of their actions and the risks and consequences they pose (Triebel et al., 2009; Wood & Liu, 2012). Financial capacity is the ability to understand financial concepts and transactions ranging from the ability to count change to retirement planning.

MEASURING CAPACITY

Protecting the rights and safety of people with cognitive impairments requires that the disabilities associated with impairments are clearly understood and can be demonstrated. Cognitive assessment tools for doing so are becoming increasingly specialized. The Montreal Cognitive Assessment tool (MOCA), for example, was developed to detect MCI (Nasreddine et al., 2005). The Assessment of Capacity for Everyday Decision-Making (ACED) identifies four elements related to financial capacity: (a) having basic monetary skills, (b) carrying out cash transactions, (c) managing a checkbook and bank statement, and (d) exercising financial judgment (Lai et al., 2008). Another tool, the Financial Capacity Instrument, adds the domain of "financial conceptual knowledge" (Marson et al., 2009). The Lichtenberg Financial Decision Rating Scale (LFDRS) builds on these tools but assumes that financial capacity depends not only on intellectual factors but on "contextual factors" and long-held personal values (Lichtenberg, Stoltman, Ficker, Iris, & Mast, 2015). It proposes "person-centered principles" to understand financial decisions and abuse.

The scope and depth of cognitive assessments that are performed in specific instances reflect the nature of the decisions in question. The more consequential the decisions, the more exacting the tools that are used. For example, in determining whether someone has the requisite capacity to consent to (or deny consent for) social or support services, decisions are rarely questioned when clients consent, because the consequences of receiving unnecessary services are not considered to be great. Decisions are more likely to be questioned when people refuse services that are considered essential or consent to anything that is offered.

CLINICAL AND LEGAL ASSESSMENTS

Cognitive assessments fall into one of two categories: clinical and legal. Clinical assessments, which are typically conducted by psychologists or physicians, examine cognitive and psychological changes that affect people's actions and decisions. Although critical to identifying deficits, the information yielded by clinical assessments is not readily meaningful in the legal context. A determination that someone has deficits in executive function, for example, does not necessarily mean that he or she is incapable of consenting to surgery. Rather, deficits need to be examined in light of specific tasks or decisions.

Legal capacity refers to legally recognized standards for making decisions like choosing others to act on one's behalf, agreeing to the terms of contracts, executing wills, or getting married. Testamentary capacity, the standard used to decide if someone has the capacity needed to execute a will, is described later. There are also agreed-upon standards for decisions about contracts (capacity to contract), giving gifts (donative capacity), and imposing involuntary protective services. Legal determinations are also used to trigger involuntary protective interventions and fend off unnecessary intrusions or interference.

The legal system differentiates the capacity required for financial matters from that which is required for personal matters. There are, for example, "guardianships of person" and "guardianships of estate." Similarly, there are POAs for finances and estate. As described earlier, there is general agreement about how to define financial capacity, and multiple tools exist to measure it. There is also agreement about how to define and evaluate capacity for medical treatment decisions. There is less agreement, however, about how to define and measure such deeply personal matters as the capacity to marry or consent to sexual relations. Getting it right in these instances is critical since it can mean the difference between exposing people to exploitation and interfering in what is nobody else's business. Other judgments about capacity require balancing individual rights and public safety, as is the case in determining if someone has the mental skills and judgment needed to drive or use firearms responsibly.

TRANSLATING CLINICAL ASSESSMENTS INTO THE LEGAL CONTEXT

The gap between clinical judgments and legal standards of decision-making capacity prompted the ABA, the APA, and the National College of Probate Judges to produce a series of handbooks for judges, psychologists, and lawyers that explore the implications of cognitive deficits on legal standards of decision making, acquaint lawyers and judges to the field of neuropsychology, familiarize psychologists with legal concepts related to decision making, and provide an overview of scientific knowledge related to capacity and decision making (ABA & APA, 2005, 2008; American Bar Association et al., 2006).

Principles of Decision Making

The American justice system assumes that adults have decision-making capacity; their right to make decisions can only be revoked or denied when others convincingly demonstrate that they do not. Corollaries to this assumption include:

- There is no single standard for capacity; it is situation specific. Someone who is able to make rational decisions about surgery may not be able to make financial decisions.
- The "burden" for determining whether someone lacks capacity is with those alleging incapacity. For example, if adult offspring want to assume responsibility for their parents' finances against the parents' will, it is up to them (the children) to demonstrate their parents' incapacity. The onus is not on the parents to defend their capacity (and rights).
- Diagnosis does not constitute incapacity; neither does impairment. It cannot be assumed, for example, that a person diagnosed with Alzheimer's disease or a specific impairment lacks decision-making capacity.
- The greater the consequences and repercussions of decisions that are in question, the greater the need and urgency to substantiate capacity, the higher the level of capacity needed, and the greater the level of certainty that is required. For example, assessments for determining whether guardianship is needed ranks among the most rigorous because of the severe restrictions guardianships place on personal freedom and self-determination (Falk & Hoffman, 2014). When guardianship is being

considered, courts typically consult with experts or order comprehensive batteries of tests.

UNDUE INFLUENCE AND OTHER FACTORS UNDERMINING FREE WILL

Factors other than cognitive impairment may undermine people's ability to exercise choice, free will, and autonomy. Undue influence, in particular, has been a focus of attention in recent decades. Unlike cognitive impairments that are associated with individuals' mental skills, undue influence is a psychological process by which people in positions of power unfairly persuade or manipulate others to do things they would not have done otherwise to benefit persuaders at the expense of the persuaded. It has been described by psychologists (often referred to in the psychology literature as unfair or coercive persuasion) in a broad range of contexts. A literature review commissioned by the San Francisco Superior Court identified the following contexts or settings that have been explored to explain how people's free will is subordinated (Quinn, Goldman, Nerenberg, & Piazza, 2010):

A. How totalitarian regimes exercise social control;

B. How captors induce prisoners of war to denounce their countries, collaborate with captors, or turn on fellow prisoners;

C. How cults recruit and maintain members;

D. Why victims of domestic violence align with abusers and refuse to leave or take action against them;

E. How caregivers maintain control over those they care for;

F. Why hostages bond with their captors (Stockholm syndrome);

G. How professionals exploit relationships of trust and confidence toward clients; and

H. How white collar criminals and con artists manipulate and deceive.

The legal system has long recognized undue influence as a threat to the legitimacy of wills or contracts (Hall, Hall, Myers, & Chapman, 2009; Nievod, 1992). A study of testamentary capacity found signs of undue influence in 56% of the cases in which concerns about capacity had been raised (Shulman, Cohen, Krish, Hull, & Champine, 2005). Undue influence is also among the threats to free will that often suggest the need for guardianship. The aforementioned San Francisco Superior Court study revealed that a significant number of conservatorship (California's term for adult guardianships) petitions cited undue influence among the reasons for which conservatorship was being requested.

The Restatement of Contracts, a nonbinding but widely recognized and cited legal authority in common law, defines undue influence as:

> Unfair persuasion of a party who is under the domination of the person exercising the persuasion or who by virtue of the relation between them is justified in assuming that that person will not act in a manner inconsistent with his welfare. (Restatement [Second] of Contracts § 177 (1) [1981])

Although there are no validated tools available to measure undue influence or susceptibility to it, a number of models and screening tools have drawn from laws, case law, and the literature on undue influence and elder abuse to provide guidance to professionals in identifying and documenting it (Bernatz, n.d.; Blum, 2003; Quinn, Nerenberg, Navarro, & Wilber, 2017).

Other emotional and psychological factors that are believed to affect judgment and decision making include individuals' risk tolerance and the effects of abnormal or extreme conditions, environments, or circumstances such as isolation, sensory deprivation or overload, sleep deprivation, disorientation, humiliation, coercion, or duress.

Older people's capacity may also come into question when those who are alleged to have committed crimes or mistreatment are believed to have cognitive impairments. In these cases, determining capacity focuses on whether they are in fact culpable, (Did they understand and appreciate the impact and implications of their actions?) Other considerations include whether they pose ongoing threats to others and whether their behaviors can be controlled or modified.

INCAPACITY AND UNDUE INFLUENCE AS THREATS TO INDIVIDUAL RIGHTS

Cognitive impairments and undue influence can pose serious threats to individuals' rights and liberties. The following sections explore these threats with respect to:

- Autonomy
- Vulnerability to elder abuse
- Threats to legacies
- The right to die

Threats to Autonomy

Judgments of incapacity may be used to deprive people of the right to make decisions and choices. This includes the right to exercise consent for admission into health and social programs, for entering into agreements, for executing contracts and advance directives, and for making medical decisions.

Limiting the individual rights of incapacitated people may be justified when they pose a danger to themselves or others or are unable to meet their own needs or protect themselves from harm. Unjustified limitations may be imposed, however, that violate their rights and privacy. They may be unnecessarily institutionalized, have advance directives ignored, or be prevented from associating with those they choose to. These measures may be imposed by overly cautious but well-meaning family members, friends, and others who do not understand the person's abilities or rights.

Frequently alleged violations of individual rights include the involuntary use of antipsychotic drugs in nursing homes. Patients and watchdog organizations report that nursing homes often give antipsychotic drugs without seeking proper informed consent or in dosages that are too high. They may also use the drugs to inappropriately sedate residents for the convenience of staff. According to a *Human Rights Watch* report, "In an average week, nursing facilities in the United States administer antipsychotic drugs to over 179,000 people who do not have diagnoses for which the drugs are approved. The drugs are often given without free and informed consent" (Flamm, 2018, para. 1). Studies show that the use of antipsychotic drugs nearly doubles the risk of death among older people with dementia. The use of surveillance cameras and monitoring devices without consent has raised new questions and concerns about privacy.

Vulnerability to Abuse

People with cognitive impairments are at heightened risk for abuse, neglect, exploitation, and undue influence. The extent to which this is true, however, is unknown, due at least in part to the fact that research subjects must give consent to participate in studies, which those with impairments are typically incapable of giving. Abuse against people with cognitive impairments were not, for example, included in the National Elder Mistreatment Study (Acierno et al., 2010), the largest and most comprehensive prevalence study to date.

Victims' cognitive functioning may determine whether abuse has, in fact, even occurred. Giving large gifts is perfectly proper as long as donors understand the nature and ramifications of their gifts. If not, and the transfer was made at the urging of others who stand to gain, it is likely to be considered misconduct.

Mosqueda et al. (2016) found that people with cognitive impairments are more likely to experience certain forms of abuse and that different stages of cognitive impairment create different vulnerabilities. They suggest, for example, that early dementia heightens the risk for financial abuse but as dementias progress to the moderate stage, patients become more vulnerable to physical abuse and those in the advanced stages are at greater risk for neglect. The risk for psychological abuse appears to exist throughout the stages. Abuse by surrogates ranges from disregard for dementia sufferers' wishes to the plundering of their assets, to unnecessary restraints and neglect.

Threats to Legacies

Legacies are what people leave behind when they die. Most basically, it refers to the money and property they leave to heirs or charities. Seen more expansively, legacies are enduring reflections of peoples' histories and values, which is why leaving legacies is one of life's most valued and gratifying rights.

Author and sociologist Ruth Dixon-Mueller observes that legacy planning often is dominated, at the urging of financial planners or family members, by financial concerns such as figuring out ways to avoid taxes (Dixon-Mueller, 2017). She sees it as an opportunity to consider philosophical questions about individual freedom and to express one's values about fairness with respect to one's family, community, and society. What may be considered as fair in an estate plan, such as dividing assets equally among one's children, may fail to acknowledge other factors that characterize the parties involved and their relationships, including individuals' needs and aspirations, and the contributions they have made to others. She calls for those engaged in end-of-life planning to use the opportunity to consider what their legacies will say about their values and how they will affect those left behind. She urges lawyers to do the same.

The Right to Die

Death itself is at once the most personal of experiences and the most universal. People's choices about death and what happens leading up to and following it are among the most profound expressions of one's values and beliefs. Choices about how and where people want to die and with whom, how they want to be remembered, and to whom they want to leave their possessions are also shaped by their cultural and religious traditions, morals, and faith.

Societies too distinguish themselves by how they address death. Values and beliefs about death are reflected in art and culture as well as in more mundane matters like tax codes and inheritance laws. They are the subject of ethical and moral debates, including whether society has a right or duty to override personal choices about death or end-of-life care. Collective attitudes and beliefs about these issues dictate how societies allocate resources, as is the case in determining whether public funds should be used to prolong the lives of those who no longer want to live when they could be used to prolong the lives of those who do.

Discussions about end-of-life decisions, including the "right to die" and "death with dignity" laws, are particularly controversial. Stanford and Rivas (2017) point out that some consider suicide the ultimate human and civil right and that society does not have the right to interfere with a person's decision to commit suicide. In a truly free society, they contend, one has the right to take his or her life as long as the rights of others are not violated. The Death with Dignity National Center (formerly called the Hemlock Society) puts it this way: "The greatest human freedom is to live and die according to our own desires and beliefs" (n.d.).

The right to get and give help in ending life is more controversial still, striking a nerve for many, and arousing passion and outrage. Even states that allow terminally ill patients to decline life-sustaining medical assistance typically do not permit others to assist. Only a few states—California, Colorado, Montana, Oregon, Vermont, and Washington, and the District of Columbia—have authorized medically assisted suicide.

Some opponents of aid in dying laws fear that they raise the risk of abuse, and that vulnerable people, including isolated older people, those with disabilities, and those who are depressed and overcome with hopelessness, can potentially be pressured or unduly influenced to end their lives. Physicians, who play a major role in making decisions in individual cases, have historically been among the most vocal opponents of medical aid in dying. Official opposition from the medical field has declined, however, with state medical societies increasingly moving from opposition to neutral stances (Bailey, 2018).

Questions about "who should decide?" dominate these debates. These range from discussions about liability (Will I be sued for ending treatment?) to contemplating unlikely hypotheticals about beating the odds of death and terminal illnesses. They may become highly charged and political.

Such was the case with Terri Schiavo, a Florida woman who spent nearly 15 years on life support in a vegetative state after sustaining a cardiac arrest in 1990 that left her brain-dead at the age of 26. A legal battle ensued between her husband, who wanted the life support removed, and her parents, who wanted it continued. Schiavo's husband prevailed and the tube was removed. The then governor Jeb Bush, however, issued an executive order to put the feeding tube back in, which led to 14 appeals and numerous motions, petitions, and hearings in the Florida courts; five suits in federal district court; extensive political interventions by the Florida state legislature and Congress; and four denials of requests for review from the Supreme Court. Schiavo died in 2005 after a federal court upheld the original decision to remove the feeding tube (Lepore, 2009).

METHODS AND TOOLS FOR ENHANCING AUTONOMY IN THE FACE OF INCAPACITY AND DEATH

Concerns about the ethical, legal, moral, and medical implications of end-of-life decisions, and their implications for autonomy and choice, have heightened attention to advance care planning and advance directives. Advance care planning typically refers to the process of discussing end-of-life choices, executing advance directives, selecting surrogates, and ensuring that plans will be followed.

Advance directives are legal documents that are executed by capable people to memorialize their choices. Some take effect immediately, while others go into effect at the onset of disability or death. They can be updated as long as those executing them have capacity. Advance directives work in two basic ways. They may spell out specific wishes or designate surrogates. They may also do both.

ADVANCE DIRECTIVES

WILLS

Wills are among the best known and understood advance directive. Testators (those who execute wills) instruct others in what to do with their property after they die and may name "executors" to carry out their wishes. They may also name guardians for children and provide for pets.

Because people have been writing and contesting wills from time immemorial, there is general consensus about "testamentary capacity," the standard used to decide if someone has the capacity needed to execute a will. Testators have to understand what wills are and the extent of their property. They must further recognize or identify their heirs. Testators must be acting freely without duress or coercion from others.

(*continued*)

Wills can and often are invalidated when it can be shown that testators were not acting freely.

Wills are often prepared by lawyers although they do not have to be. There are books, software, and websites that provide instructions and documents; however, they must be signed in front of two witnesses. Most states recognize "holographic" wills, or wills that are not signed by witnesses, in some circumstances. They are, however, much more likely to be challenged.

POWERS OF ATTORNEY

POAs are legal documents by which people authorize others to act on their behalf. The people granting the authority are called *principals* and those appointed to act on their behalf are *attorneys-in-fact* or agents. The authority granted can pertain to principals' finances (also called estates), medical (or health) care, or both, and can spell out specific wishes, assign surrogates, or both. Medical or healthcare POAs grant authority over medical treatments; life-sustaining interventions, including the use of ventilators, artificial nutrition (tube feeding), or hydration (intravenous fluids); and pain relief. "POAs of estate" typically grant authority over financial matters and provide access to financial accounts to pay bills, file taxes, make investment decisions, collect debts, manage property, and apply for public benefits.

Some states have *living wills*, which are written statements in which people make their healthcare wishes known in certain medical circumstances. They are similar to POAs for healthcare and are often signed at the same time. By themselves, they do not provide for the appointment of surrogate decision makers.

ADVANCE DIRECTIVES FOR EMERGENCY AND END-OF-LIFE CARE

POAs for medical care are not always abided by during emergencies, often because emergency response personnel are not aware that they exist. The Physician Orders for Life-Sustaining Treatment (POLST) was created in response to this problem (some states use the term Medical Orders for Life-Sustaining Treatment, or MOLST). Completed by healthcare professionals, they serve as medical orders to ensure that dying patients' wishes regarding heroic, intrusive, lifesaving measures are adhered to during medical emergencies.

TRUSTS

Trusts are written agreements, typically created by attorneys, that authorize financial institutions, professional fiduciaries, friends, or families to manage others' assets and property. "Trustees," those entrusted with the authority, have a "fiduciary relationship" to "settlors" (also called "trustors"), which means that they must act in settlors' best interest.

There are several types of trusts, the most common of which are testamentary trusts and living trusts. Testamentary trusts do not go into effect until after the death of the settlor. Living trusts go into effect during the lifetime of the settlor and give trustees authority to manage the settlor's property. They can be changed as long as the settlor has capacity (unless it is an irrevocable trust). Trustees can continue to manage assets even if the settlor becomes incapacitated and can make distributions after the settlor's death without going through probate.

LIMITATIONS OF ADVANCE DIRECTIVES AND PLANNING

Among the most frequent complaints about advance directives is that they are often disregarded and there are few consequences for those who knowingly do so. Few states require any type of registration of POAs and most do not require lawyers' involvement in their drafting. Their signing does not need to be witnessed to ensure that agents have mental capacity and are not being coerced. Notarization may be required but notaries' role is limited to ensuring that the parties are who they claim to be.

Because there is no requirement that principals be notified when POAs are used, even principals who have capacity may not be able to monitor the actions of attorneys-in-fact. Without guidance, many elders do not realize the extent of the authority they are assigning to chosen agents.

Those in the field of elder abuse prevention understand how advance directives can easily become licenses to steal. Reported abuses by attorneys-in-fact include:

- The requirements for signing are not met (e.g., principals lack sufficient mental capacity).
- Principals are coerced or tricked into signing.
- Attorneys-in-fact use the powers after they have terminated or been revoked.

- Attorneys-in-fact use POAs for purposes other than those for which they were intended.
- Attorneys-in-fact transfer principals' property to themselves without authorization to do so.
- Attorneys-in-fact do not act solely in the interests of principals.
- Attorneys-in-fact fail to keep principals' property separate and distinct from their own.
- Attorneys-in-fact use POAs to give themselves gifts.
- Attorneys-in-fact fail to carry out responsibilities (e.g., pay bills).

Intentional failures to abide by advance directives involving money and property are often challenged, typically by those who stand to gain or lose. Much rarer are sanctions for failures to abide by advance directives involving health and medical care. There are exceptions, however, as was the case in *Stewart v. Superior Court* (Cal. Ct. App. - Oct. 12, 2017). San Francisco attorney John O'Grady (2018) describes the case this way:

On February 1, 2012, St. Mary's Medical Center of San Bernardino County admitted Anthony Carter, 78, into its care. Confused, Carter communicated only with grunts and mumbles and had gaps in his heartbeat. Maxine Stewart, a licensed nurse and Carter's lawful health care agent, refused to consent when Carter's doctor wanted to insert a gastronomy tube. The hospital ethics committee approved the surgery which occurred without Stewart's knowledge or consent. Later that day, Carter went into cardiac arrest, causing brain damage. He required acute nursing care until passing on April 15, 2013. Stewart sued. The trial court dismissed her claims that the hospital committed elder abuse, medical battery, and fraudulent concealment. The Court of Appeal reinstated these claims. The Court's recitation of the facts froths with indignation and scorn for the Catholic hospital's defenses. It said that Carter exercised his fundamental and autonomous right to refuse surgery through Stewart, his lawfully designated surrogate. (Reproduced by permission of the author)

States have attempted to remedy these problems through legislation, many adopting provisions contained in the Uniform Power of Attorney Act, created by the National Conference of Commissioners on Uniform State Laws (NCCUSL). NCCUSL is an organization of lawyers, judges, and law professors who are appointed by states to draft proposals for uniform and model laws and work toward their enactment. The act, which was created in 1987 and updated in 2006, contains safeguards for protecting incapacitated principals' right to determine the extent of the authority they are granting and principles for guiding decisions. It also includes remedies for abuse and sanctions for those who fail to honor them.

SURROGATES

Surrogates appointed to make decisions on behalf of people with cognitive impairments include friends, family members, attorneys, attorneys-in-fact, trustees, and many others. They may be designated by those whose interests they represent, as is the case with attorneys-in-fact, or by courts, as is the case with guardians. Representative payees are people or organizations that are authorized by government entities to receive and manage public benefits, including Social Security payments, Supplemental Security Income (SSI), veterans' benefits, and civil service and railroad pensions for others.

Ethicists and lawyers have developed a hierarchy of preferred approaches to surrogacy, based on the extent to which they preserve the autonomy of those they are intended to protect:

- **Explicit directives.** Whenever possible, surrogate decision makers should make decisions based on the expressed wishes (explicit directives) of those they represent, as relayed in past discussions or memorialized in documents like POAs.
- **Substituted judgment.** This standard is used when explicit directives do not exist. It refers to decisions based on what surrogates believe those they represent would have wanted. It therefore requires knowledge of the person's values, such as his or her attitudes about autonomy, dependence, and confinement. Knowledge about the person's lifestyle, past patterns of spending or giving gifts, and social networks may also be relevant.
- **Best interest.** This standard is resorted to when the impaired person's history, wishes, and values are unknown. It is generally based on what a reasonable person in the situation would want.

GUARDIANSHIP AND CONSERVATORSHIP: WHEN ALL ELSE FAILS

When adults with cognitive impairments are unable to provide for their own needs or protect themselves against grave danger and threats to their safety and security, and they lack advance directives and surrogates, courts may intervene through adult guardianships (called "conservatorship" in some states). Guardianship is a legal process by which courts appoint trustworthy individuals or institutions to act on others' behalf. In doing so, they are exercising *parens patriae*, states' authority to protect those who are unable to protect themselves (see Chapter 3).

Guardians include incapacitated people's family members or friends, private professionals, businesses, and nonprofit agencies. Public guardians, often considered the option of last resort, are public programs that serve as guardians.

Those in need of guardians include people with severe cognitive impairments who lack advance directives or responsible parties, sometimes referred to as *unbefriended* or *unrepresented* individuals (Moye, Catlin, Kwak, Wood, & Teaster, 2017). In the past, those for whom guardians were appointed were referred to as wards, a term that has been rejected as stigmatizing and replaced with others, including "alleged incapacitated persons" and "subjects of guardianships," which have yet to be widely adopted.

As is the case with POAs, there are two general types of guardianship, which reflect the nature of the authority they convey: "Guardians of estate (or property)" manage financial affairs and "guardians of the person" make decisions about personal matters.

Although laws vary from state to state, the process typically involves determining if: (a) the person in question is incapable of acting in his or her best interest, (b) there is a compelling reason to assign authority to another (e.g., to stop abuse or authorize medical treatment or services), and (c) the proposed guardian is trustworthy and willing and able to do what is needed.

Guardians are typically appointed when decisions are needed regarding incapacitated people's finances, medical treatment, or care. Examples include decisions about estates, housing, bank accounts, taxes, investments, or real estate transactions. Some need guardianship because they are no longer able to care for themselves or their homes or property, or because they are at risk for eviction, homelessness, illness, or decline.

Quinn (2005) describes situations in which guardianship is used to stop or prevent elder abuse:

- When severely impaired victims are unable to grasp the severity of their situations and refuse needed protective services
- When family members are in conflict over the custody or assets of an impaired elder
- When adult children want to claim inheritances prematurely or influence older family members to make new wills
- When other devices like durable POAs or trusts have been misused

Specific actions that guardians of estate can take to stop abuse include recovering misappropriated assets and removing control from wrongdoers (e.g., revoking POAs that have been used to exploit), evicting wrongdoers from elders' residences, selling property, initiating lawsuits to recover misappropriated assets or property, and purchasing needed services. Guardians of person can authorize medical treatment and arrange for elders to live in safe places.

GUARDIANSHIP CRITICISMS AND CONTROVERSIES

Guardianship has been the target of harsh criticism for its sweeping scope, susceptibility to abuse, and lack of oversight. The late Congressman Claude Pepper famously said, "the typical ward has fewer rights than the typical convicted felon" (U.S. House of Representatives, 1987, p. 4). Those under guardianship lose the right to choose where they live, how they spend their money, and with whom they associate. They cannot enter into contracts or make decisions about their own health.

The media has played a major role in highlighting guardianship problems and abuses, going back to a scathing exposé by the Associated Press, *Guardianship: Few Safeguards* which examined 2,200 randomly selected guardianship court files and concluded that the guardianship system was "a dangerously burdened and troubled system that regularly puts elderly lives in the hands of others with little or no evidence of necessity, then fails to guard against abuse, theft and neglect" (U.S. House of Representatives, 1987, p. 15). It claimed that courts "routinely take the word of guardians and attorneys without independent checking or full hearings" and "ignore their wards" (U.S. House of Representatives, 1987, p. 33) The article prompted a hearing by the U.S. Senate Special Committee on Aging titled "Abuse of Power: Exploitation of Older Americans by Guardians and Others They Trust" (U.S. House of Representatives, 1987).

More recently, a 2017 issue of *The New Yorker* contained an article about guardianship entitled "How the Elderly Lose Their Rights" that set off a firestorm of allegations purporting that guardians were actively seeking out subjects, making surprise visits to their homes, and assuming control over their lives without justification (Aviv, 2017).

Vocal advocacy groups, backed up by media accounts like these, have accused judges, court investigators, guardians, lawyers, and others of overreach, collusion with self-interested parties, lack of respect for cultural values and traditions, and corruption. They call for more robust representation for those whose rights are at stake and better oversight of the guardianship systems.

Government reports have substantiated many of the claims. A 2010 Government Accountability Office (GAO) report identified hundreds of allegations of physical abuse, neglect, and financial exploitation by guardians in

45 states and the District of Columbia between 1990 and 2010. It charged that lack of information about guardianship was part of the problem. "We could not locate a single Web site, federal agency, state or local entity, or any other organization that compiles comprehensive information on this issue" (GAO, 2010, para. 8).

A survey of judges and court personnel conducted by the National Center for State Courts to explore court monitoring of guardianships found that many courts lacked the resources needed to track whether guardians in fact submitted required inventories, accountings, and reports. It also found that even courts that monitor guardianships tend to focus on incapacitated people's finances as opposed to their well-being (Solomon-Cuthbert, n.d.).

Many have criticized guardianship for its heavy-handedness. Although some states require petitioners to consider less restrictive alternatives, few alternatives actually exist for the many circumstances in which they may be needed. These include situations in which single decisions or transactions would suffice to solve problems, such as authorizing a single medical treatment or service, revoking a POA, freezing assets that are in jeopardy during an abuse investigation, and hospitalizing a gravely ill person in order to assess his or her physical and cognitive status (Quinn & Nerenberg, 2005). Those that do exist, including supported decision making (SDM), which is described later, have not been adequately evaluated.

There is also evidence to suggest that guardians routinely rely on the "best interest" standard rather than "substituted judgment" in making decisions. Forlik and Whitton (2012) found that in states requiring the substituted judgment standard, guardians were more likely to engage in discussions with subjects of guardianship about their care but continued to do what they felt was best anyway and were rarely challenged for doing so.

International human rights and disability rights advocates have even questioned the very legitimacy of guardianship itself (Steinert, Steinert, Flammer, & Jaeger, 2016). The United Nations (UN) Convention on the Rights of Persons with Disabilities (CRPD)[1] asserts that everyone, regardless of mental disability or cognitive impairment, is entitled to make decisions and have those decisions recognized under the law. It further asserts that governments may not deprive individuals of their right to make decisions and have those decisions recognized on the grounds of disability or impaired decision-making skills. They advise that cognitive and other mental disabilities should instead trigger a right to *support* in decision making, including assistive technologies and SDM.

---

[1] It should be noted that the United States has not ratified the convention.

REFORMING GUARDIANSHIP

Efforts to reform guardianship have been ongoing since the 1987 Associated Press report mentioned earlier. Among the most significant is the landmark multidisciplinary guardianship symposium Wingspread of 1988, which was sponsored by the ABA Commission on Law and Aging (COLA) and the Commission on Mental and Physical Disability Law. The event brought together 38 experts from across the country to review the current status of guardianship and adopt recommendations to improve the system. The group offered 31 sweeping recommendations, which became known as the Wingspread recommendations. They include training and technical assistance for guardians, standards of practice and certification, routine accountings of wards' finances and personal care, and other measures to ensure accountability and reduce the risk of abuse (Hurme & Wood, 2002). These led to the creation of the National Guardianship Association (NGA), founded in 1989, which established standards of practice and a code of ethics, and now operates certification and training programs.

These developments and others prompted state legislatures to pass reforms that include due process protections such as hearings, the right to counsel, and court monitoring. Other protections include the use of "functional" measures to demonstrate incapacity, as opposed to diagnoses, and requiring petitioners to demonstrate that subjects cannot perform tasks or make decisions that directly relate to the circumstances prompting guardianships. Many states went further in requiring courts to tailor guardianships to only give guardians those powers necessary to meet specific needs, ensuring that subjects retain other rights. Some states require petitioners to consider less restrictive alternatives.

Mary Joy Quinn, former director of the San Francisco Superior Court's Department of Probate, and Judge Isabella Grant (now deceased), who presided over the court for many years, recommended in granular detail options that individual courts can take to stop or prevent elder abuse. These include scheduling future inventories, appraisals, and accountings at the time that guardians are appointed, with failures to appear resulting in serious consequences, such as being ordered to show cause why they should not be removed, suspension of their powers, appointment of temporary successor guardians, frequent status hearings, and the issuing of bench warrants for guardians' arrest for particularly egregious conduct.

The Uniform Guardianship, Conservatorship, and Other Protective Arrangements Act (UGCOPAA), which was updated by NCCUSL in 2017, introduces the concepts of person-centered planning into guardianship, placing persons subject to guardianships at the center of decision making. It protects subjects' right to receive independent legal counsel, to have orders modified or terminated when appropriate, and to receive visits or communications from family and friends (National Conference of Commissioners on Uniform State Laws, 2017). The act also promotes the use of SDM and limited protective arrangements.

The Working Interdisciplinary Networks of Guardianship Stakeholders (WINGS) was created by the ABA COLA in partnership with other organizations to engage stakeholders in improving their states' guardianship systems. Under the WINGS model, states' chief justices convene stakeholder groups that identify issues surrounding guardianship and develop strategies to respond. Some states have been provided with seed funding and technical assistance. Among their activities are:

- Distributing information on nursing home residents' rights to new guardians
- Facilitating coordination between court administrative offices and regional Social Security offices (which are responsible for representative payeeship)
- Promoting family guardian participation in state guardianship associations
- Convening meetings or presentations on SDM

Despite initiatives like these, progress has been slow. Efforts to regulate or license professional guardians, some supported by guardians themselves, have been rejected in some states. Where courts have set up registries to track abusive or unqualified guardians, judges have tended not to use them or to only check histories of poor performance or wrongdoing occurring within their own jurisdictions.

Amid the cacophony of guardianship criticism, success stories are rarely heard. These include the many instances in which guardians protect vulnerable people from painful, degrading, and futile medical treatments or care they do not want; defend their wishes to live and die at home; and recover stolen homes and properties. Guardians also frequently protect older people against unwanted intrusions into their lives, as is the case when worried families want to infringe on personal choice and freedom in the interest of safety. Guardianship can provide a bulwark against ageism and paternalism when it fulfills its promise.

There is little data available about either the negative or positive outcomes and impact of guardianship or even how often it is used and under what circumstances. Clearly this information is needed to guide reform without sacrificing the power that guardianship has to undo wrongs and protect individual rights.

SUPPORTED DECISION MAKING

As concerns over preserving autonomy and individual rights at the end of life mount, they have led to growing interest in SDM, which is a process for providing guidance to people with limited or failing capacity. The concept was proposed by members of the disability rights community in Canada during the 1990s as an alternative to guardianship (Diller, 2016). It involves explaining the benefits and drawbacks of decisions to decision makers in plain language, providing advice and recommendations, and finding ways to help those who have communication barriers express and carry out their wishes and choices.

More recently, the approach has gained traction in the United States. In recent years, the Administration for Community Living (a division of the Department of Health and Human Services) started funding a national resource center on SDM and supporting pilot projects to evaluate the approach. The ABA is urging states to consider requiring SDM as an alternative before guardianships are granted.

Counterbalancing this enthusiasm are concerns by some in the aging services field that SDM is not as transferable to older people as originally imagined. Among these concerns is that decisions that older people with diminished mental capacity face may be significantly more complicated than those of younger people with intellectual disabilities, for whom the approach was designed. Older people, for example, are much more likely to own homes and have assets, which makes them targets for exploitation and creates a greater need for financial safeguards and remedies, which may be complex. Older people are more likely to suffer from physical disabilities or frailty that render them less resilient to accidents, lapses in care, and neglect. In other words, the stakes for errors or abuse may be greater.

CONCLUSION

Earlier chapters introduced the concept of a functional interpretation of the "right to life" as the right to a full life and one worth living. Under this interpretation, government plays a role in providing life-sustaining necessities and reducing disparities in life expectancy, disease and disability, and quality of life. It is a role that is highly compatible with the elder justice paradigm offered in this book.

This chapter has suggested the need for a corollary: the right to die in ways that preserve autonomy, dignity, and choice. It calls for an end-of-life perspective that focuses on the individual rights of those with severely diminished capacity, the dying, and the deceased. This includes the use and enforcement of advance directives, autonomy-based dementia care, ensuring that trustworthy surrogates are available to those who need them, maintaining high standards for surrogates, supporting death with dignity policy, and ensuring that decedents' legacies are preserved according to their wishes. Adopting an elder justice approach to end of life further requires limiting the role of medical professionals in decisions that are best left to the dying, their families, and trusted advisors, and that align with their moral beliefs and values as opposed to being based on determinations of medical futility.

From an elder justice perspective, end of life discussions need to go beyond individual rights to include fairness considerations. Because innovations in life-extending technologies that only the wealthy can afford pose a threat to social equality and may fuel intergenerational conflict, a justice-based approach needs to define government's role in regulating life-extending technologies, basing decisions on the public good. Key questions that need to be addressed are whether extending the lives of some comes at the expense of others. Just as proponents of the right to life have expounded on when life begins, proponents of the right to die with dignity may need to offer a parallel marker of when life ends and what efforts and resources are justified to prolong it.

But is the public ready to make the switch from a health and long-term care system that treats old age as a disease to one that promotes quality of life, choice, and autonomy? Is it ready to reject the notion of death as the failure of medicine? Discussions about end of life care reveal deeply embedded anxiety about government overreach and malevolent motives, giving rise to apocalyptic fears that physician-assisted suicide and right to die laws, or even end-of-life care, will be used as pretexts for withholding care and discriminating against the disenfranchised.

These anxieties were clearly evident a decade ago in the firestorm about "death panels" that were ignited by proposals for Medicare to cover voluntary discussions between patients and doctors about advance directives and end of life treatment preferences as part of the Affordable Care Act. The fact that these provisions were quietly added later with little resistance suggests that public sentiment may be changing. Still, more needs to be done to reject the fear-mongering that has characterized discussions about end of life and to promote rational debate about these fundamental issues.

REFERENCES

Acierno, R., Hernandez, M. A., Amstadter, A. B., Resnick, H. S., Steve, K., Muzzy, W., & Kilpatrick, D. G. (2010). Prevalence and correlates of emotional, physical, sexual, and financial abuse and potential neglect in the United States: The National Elder Mistreatment Study. *American Journal of Public Health, 100*(2), 292–297. doi:10.2105/ajph.2009.163089

Alzheimer's Association. (2018). *2018 Alzheimer's disease facts and figures: Includes a special report on the financial and personal benefits of early diagnosis.* Retrieved from https://www.alz.org/media/HomeOffice/Facts%20and%20Figures/facts-and-figures.pdf

American Bar Association & American Psychological Association. (2005). *Assessment of older adults with diminished capacity: A handbook for lawyers.* Retrieved from https://www.apa.org/pi/aging/resources/guides/diminished-capacity.pdf

American Bar Association & American Psychological Association. (2008). Assessment of older adults with diminished capacity: A handbook for psychologists. Retrieved from https://www.apa.org/pi/aging/programs/assessment/capacity-psychologist-handbook.pdf

American Bar Association, American Psychological Association, & National College of Probate Judges. (2006). *Judicial determination of capacity of older adults in guardianship proceedings: A handbook for judges.* Retrieved from https://www.apa.org/pi/aging/resources/guides/judges-diminished.pdf

Aviv, R. (2017, October 9). How the elderly lose their rights. *The New Yorker.* Retrieved from https://www.newyorker.com/magazine/2017/10/09/how-the-elderly-lose-their-rights

Bailey, M. (2018, January 26). As doctors drop opposition, aid-in-dying advocates target next battleground states. *Kaiser Health News.* Retrieved from https://khn.org/news/as-doctors-drop-opposition-aid-in-dying-advocates-target-next-battleground-states

Bayles, F., & McCartney, S. (1987, September 27). Guardianship: Few safeguards. *Associated Press.* Retrieved from http://articles.latimes.com/1987-09-27/news/mn-10389_1_guardianship-petitions

Bernatz, S. (n.d.). The Scam™ model. Retrieved from http://www.bernatzexperts.com/areas-of-expertise/scam%E2%84%A2-model

Blum, B. (2003). The "undue influence worksheet" and "IDEAL" protocol—An introduction. *NCPJ Life & Times, 2*(7). Retrieved from http://www.bennettblummd.com/sitebuildercontent/sitebuilderfiles/undueinfluence.pdf

Death with Dignity National Center. (n.d.). About us. Retrieved from https://www.deathwithdignity.org/about

Denburg, N. L., Cole, C. A., Hernandez, M., Yamada, T. H., Tranel, D., Bechara, A., & Wallace, R. B. (2007). The orbitofrontal cortex, real-world decision making, and normal aging. *Annals of the New York Academy of Sciences, 1121,* 480–498. doi:10.1196/annals.1401.031

Diller, R. (2016). Legal capacity for all: Including older persons in the shift from adult guardianship to supported decision-making. *Fordham Urban Law Journal, 43*(3), 495–538. Retrieved from https://ir.lawnet.fordham.edu/cgi/viewcontent.cgi?article=2657&context=ulj

Dixon-Mueller, R. (2017). *Passing on: What's fair in family inheritance?* Scotts County, CA: Author.

Falk, E., & Hoffman, N. (2014). The role of capacity assessments in elder abuse investigations and guardianships. *Clinics in Geriatric Medicine, 30*(4), 851–868. doi:10.1016/j.cger.2014.08.009

Flamm, H. (2018). *"They want docile": How nursing homes in the United States overmedicate people with dementia.* Retrieved from https://www.hrw.org/report/2018/02/05/they-want-docile/how-nursing-homes-united-states-overmedicate-people-dementia

Forlik, L. A., & Whitton, L. S. (2012). The UPC substituted judgment/best interest standard for guardian decisions: A proposal for reform. *University of Michigan Journal of Law Reform, 45,* 739–760. Retrieved from https://repository.law.umich.edu/mjlr/vol45/iss4/1

Government Accountability Office. (2010). *Guardianships: Cases of financial exploitation, neglect, and abuse of seniors* (Report No. GAO-10-1046). Retrieved from https://www.gao.gov/assets/320/310745.html

Hall, R. C. W., Hall, R. C. W., Myers, W. C., & Chapman, M. J. (2009). Testamentary capacity: History, physicians' role, requirements, and why wills are challenged. *Clinical Geriatrics, 17*(6). Retrieved from http://www.cfmal.com/PDFs/Testamentary%20Capacity.pdf

Hurme, S. B., & Wood, E. (2002). Guardian accountability then and now: Tracing tenets for an active court role. *Stetson Law Review, 31*, 867–929. Retrieved from https://www.stetson.edu/law/lawreview/media/guardian-accountability-then-and-now-tracing-tenets-for-an-active-court-role.pdf

Lai, J. M., Gill, T., Cooney, L. M., Bradley, E. H., Hawkins, K. A., & Karlawish. J. (2008). Everyday decision-making ability in older persons with cognitive impairment. *American Journal of Geriatric Psychiatry, 16*(8), 693–696. doi:10.1097/jgp.0b013e31816c7b54

Lepore, J. (2009, November 30). The politics of death: From abortion to health care—How the hysterical style overtook the national debate. *The New Yorker*. Retrieved from http://www.newyorker.com/magazine/2009/11/30/the-politics-of-death

Lichtenberg, P. A., Stoltman, J., Ficker, L. J., Iris, M., & Mast, B. (2015). A person-centered approach to financial capacity assessment: Preliminary development of a new rating scale. *Clinical Gerontologist, 38*(1), 49–67. doi:10.1080/07317115.2014.970318

Marson, D. C., Martin, R. C., Wadley, V., Griffith, H. R., Snyder, S., Goode, P. S., . . . Harrell, L. E. (2009). Clinical interview assessment of financial capacity in older adults with mild cognitive impairment and Alzheimer's disease. *Journal of the American Geriatrics Society, 57*(5), 806–814. doi:10.1111/j.1532-5415.2009.02202.x

Mosqueda, L., Burnight, K., Gironda, M. W., Moore, A. A., Robinson, J., & Olsen, B. (2016). The abuse intervention model: A pragmatic approach to intervention for elder mistreatment. *Journal of the American Geriatrics Society, 64*(9), 1879–1883. doi:10.1111/jgs.14266

Moye, J., Catlin, C., Kwak, J., Wood, E., & Teaster, P. B. (2017). Ethical concerns and procedural pathways for patients who are incapacitated and alone: Implications from a qualitative study for advancing ethical practice. *HEC Forum, 29*(2), 171–189. doi:10.1007/s10730-016-9317-9

Nasreddine, Z. S., Phillips, N. A., Bédirian, V., Charbonneau, S., Whitehead, V., Collin, I., . . . Chertkow, H. (2005). The Montreal Cognitive Assessment, MoCA: A brief screening tool for mild cognitive impairment. *Journal of the American Geriatrics Society, 53*(4), 695–699. doi:10.1111/j.1532-5415.2005.53221.x

National Conference of Commissioners on Uniform State Laws. (2017). Uniform guardianship, conservatorship, and other protective arrangements act. Retrieved from https://my.uniformlaws.org/committees/community-home?CommunityKey=2eba8654-8871-4905-ad38-aabbd573911c

Nievod, A. (1992). Undue influence in contract and probate law. *Journal of Questioned Document Examination, 1*(1), 14–26. Retrieved from https://www.icsahome.com/articles/undue-influence-in-contract-and-probate-law-nievod

O'Grady, J. (2018). Court champions elder rights over hospital wrongs. Retrieved from https://www.elderjusticecal.org/news--updates--marchapril-2018.html#Cal3

Quinn, M. J. (2005). *Guardianships of adults: Achieving justice, autonomy, and safety.* New York, NY: Springer Publishing.

Quinn, M. J., Goldman, E., Nerenberg, L., & Piazza, D. (2010). *Undue influence: Definitions and applications.* San Francisco, CA: San Francisco Superior Court. Retrieved from http://www.courts.ca.gov/documents/UndueInfluence.pdf

Quinn, M. J., & Nerenberg, L. (2005). *Improving access to the San Francisco Superior Court (Probate and Unified Family Courts) for elders: Final report.* San Francisco, CA: San Francisco Superior Court.

Quinn, M. J., Nerenberg, L., Navarro, A. E., & Wilber, K. H. (2017). Developing an undue influence screening tool for Adult Protective Services. *Journal of Elder Abuse & Neglect, 29*(2–3), 157–185. doi:10.1080/08946566.2017.1314844

Restatement (Third) of Prop.: Servitudes § 6.2(1) (Am. Law Inst. 1981). Retrieved from https://www.nylitigationfirm.com/files/restat.pdf

Shulman, K. I., Cohen, C. A., Kirsh, F. C., Hull, I. M., & Champine, P. R. (2007). Assessment of testamentary capacity and vulnerability to undue influence. *American Journal of Psychiatry, 164*(5), 722–727. doi:10.1176/ajp.2007.164.5.722

Solomon-Cuthbert, W. A. (n.d). *Guardianship monitoring: Helping the forgotten speak.* Williamsburg, VA: National Center for State Courts. Retrieved from https://www.ncsc.org/~/media/files/pdf/education%20and%20careers/cedp%20papers/2011/guardianship%20monitoring.ashx

Stanford, E. P., & Rivas, E. E. (2017). Where do older adults fit in the evolution of civil rights in America? *Aging Today, 38*(3), 1, 4. Retrieved from https://www.asaging.org/blog/where-do-older-adults-fit-evolution-civil-rights-america

Steinert, C., Steinert, T., Flammer, E., & Jaeger, S. (2016). Impact of the UN convention on the rights of persons with disabilities (UN-CRPD) on mental health care research: A systematic review. *BMC Psychiatry, 16*, 166. doi:10.1186/s12888-016-0862-1

Triebel, K. L., Martin, R., Griffith, H. R., Marceaux, J., Okonkwo, O. C., Harrell, L., . . . Marson, D. C. (2009). Declining financial capacity in mild cognitive impairment: A 1-year longitudinal study. *Neurology, 73*, 928–934. doi:10.1212/wnl.0b013e3181b87971

U.S. House of Representatives. (1987). Abuses in guardianship of the elderly and infirm: A national disgrace. A briefing by the chairman of the Subcommittee on Health and Long-Term Care of the Select Committee on Aging, One Hundredth Congress, First Session. Retrieved from https://archive.org/details/ERIC_ED294080/page/n35

Wood, S., & Liu, P. (2012). Undue influence and financial capacity: A clinical perspective. *Generations, 36*(2), 53–58. Retrieved from http://www.pijumarianliu.com/wp-content/uploads/2015/06/Undue-Influence-and-Financial-Capacity.pdf

11

Moving Forward

INTRODUCTION

As described throughout this book, elder justice has emerged from multiple fronts. It comes from researchers who are discovering that chronic illnesses, disability, and elder abuse are linked to poverty, discrimination, and social exclusion. It comes from those in the field of long-term care who have recast care users as "consumers" and affirmed their right to greater choice and control over their care. It is implicit in the infusion of public health principles and approaches into aging and elder abuse prevention, which has heightened awareness about health equity and ways to achieve it. It comes from the international aging rights movement, which offers expansive new perspectives and approaches. Heightened attention to ageism has further led advocates to reject paternalistic approaches that overrely on protective interventions and cede decisions about deeply personal matters to professionals.

Elder justice offers a comprehensive and overarching framework for addressing these and other issues and developments. It explains how social and economic forces contribute to problems confronting older people and, in particular, older people of color; women; members of religious minorities; lesbian, gay, bisexual, and transgender (LGBT) elders; and those with disabilities. It explains how discrimination and exclusion compound over time, lowering life expectancy and leading to disability, insecurity, poverty, and abuse.

Elder justice further provides a rallying call and driving force for change. It can animate stakeholders, inspire public support and participation, and lead to new partnerships between the aging and human rights networks. It highlights the critical role that older people and their allies and advocates can play in responding to the unprecedented political, social, economic, and

© Springer Publishing Company DOI: 10.1891/9780826147578.0011

technological changes that America faces today and in creating a more just society for people of all ages.

OLD ASSUMPTIONS AND UNFINISHED BUSINESS

Crafting a new paradigm of elder justice begins by revisiting assumptions that undergird the fields of aging and elder abuse prevention. Whereas some of these assumptions led to enormously impressive progress and achievements, others were based on wishful thinking and unrealistic expectations, leading to gaps, omissions, unfulfilled promises, and unintended consequences.

- **Assumption 1.** From the beginning, Medicare proponents like Congressman Claude Pepper had envisioned universal government-funded health coverage. After years of debate, a compromise was offered that adopted an incremental approach whereby older adults would be covered first, thereby pushing universal coverage into the future (Rich & Baum, 1984). As a result, dramatic disparities exist in health status, life expectancy, and rates of disease and disability.
- **Assumption 2.** Social Security would provide a "safety net," shielding retirees from extreme poverty and reducing disparities. Although Social Security has radically reduced poverty, the rates among certain groups today remain unacceptably high. The risk of poverty and income insecurity are greatest among those who experienced discrimination, exclusion, and lower workforce participation earlier in life.
- **Assumption 3.** Ageism would take its place alongside other "isms" as a social justice issue aligned with the human rights movement. As such, it would have broad public appeal and support. Despite the efforts of leaders like Maggie Kuhn and Robert Butler, ageism is not seen on par with other "isms" by older people, their advocates, the broader human rights network, or the public.
- **Assumption 4.** The "discovery" of elder abuse and neglect would result in public outrage and demands for action and funding. This assumption prompted providers of mental health and protective services to align themselves with elder abuse prevention in hopes of reaping these benefits. Toward that end, they attached the stigmatizing label of "self-neglect" to problems stemming from substance abuse, dementia, depression, mental illness, trauma, poverty, and discrimination. Programs to combat all of these problems remain critically underfunded.

- **Assumption 5.** Patterning Adult Protective Services (APS) after Child Protective Services (CPS) would elevate the stature of APS programs and lead to increased funding, higher professional standards, and enhanced regulation, oversight, and legal authority. Instead, APS remains underfunded and lacks stringent standards, regulation, and oversight. The program does not have broad public support and is poorly understood by the public and many professionals.
- **Assumption 6.** Block-granting APS would foster innovation in how protective services were delivered across the country. Instead, with the exception of New York, states took a "follow the leader" approach to adopting mandatory abuse reporting and, with few exceptions, alternatives have not emerged. Information about variations within states and approaches adopted in other countries have not received significant attention.
- **Assumption 7.** Designating aging and elder abuse as public health issues would raise their visibility, attract funding, offer new research methods, and shift the focus of healthcare toward disease prevention and health promotion. Epidemiological studies have, in fact, significantly broadened understanding of risk factors for age-related conditions and elder abuse and suggested myriad opportunities for prevention. The concepts of health promotion and healthy aging have been widely accepted. However, not all aspects of public health theory and practice have been fully embraced by the aging and elder abuse prevention fields. Programs that have adopted public health approaches generally focus on primary and secondary prevention at the individual and interpersonal levels with little attention paid to systemic risk factors, social determinants of health, and large-scale systemic approaches to prevention.
- **Assumption 8.** The Elder Justice Act (EJA) would provide a national structure for elder abuse prevention, leading to increased funding for services and improved coordination among federal departments, states, and communities. Only a small portion of the funding called for in the EJA has been forthcoming. Although the Elder Justice Coordinating Council is raising awareness and improving coordination at the federal level, this has not filtered down to states and local communities. Provisions for promoting public engagement, including the Advisory Board on Elder Abuse, Neglect, and Exploitation, which was called for in the EJA, have not been implemented.
- **Assumption 9.** The Patient Protection and Affordable Care Act (ACA) would vastly extend access to healthcare, ban unfair practices by insurance companies, reduce health disparities, and rebalance health

resources to provide more community-based long-term services and supports (LTSS). Although the ACA was successful in achieving many of its objectives, important features, including provisions for long-term care, were not enacted and others have been overturned or weakened.

NEW DEVELOPMENTS CREATE NEW NEEDS

The need for a broader, more inclusive, and better defined model of elder justice is increasingly urgent in light of new challenges, which include:

- **Calls for Medicare and Social Security reform.** Policy makers across the political divide agree that structural changes are needed to ensure the solvency of these programs. Some of the strategies under consideration, however, would result in greater health and wealth disparities by disproportionately benefitting some groups while penalizing others and undermining public trust by reneging on past promises. Proposals for raising the age of eligibility, for example, would disadvantage groups with shorter life expectancies whose members are also likely to experience age-related disabilities at an earlier age.
- **Threats to the ACA and safety net programs.** Continuous efforts to repeal or weaken the ACA threaten the enormous progress that has been made to date and further render uncertain the future of the EJA, which it contains. Retrenchments to Medicaid, Supplemental Security Income, and Social Services Block Grants, as well as unrealistic eligibility criteria (e.g., work requirements), threaten to increase health and wealth disparities, poverty, housing insecurity, abuse and neglect, disease, and disability.
- **Threats to consumer rights.** Recent and proposed measures limit protections for consumers of healthcare, LTSS, housing, and financial products, exposing them to new risks and reducing options for recourse at a time when fraud and abuse are at epidemic levels. These include ongoing threats to the Consumer Financial Protection Bureau (CFPB).
- **The weakening of civil rights divisions and responsibilities within federal agencies.** Among the agencies that have special divisions charged with investigating rights violations and discrimination that could be in jeopardy are the Equal Employment Opportunity Commission; the Environmental Protection Agency; and the Departments of Justice, Labor, Health and Human Services, and Housing and Urban Development. The changes could weaken important protections against age-based as well as other types of discrimination in housing, employment, healthcare, environmental safety, and emergency preparedness.

- **Heightened attention to end-of-life issues.** As new state and national policies are enacted addressing "right to die," advance directives, and guardianship, their implications for human rights and social justice need to be fully scrutinized and discussed by the public and policy makers to guard against unintended consequences.
- **Technological innovations.** Human rights and social justice concerns posed by technology include medical innovations that extend the length and quality of life for the wealthy at the expense of others. Telemonitoring, enhanced surveillance, and the Internet of things—while holding promise for vastly increasing the independence, security, and safety of frail older people—also pose enormous threats to privacy and autonomy.

IN PURSUIT OF ELDER JUSTICE

Although adopting an elder justice paradigm or ethos may seem daunting, the process, to a great extent, has already begun, fueled by growing attention to social justice and calls for reinforcing America's basic institutions. Formalizing these efforts and raising awareness about them can potentially enrich the field by bringing in new voices while reviving the spirit and wisdom of past generations of advocates and activists. It will require the following steps:

1. Defining elder justice
2. Developing a conceptual framework
3. Developing guiding principles for policy and practice
4. Applying an elder justice lens to existing and proposed policy
5. Ensuring accountability
6. Creating a culture of elder justice

1. Defining Elder Justice

Elder justice can be seen as the infusion of social justice goals and principles into aging services and policy. Elder justice policy must, therefore, meet two criteria:

- Affect older people
- Seek to achieve justice and human rights goals

Defining "elders" may seem straightforward. Chronological age thresholds have been set for everything from public entitlement programs to early bird specials. But these thresholds have social justice implications that need to be considered. As described in Chapter 8, the age at which people experience age-related disabilities and impairments reflects their economic and social status and life course. As a result, the higher the age threshold used to determine eligibility for services and resources, the more it disadvantages already disadvantaged groups; the lower the threshold, the more non-needy people benefit, rendering programs costlier and more politically vulnerable. Decisions about who is old need to be made carefully to balance these potential consequences.

"Aging policy" has traditionally meant policies and programs that were specifically designed for older people, including Medicare, Social Security, and Older Americans Act programs. But older people are significantly, and often disproportionately, affected by other policies and programs. These include policies pertaining to such far-ranging issues as natural disasters, immigration and migration, food policy and programs, transportation, zoning laws, housing, and many others. Elder justice policy, therefore, needs to include "mainstream" policies to the extent that they affect older people. Techniques for doing so include "mainstreaming" or "affirmative action," as used by international aging rights advocates (see Chapter 5).

On the "justice" side of the equation, elder justice policies and programs must protect individual rights and seek to achieve social justice goals. These include provisions that are currently recognized in law as well as aspirational goals that reflect current thinking and public sentiment. Legal rights include equal protection under the law, due process, least restrictive alternatives, and reasonable accommodation for those with disabilities. Rights proposed by philosophers include Martha Nussbaum's "right to life" approach as described in Chapter 2. Advocacy organizations have also defined justice similarly to Justice in Aging, which frames justice in its mission statement as the "opportunity to live with dignity, regardless of financial circumstances—free from the worry, harm, and injustice caused by lack of health care, food, or a safe place to sleep" (Justice in Aging, n.d., "Vision"). Other ethical, moral, professional, and cultural values associated with individual rights include respect, fairness, dignity, and filial piety.

2. Developing a Conceptual Framework

Conceptual models and frameworks have been described in earlier chapters. Chapter 4, for example, described the ecological model of public health, and Chapter 5 applied the model to elder abuse prevention. Chapter 5 further explained other theories that have been applied to elder abuse and points out the importance of conceptual frameworks in general for shaping how we think about problems, formulate solutions, predict outcomes, and identify biases.

The ecological model offers a logical starting point for conceptualizing elder justice policy, practice, and research that can build on past work. Other theories that may be relevant include the social exchange theory, feminist and other critical theories, and change models (Pease, Allan, & Briskman, 2003). As noted in Chapter 6, social exchange theory explains the give-and-take dynamics in interpersonal relationships and between individuals and society. Applied to elder justice, it can inform thinking about society's obligations to its older members and older peoples' contributions to their families, communities, and society. Similarly, feminist theory can be applied to elder justice to explain how women's status in society contributes to poverty, disease, disability, and abuse.

Just as feminist theory blames sexism for gender-based discrimination, exploitation, and exclusion, ageism may offer a logical starting point for a critical model of elder justice. It might focus, for example, on how ageism, along with other forms of discrimination, affects the social, political, and economic lives of older people and raises the risk of poverty, insecurity, abuse, neglect, and exploitation. The approach would further align ageism with other forms of discrimination and disadvantage, highlighting parallels, connections, and common goals.

"Theories of justice" also warrant consideration. Proposed by political scientists and ethicists, these theories provide the rationale for distributive justice with respect to how societies allocate or control resources among their members.

A conceptual model of elder justice needs to go beyond explaining the approach to proposing strategies for achieving it. This can be guided by change models, which describe processes for achieving collective outcomes and goals. Referred to as road maps, blueprints, engines of change, and theories of action, there are several variations:

- The Social Change Model seeks to change physical and social conditions related to poverty, the environment, health, equality, and democracy though advocacy and public policy.
- The Policy Change Model focuses on changing communities' institutions through policy development, reform, and enforcement, and by ensuring adequate resources.

3. Developing Guiding Principles for Policy and Practice

Promoting elder justice requires translating goals and concepts into principles or guidelines for policy and practice. The following principles of elder justice, created by members of the California Elder Justice Coalition (CEJC), serve as an example.

Elder Justice Principles

- The right to live free from abuse, neglect, and exploitation, which requires heightened awareness, prevention, early detection, holding perpetrators accountable, and providing relief to victims.
- Fair access to resources, services, and benefits that promote independence and autonomy, regardless of gender, ethnicity, race, gender identification, and religion. Fair access may further require countering disparities resulting from bias, exclusion, discrimination, and disadvantage.
- Fair access to the justice system through affordable legal aid and advocacy, accessible courts, and legal remedies that reflect older victims' special needs and vulnerabilities.
- Equity in the allocation of resources for protective services and victims' assistance to reflect the needs of victims and vulnerable people of all ages.
- Consumer protections and rights that pertain to consumers of LTSS, financial products, housing, and other goods and services. Consumer rights include aggressively pursuing predators who target older people.
- Ensuring the rights of people with cognitive impairments through support in decision-making and surrogate decision-making options that offer maximum autonomy, protection, and accountability.
- Support for family caregivers and direct service workers that acknowledges their needs and the value of their contributions.

A comprehensive and holistic approach to elder justice further needs to recognize and defend older people's rights to fairness in employment, housing, and healthcare. It needs to acknowledge their rights to privacy and confidentiality; to assemble and associate with whomever they choose; to marry; to vote and engage in other political or civic activities; to designate heirs; and to execute advanced directives like powers of attorney and wills (and have them respected).

4. Applying an Elder Justice Lens to Existing and Proposed Policy

The conceptual framework and principles described earlier can provide a lens for evaluating public policy, programs, and conduct on an ongoing basis. This lens highlights: (a) how older people are affected and (b) whether or not they advance social justice goals. This, in turn, can reveal if existing policy is adequate, what is missing, and how gaps can be filled.

A. How Are Older People Affected?

Policy, programs, and interventions affecting older people need to be reviewed to determine how they work to older people's advantage or disadvantage. Doing so will require that researchers, policy makers and analysts, advocates, and others have measures for tracking the impact of policies and programs on older people's quality of life, disease and disability rates, financial and housing security, risk of abuse, and other factors. It will further require tracking their access to and participation in health, public health, legal, and protective service programs. Policies and programs also need to be reviewed to expose biases, ageism, misconceptions, and false assumptions and narratives.

Policies, programs, and interventions also need to be reviewed to determine the extent to which they acknowledge, protect, and advance older people's rights as members of specific groups, including:

- **Members of historically disadvantaged, exploited, or oppressed groups.** Elder justice needs to respond to discrimination against older people in all settings and circumstances.
- **Residents of long-term care facilities.** Elder justice requires protections against systemic abuses as well as abuse by staff, visitors, residents (toward one another), and vendors; and recourse when abuses occur.
- **Consumers.** Elder justice requires that older consumers have objective information about products and services; alternative options to choose from; protection against fraudulent, predatory, or exploitative practices; and recourse when fraud or abuse occur.
- **Victims of crime.** Elder justice requires that older victims are protected from abusers, have information about their cases and a voice in criminal proceedings, and restitution and compensation for losses.
- **Crime suspects and defendants and those who are incarcerated or on probation or parole.** The special needs and circumstances of older suspects, defendants, and those convicted of crimes need to be recognized and addressed. These include due process protections for those accused of crimes and their right to be confronted by accusers. Older prison and jail inmates' rights include Americans with Disabilities Act protections and compassionate release policies.

B. Do Policies Comply With Social Justice Goals?

Policy analysts use various methods for evaluating such factors as fairness, parity, equality, and personal freedom. In analyzing the fairness of tax policy, for example, analysts determine the extent to which taxes are regressive, proportional, or progressive. Chapter 8 described where payroll taxes, which are used to fund Social Security and Medicare, fall with respect to this criterion and points out the impact of raising the cap on payroll taxes from a fairness perspective. As pointed out earlier, raising the age of eligibility for programs also disadvantages groups whose members have shorter average life expectancies. Measures to sustain programs cannot come at the expense of those in greatest need.

Some human rights advocates call for going beyond measures that make current laws fairer to those that make up for past injustices, including "affirmative action" or "positive discrimination," as described in Chapter 5. Examples include development programs that require or encourage recipients of foreign aid to demonstrate the impact the aid will have on women and girls and to take affirmative steps to overcome past discrimination.

Applying the elder justice lens to public policy will require forums and opportunities for advocates and policy makers to come together to achieve consensus on what is fair, just, and equitable with respect to older people and how it can be evaluated. It will further require the development of mechanisms and tools such as templates or protocols that can be applied to proposed or existing policies, programs, and government actions.

5. Ensuring Accountability

To be meaningful, a plan for elder justice needs to provide for goal setting and monitoring, and hold responsible parties accountable for achieving them. The monitoring systems for United Nations (UN) conventions provide a good model for doing so. They include the setting of objectives and milestones, benchmarks, and transparent periodic reviews. Although the UN lacks authority to enforce conventions, ratifying the Inter-American Convention on Protecting the Human Rights of Older Persons would provide a framework for tracking progress in the United States. Watchdog groups are also needed to hold governments accountable. Groups like HelpAge International can serve as examples.

6. Creating a Culture of Elder Justice

As former Secretary of Aging Kathy Greenlee points out, elder justice requires culture change (see Preface). It will further require making the case that ageism is integrally connected to other forms of discrimination.

Adopting elder justice begins by rejecting the narrative that old age is a disease that needs to be cured, which has led to an over-reliance on medical treatment and institutional care. Its corollary, that death is the failure of medicine, has resulted in an inflated role for physicians in authorizing end-of-life decisions. Elder justice requires healthcare programs that reflect public health values and principles and that seek to achieve health equity, optimal functional capacity, and home- and community-based long-term care. Making the shift will not be easy, particularly in light of the special interests that have a stake in the status quo.

Elder justice also requires rejecting "generations at war" narratives and addressing the cultural divide between the old and the young. As described in Chapter 8, this requires two-directional approaches. Older people need to understand how the prosperity of young people, especially younger minorities, is vital to their future as racial minorities and immigrants make up an increasingly large part of the labor force. On the other hand, younger generations need to understand that older White voters are critical to enacting public policies that invest in the education and health of a multicultural generation. This will require educating youth about the importance of foundational programs like Medicare and Social Security and how changes to these programs will affect them. Overcoming negative attitudes further requires rejecting "greedy geezer" characterizations that suggest that older voters' support for these programs is fueled by self-interest alone.

And finally, public acceptance of elder justice requires establishing its place among other social justice movements. Because the public appears wary of equating or comparing ageism with other forms of injustice and discrimination, a more productive approach may be to focus on how age and ageism compound and intensify other forms of discrimination. Doing so further invites partnerships with other networks to combat discrimination, poverty, exclusion, hunger, and insecurity for people of all ages. It further serves to raise awareness among these groups about the special circumstances and needs of their older members.

CHALLENGES TO DEVELOPING AN ELDER JUSTICE AGENDA

Implementing a comprehensive elder justice agenda will require overcoming a wide range of barriers and challenges that include:

- **Diversity of issues.** Challenges to elder justice range from the need for criminal justice reform to sustaining entitlement programs like Medicare. Their diversity makes articulating a clear and compelling message that can generate support a formidable challenge.

- **Politics.** Elder justice-related policies fall under the jurisdictions of multiple legislative bodies and within the purviews of different regulatory and administrative entities, ranging from social welfare, to criminal justice, to consumer rights. Some reflect highly partisan principles and ideologies. Achieving comprehensive elder justice policy, therefore, requires navigating jurisdictional boundaries and partisan divides.
- **Special interests.** Elder justice advocates face powerful opponents. Hospitals, nursing homes, physicians, pharmaceutical companies, and insurance providers can be counted upon to reject any efforts that shift the balance of public funding toward community-based and public health approaches. Powerful lobbies also routinely oppose regulations, consumer protections, and meaningful penalties for poor care and abuse in institutional settings. Opposition also comes from financial institutions, providers of senior housing, and others.
- **Turf issues.** Aligning with other social justice networks will require allaying fears that elder justice advocates will capitalize on or co-opt others' work, modify or distort their visions, or compete for resources. Overcoming distrust will require conveying the message that partnerships will enhance and strengthen, rather than diminish, the work of individual partners.
- **Threats to safety net program.** Today, such fundamental safety net programs as Supplemental Security Income, Medicaid, and Social Services Block Grants are in the crosshairs of many lawmakers and special interest groups. In today's tumultuous political climate, detecting when policies, programs, and resources are at imminent risk and anticipating what the impact of changes will be is a monumental task. As calls for retrenchments increase, they will require heightened vigilance by advocates.
- **Lack of leadership.** As Polivka (2015) points out, not since Claude Pepper has there been a champion for old people who has actively fought for antiageist measures like changing Medicare to include long-term services and support.

SEIZING OPPORTUNITIES

These daunting realities have been accompanied by surprising and unprecedented opportunities at a time when the public seems poised for change. As proposals to ensure the solvency of programs like Medicare and Social Security, Supplemental Security Income, and the ACA are discussed, it creates new opportunities for raising awareness about the importance of the programs in achieving social justice.

Current upheavals have also revealed dramatically changing attitudes and sparked unprecedented engagement and activism. The response to threats to the ACA suggests that public support for the act has significantly increased, with more states adopting ACA provisions for expanding Medicaid. Some policy makers are venturing further than ever before in calling for increased access to healthcare, reviving calls for universal coverage that have not been heard for decades, and proposing "Medicare for all" as the mechanism for achieving it. Discussions about healthcare reform may provide new opportunities to confront institutional biases in healthcare. In a period of deep partisanship, some elder justice and abuse prevention initiatives are seen as nonpartisan, drawing support, albeit meager, from both sides of the aisle.

In addition to having an enormous stake in the outcomes of these changes, elder justice advocates can make immense contributions as change occurs. As calls for "Medicare for All" get louder, who better than aging advocates— those who understand the intricacies of Medicare and have piloted measures to reform and expand the program—to lead the way? Aging advocates also understand the vulnerabilities and risk factors that predict abuse, isolation, disenfranchisement, poverty, and disability and have designed programs to reduce those risks and empower the vulnerable. Many witnessed first-hand how recession-era cuts were accompanied by increased reports of elder abuse and neglect, elder homelessness, food insecurity, and disparities in health and financial security. Elder abuse prevention advocates have created statutory and procedural innovations to extend access to courts and the legal system; their insights and experiences can clearly enrich public discourse and policy development.

International elder justice advocates also have much to contribute to discussions in the United States. The Convention on the Rights of Older Persons offers a powerful model for integrating policies under a comprehensive umbrella.

CONCLUSION

The potential benefits of achieving a unified vision of elder justice are enormous. Elder justice provides an inclusive and value-driven approach to public policy. It offers a compelling rationale for shifting away from medically driven systems of care that are increasingly less justifiable from an economic or social justice standpoint. It can provide guidance and touchstones during a period of transition and uncertainty. Older people are not the only ones who stand to gain. Elder justice serves all who aspire to live long and healthy lives.

REFERENCES

Justice in Aging. (n.d.). This is Justice in Aging. Retrieved from http://www.justiceinaging .org/about-us/missionvision

Pease, B., Allan, J., & Briskman, L. (2003). Introducing critical theories in social work. In J. Allan, B. Pease, & L. Briskman (Eds.), *Critical social work: An introduction to theories and practices* (pp. 1–14). New South Wales, Australia: Allan & Unwin.

Polivka, L. J. (2015, October 22). The legacy of Claude Pepper and the future of aging advocacy [Blog post]. Retrieved from http://asaging.org/blog/legacy-claude -pepper-and-future-aging-advocacy

Rich, B. M. & Baum, M. (1984). The aging: A guide to public policy . Pittsburgh, PA: University of Pittsburgh Press.

An Elder Justice Agenda

INTRODUCTION

This agenda consolidates recommendations described in earlier chapters into five sections: (a) practice; (b) education, training, and workforce development; (c) public policy; (d) public awareness and engagement; and (e) research.[1] It suggests strategies that can be adapted by advocates, service providers, educators, planners, policy makers, and researchers, and offers examples for doing so. It is intended to generate ideas, discussion, and action.

PRACTICE

Elder justice practice refers to interventions, services, programs, and service delivery models that protect older people's individual rights and strive for fairness. Individual rights include freedom from unwarranted intrusions into people's lives, due process when those rights are restricted, and the right to be treated with dignity and respect. Fairness is sought in access to resources, protection, and opportunities.

Requirements of Elder Justice Practice

- A balanced approach that applies elder justice objectives and outcomes at each level of intervention described in the ecological model: (a) individual, (b) interpersonal, (c) community, and (d) societal:
  a. Interventions to enhance individuals' choice, autonomy, freedom, independence, privacy, self-determination, safety, and engagement

---

[1] The categories contained in the agenda roughly align with those contained in *The Elder Justice Roadmap: A Stakeholder Initiative to Respond to an Emerging Health, Justice, Financial and Social Crisis* (Connolly, Brandl, & Breckman, 2014).

b. Interventions to strengthen interpersonal relationships and reduce power imbalances that raise the risk for interpersonal violence, exploitation, neglect, undue influence, and the violation of individual rights

c. Community interventions to bring resources to underserved communities and make neighborhoods healthier, safer, and more accessible

d. Societal interventions with broad impact, including public policy and awareness campaigns that promote elder justice

- Interventions to prevent injustices and rights violations that align with the public health hierarchy of (a) primary, (b) secondary, and (c) tertiary prevention:

  a. Primary prevention includes:
    - Disseminating information about risks to older people's rights, safety, security, privacy, autonomy, and independence
    - Services to prevent or reduce discrimination, crime and abuse, isolation, food and housing insecurity, dementia, disease and disability, substandard care and neglect in nursing homes, and environmental dangers
    - Removing barriers to justice through:
      - Targeted, culturally specific outreach to underserved communities
      - The use of community health workers, "navigators," health interpreters, health educators, and advocates to help clients navigate service delivery systems

  b. Secondary prevention includes:
    - Screenings for discrimination, hunger, home loss and homelessness, physical and cognitive decline and disability, elder abuse, extreme poverty, and isolation
    - Adjusting thresholds for health screening (the recommended age at which they start) that reflect the earlier onset of disease and disabilities for certain groups including the poor, people of color, and the homeless and incarcerated

  c. Tertiary prevention includes:
    - Interventions to stop and prevent recurrences of discrimination, abuse, preventable decline, isolation, and other elder rights violations
    - Harm reduction to mitigate the impact of elder justice violations and abuse
    - Interventions to reduce disparities in access to treatment and services

- Practice in elder justice must acknowledge older people's individual and collective experiences with trauma, deprivation, social isolation, and discrimination, as well as barriers between clients and professionals. Examples include:
  - ○ Trauma-informed practice that acknowledges how trauma influences beliefs, mental and physical health, coping, resilience, and trust in institutions and service providers. Trauma-informed practice seeks to empower clients and reinforce strengths
  - ○ "Cultural humility," which requires self-reflection by advocates and service providers to understand how their own histories, values, biases, and experiences shape the way they perceive and interact with clients and colleagues
  - ○ Strategies that empower clients to exercise choice, autonomy, and self-determination, including autonomy-based dementia care, supported decision making, client-centered practice, and goal attainment measures
- Systemic interventions that affect large numbers of people and address the needs of underserved groups
- Community needs assessments to identify and respond to specific circumstances, leadership, resources, strengths, barriers, and underserved groups

---

EXAMPLE: APPLYING ELDER JUSTICE TO ELDER ABUSE PREVENTION

- Develop and employ elder abuse screening and assessment tools that identify social determinants and risk factors, including low social support and previous traumatic event exposure.
- Reject approaches that pressure victims into taking actions they find unacceptable.
- Expand the use of restorative justice (e.g., conferencing and mediation).
- Expand the use of harm reduction. Examples include:
  - ○ Securing the safety, housing, and major assets of victims who choose to maintain contact with abusers
  - ○ Restoring or establishing social support
  - ○ Addressing health and mental health problems and injuries
- Encourage multidisciplinary teams to identify and address conflicts of interest among professionals and ensure that checks and balances exist (e.g., when advocates' goals of protecting choice conflict with law enforcement's mandate to enforce laws when victims do not want to press charges against abusive family members).

EXAMPLE: APPLYING ELDER JUSTICE TO LEGAL ASSISTANCE

- Provide assistance/advocacy to:
  - Those who have experienced age-based discrimination in the workplace, health and long-term care, housing, the criminal justice system, victim services, and prisons
  - Subjects of guardianships and other protective arrangements
  - Ensure that advance care and estate plans are "safe"; that is, they contain provisions to increase the likelihood that they will be adhered to
  - Ensure that advance care and estate plans reflect the personal values and beliefs of those executing them
- Prioritize cases with broad public impact, such as class action lawsuits against abusive nursing home chains.
- Adopt supported decision making, conflict resolution, mediation, and other techniques that support choice and autonomy when doing so does not pose unacceptable risks to safety and security.
- Use specialized screening and assessment tools to detect when incapacity, undue influence, or other impediments to choice pose unacceptable risks to individual rights.

ELDER JUSTICE–FOCUSED EDUCATION, TRAINING, AND WORKFORCE DEVELOPMENT

Ensuring an "elder justice–informed" workforce requires that those who work with older people in diverse settings—including professionals and advocates in the fields of aging, public health, human rights, elder abuse prevention, disability rights, legal assistance, social work, law enforcement, victim rights, and consumer rights—understand elder justice principles and have competency in elder justice techniques. Elder justice competencies include:

- Knowledge about:
  - Social justice concepts, including individual rights, health and social equity, social determinants, intersectionality, cumulative disadvantage, and ageism
  - Public health concepts, including the relationship between health and income disparities across the life span; social determinants of health, risk factors and risk reduction, the ecological model, the three levels of prevention, and *Healthy Aging 2020* goals, objectives, and methods

○ How social justice and individual rights apply to specific groups, including nursing home residents, consumers of long-term services and supports, people with disabilities, and victims of crime

○ Conflicts of interest in workers' roles with respect to the rights and interests of older people vis-à-vis their caregivers, family members, and abuse perpetrators

○ The impact of diminished capacity and undue influence in choice and decision making

- Skills in:
  ○ "Across the life span" approaches to health, economic security, and other aspects of people's lives
  ○ Trauma-informed and client-centered practice
  ○ Cultural humility
  ○ Interventions to prevent and respond to discrimination and other rights violations

- Promising methods for infusing elder justice content into education, training, and workforce development include:
  ○ Incorporate elder justice into educational requirements and competencies for professionals who work with older adults in diverse fields and settings.
  ○ Encourage academic and training institutions (e.g., schools of social work, public health, law, nursing, medicine, gerontology, police academies) to include elder justice content, classes, certificates, and degrees.
  ○ Convene multidisciplinary forums of advocates, professionals, and stakeholders to develop content and identify best practices, opportunities, and resources.
  ○ Provide on-the-job and in-service trainings and training events to increase professionals' awareness of elder justice and encourage them to integrate it into their work.
  ○ Develop programs to encourage students to consider careers or specializations that promote elder justice (e.g., encourage law students to specialize in elder law and develop expertise in social impact law, age discrimination, and elders' rights).
  ○ Create and expand on existing opportunities for older workers by combatting discrimination, promoting flexible work schedules and age-friendly work settings, and offering ongoing training and retraining.

PUBLIC POLICY

Elder justice policy includes laws, statutes, regulations, and government actions that align with elder justice principles.

Requirements of Elder Justice–Informed Policy

- Review policies pertaining to older people and reject those that reflect ageism, restrict elders' rights, unfairly disadvantage subgroups, or increase disparities. Examples of how this has been done by UN affiliated entities and other international bodies, as described in Chapter 5, can serve as examples:
  - Enhance intergenerational equity and parity among elders with respect to opportunities, protection, and resources. Examples include funding formulas for protective services that take into account the needs of children, adults with disabilities, and older adults.
  - Address disparities resulting from discrimination. Examples include adjusting Social Security payments to reflect the lower earnings of women and members of minorities earlier in life.
  - Enhance individual rights. Examples include strengthening due process protections in involuntary hospitalizations and guardianship.
  - Ensure that non–age specific policies and regulations are not implemented in ways that disadvantage older people. This includes, for example, ensuring that protections and resources provided under the Victims of Crime Act, the Violence Against Women Act, and the Civil Rights Act are extended to older people.
- Apply individual rights and fairness "tests" or templates developed by courts or legal scholars to review policy affecting older adults. Examples include the application of the "Westinghouse Test" to evaluate the constitutionality of state mandatory elder abuse reporting laws with respect to privacy as described in Chapter 7.
- Methods and mechanisms for achieving elder justice policy goals include:
  - Bring together stakeholders, researchers, advocates, legal scholars, policy analysts and developers, and professionals in the fields of aging, elder abuse, social justice, and public health to establish goals, objectives, benchmarks, timelines, and monitoring systems.
  - Support the development of advocacy and watchdog groups to participate in and oversee policy implementation. These groups can hold public hearings, issue "report cards," produce plans or blueprints, and schedule systematic reviews.

○ Employ "mainstreaming" and/or "affirmative action,"[2] as used by United Nations (UN) entities and international advocacy groups to identify and respond to biases and disparities impacting older people (see Chapter 5).

○ Establish mechanisms to coordinate elder justice policy development at the local, state, and national levels to enhance communication, coordination, and collaboration. Examples include national associations of state and local advocacy groups to exchange information and advocate for national action. This may include, for example, advocating for the implementation of the "Advisory Board on Elder Abuse, Neglect, and Exploitation," as called for in the Elder Justice Act. The Advisory Board was envisioned to "create short- and long-term multidisciplinary strategic plans for the development of the field of elder justice and to make recommendations to the Elder Justice Coordinating Council."

○ Develop ongoing and dynamic mechanisms for policy discussion among policy makers, advocates, professionals, policy analysts and developers, researchers, and stakeholders about the benefits and drawbacks of existing and proposed policy:

- At the national level, potential topics for discussions may include the benefits and drawbacks of a constitutional amendment for victim rights, constitutional issues raised by existing or proposed policies, the need for model state statutes and programs, and U.S. participation in international treaties and forums.

- At the state level, discussions related to elder justice may include comparisons of state approaches to elder rights, justice, and abuse prevention; and the need for federal law, policies, guidance, and resources.

- Policy-focused multidisciplinary teams to identify policy needs, vet proposals, and craft policy solutions are desired. Sources of referrals could include local case review teams that have encountered systemic barriers they are not equipped to address and requests from policy makers for stakeholder input (California Elder Justice Coalition, 2016).

---

[2] As described in Chapter 5, "mainstreaming" involves ensuring age equity and that the needs and perspectives of old people are reflected in program and policy development, research, advocacy/dialogue, legislation, and resource allocation. "Affirmative action" is sometimes referred to as positive discrimination in favor of older people through institutional preferences to compensate for past inequalities.

EXAMPLE: ELDER JUSTICE APPROACHES TO HEALTH POLICY

- Promote policies that reduce health disparities by extending access to healthcare or health insurance to underserved groups (e.g., Medicaid expansion).
- Shift the focus of healthcare from its current institutional and medical orientation toward one that prioritizes public health approaches and home- and community-based care:
  - Promote the expansion of long-term services and supports.
  - Promote health policy that:
    - Addresses the social determinants of health
    - Focuses on functional as well as medical outcomes
    - Reflects *Healthy People 2020* goals
    - Promotes independence, autonomy, and choice
  - Ensure that the health needs of older people are reflected in public health policies, guidelines, and standards (e.g., ensuring that advocates for older people participate on the U.S. Preventive Services Task Force).

EXAMPLE: ELDER JUSTICE APPROACHES TO ELDER ABUSE POLICY

- Reduce disparities in public resources for protective services, victims' services, and crime prevention. Examples include extending victim compensation to older victims of financial crimes.
- Ensure that elder abuse laws, including mandatory reporting laws, do not violate individual rights.
- Respond to special needs, such as ensuring that restraining orders are available for those who are unable to contact law enforcement on their own if orders are violated.

EXAMPLE: ELDER JUSTICE APPROACHES TO CONSUMER RIGHTS POLICY

- Ensure that older consumers have acceptable options to choose from. This may require expanding the range of services and goods covered under entitlement programs.

- Ensure that older consumers can make informed decisions about services and products. This requires defining capacity with respect to making decisions about goods and services and appointing advocates or surrogates to exercise choice on behalf of those who are unable to do so on their own. It further requires that consumers have information about service providers on which to base hiring decisions, such as background information about caregivers.
- Ensure that older consumers' rights are protected. Examples include:
  - Actively pursue perpetrators of consumer fraud and exploitation who target elders.
  - Reject the use of binding arbitration agreements that unreasonably block recourse against substandard products and services and abuse by service providers.
  - Enforce regulations for government-funded services, including hospital and nursing home care, and tie reimbursement to quality and outcome measures.
  - Impose duties on providers of goods and services to act fairly and in consumers' interests when failure to do so poses unacceptable risks to older consumers.

EXAMPLE: ELDER JUSTICE APPROACHES TO DIMINISHED CAPACITY AND END-OF-LIFE POLICY

- Establish criteria for end-of-life decisions that emphasize autonomy, choice, and quality of life as opposed to medical futility.
- Ensure that hospice care, comfort care, and palliative care are available and meet quality care standards.
- Craft protections to ensure that end-of-life decisions are made freely.
- Promote provisions contained in the Uniform Law Commission's Uniform Guardianship, Conservatorship, and Other Protective Arrangements Act and reports by the Independent Expert on the Enjoyment of All Human Rights by Older Persons including guardianships that are limited in their scope of authority and duration.
- Define legal standards for decision-making capacity for circumstances in which questions commonly arise. This includes consenting to services; exercising choice in long-term care, financial services, loans, and so on; and personal decisions pertaining to marriage, adult adoptions, and sexual relations.

EXAMPLE: ELDER JUSTICE APPROACHES TO LEGAL SYSTEM AND COURT POLICY

- Expand the range and availability of legal assistance and remedies for nonaffluent and other underserved groups. Examples include creating incentives for private attorneys to accept cases and exploring the expanded use of small claims courts to address financial crimes when their associated losses do not meet minimum monetary thresholds for prosecution.
- Promote the use of elder courts.
- Remove barriers to legitimate class action lawsuits.
- Ensure that older crime victims are eligible for victim assistance and compensation.
- Draw from the *Report of the Expert Group Meeting "Rights of Older Persons"* with respect to older people's legal rights (United Nations Department of Economic and Social Affairs, 2009). Examples include providing support for strategic litigation to create legal precedents and change laws (e.g., to combat discrimination in public benefit programs).

EXAMPLE: ELDER JUSTICE POLICY APPROACHES TO PRISON AND JAIL INMATES

- Review and adopt the Inspector General's (Bureau of Prisons) recommendations to improve the treatment of older inmates. Specific recommendations include appointing independent authorities to monitor prison conditions, enforcing minimal standards of health and safety, improving the oversight and training of inmate companions, and reviewing requirements for compassionate release.

FROM PUBLIC AWARENESS TO PUBLIC ENGAGEMENT

Achieving elder justice requires going beyond raising public awareness to changing counterproductive attitudes and mobilizing the public to defend older adults' rights. It requires helping the public understand elder justice principles, applications, barriers, and solutions; combatting ageism and divisive narratives; directing the public to services that promote individual rights and social justice; and letting stakeholders and concerned citizens know what they can do. Specifically, campaigns can:

- Incorporate elder justice themes into campaigns to prevent elder abuse, reduce poverty and homelessness, and promote new services.
- Help the public understand:
  - Discrimination across the life span, including:
    - Ageism and its impact on individual rights and social justice
    - Intersectionality and how injustices experienced earlier in life may intensify and compound across the life course, threatening older people's health, security, and independence
  - Underserved groups and areas of need
  - Systemic threats to justice such as failures to enforce nursing home regulations and negative consequences associated with the privatization of long-term care
  - Services and benefits that enhance individual rights and social justice, including:
    - Benefits and services they are entitled to and how to access them. This includes creating realistic expectations about what agencies do and clearly describing their eligibility requirements. Policies pertaining to government restrictions related to immigration status and criminal backgrounds must be explained
    - Threats to services and elder justice and what they can do about them
  - International elder justice initiatives and events, including age-friendly cities, the convention for the rights of older people, World Elder Abuse Awareness Day, and UN declarations
- Change attitudes and combat counterproductive narratives. Campaigns can help the public:
  - Reject ageism by:
    - Countering the view that old age is a medical problem in need of treatments and cures
    - Emphasizing the seriousness of ageism and its consequences for health, security, and autonomy
    - Explaining the role of ageism and special interests in perpetuating lax regulation, oversight, and enforcement of abuse laws, regulations, and policies
  - Overcome denial about disability (e.g., emphasize that most Americans will both need and provide care).

- Raise awareness about intersectionality to highlight the importance of alliances with other social justice networks (e.g., the impact of sexism and racism continues into old age and may become compounded and intensified).
- Reject the "generations at war" narrative, calling instead for intergenerational unity through messages that:
  - Highlight shared goals and interdependencies among generations.
  - Promote intergenerational respect and exchange.
  - Convey to nonelders that programs like Medicare and Social Security are not "aging programs" but, in fact, ensure the security of all Americans.
  - Convey to older people that their well-being depends on the prosperity and security of younger people, and minority youth in particular.
- Encourage public engagement through messages that link elder justice ideas to solutions and actions. Examples include the following:
  - "Health justice is social justice" conveys the idea that healthcare is a right and speaks to the need for public health approaches.
  - "Healthy aging begins now" emphasizes that reducing the risk of age-related diseases and disabilities can begin at any age.
  - "Financial security begins now" emphasizes that lowering the risk of economic insecurity in advanced age needs to begin earlier in life.
  - "The health and prosperity of young and old depend on each other" promotes intergenerational exchange and appreciation.
  - "Elder abuse is a violation of human rights" appeals to Americans' sense of justice. The message also applies to elder homelessness, extreme poverty, and ageism.
- Provide opportunities for people to get involved in political action and advocacy.
  - Convene forums, town halls, hearings, and summits on elder justice and human rights.
  - Alert advocates and stakeholders to opportunities for influencing policy and provide tools for doing so. This can be accomplished by producing fact sheets, legislative timelines and schedules, analyses of policy proposals, descriptions, and contact information for key decision makers, thought leaders, and administrative officials.
- Develop a broad base of support for elder justice through the following:
  - Partner with advocates for the rights of consumers, nursing home residents, people with disabilities, crime victims, and other underserved groups.

○ Align with state, federal, and international human rights groups that promote the rights of women, people of color, LGBT (lesbian, gay, bisexual, and transgender) individuals, people with disabilities, and others, and encourage them to address the needs of older members.

○ Enlist the participation of professional associations; advocacy organizations representing various professions (e.g., the American Bar Association [ABA], National Adult Protective Services Association [NAPSA]); interdisciplinary organizations; and international professional and advocacy organizations in promoting policies, identifying needs, and generating support.

○ Encourage advocacy organizations, including AARP, the Gray Panthers, the Older Women League, the League of Women Voters, and others to adopt elder justice messages.

○ Promote awareness events commemorating the Americans with Disabilities Act, the Olmstead decision, the Violence Against Women Act, the Victim of Crimes Act, and other human rights accomplishments, highlighting how they have benefited older people.

○ Encourage human rights and social justice organizations to address the needs of older constituents.

○ Enlist the faith community and civic organizations.

RESEARCH

Research in elder justice is needed to inform policy, practice, training, and public engagement. Key components of an elder justice—informed research agenda include a conceptual research framework, descriptive and epidemiological studies, evaluations of interventions, and demonstration projects. It should contribute to the knowledge base and reflect the needs of stakeholders, including policy analysts and advocates, program developers, and service providers.

- A conceptual research model is needed that:
  ○ Builds on the ecological model and incorporates adaptations of it that are used in public health, elder abuse prevention, and other related areas. It should "fill in the blanks" by focusing attention on areas of knowledge that have not been explored with respect to community and societal dimensions of elder justice.
  ○ Is informed by other models, including critical theories and models of social change.
  ○ Incorporates elements and recommendations from earlier initiatives, including research agendas, past studies, and government reports

- ○ Identifies markers of elder justice and injustice with respect to housing and income security, access to services and resources, exposure to risks, life expectancy, health status, and dependence.
- ○ Defines and predicts what success looks like in terms of individual rights and social justice (e.g., increased participation in public benefit programs by underserved groups; clients' success in achieving personal goals).
- Descriptive and epidemiological studies are needed to:
  - ○ Establish incidence and prevalence rates for disease, disability, abuse, poverty, homelessness, and other threats to health and well-being.
  - ○ Define, identify, and measure risk and protective factors related to social justice, including social determinants associated with life expectancies; the prevalence of disease and disability, abuse, and neglect; and income and housing insecurity. Factors to consider include social isolation, individual and collective trauma, discrimination, occupation, education, and living environment.
  - ○ Identify high-risk individuals, groups, and communities, as well as disparities in risk across groups.
  - ○ Inform policy and practice. Elder justice—focused research is needed to:
    - ▪ Target services and interventions to underserved groups.
    - ▪ Measure the impact of systemic interventions on incidence and prevalence.
    - ▪ Provide evidence of the need for policy and services.
    - ▪ Inform decisions about how resources can be used to reduce disparities.
- Evaluations of programs, policies, and response systems to:
  - ○ Measure the impact and efficacy of primary, secondary, and tertiary interventions at the individual, interpersonal, community, and societal levels in achieving elder justice goals.
  - ○ Measure the impact of programs and services that are presumed to enhance elder justice, including supported decision making, harm reduction, and restorative justice programs.
  - ○ Identify barriers to access to services and resources, including:
    - ▪ Personal barriers to services such as lack of knowledge about or trust in services; concerns about privacy, liability, and retribution; inability to use services resulting from lack of transportation, literacy, physical limitations, and other factors.
    - ▪ Systemic barriers, which include lack of resources leading to shortages in the supply of services, failure to fully implement existing programs, failure to locate services in accessible locations, and lack of transportation for clients.

- o Provide information on program administration that can be used for planning and resource allocation and to identify policy, regulation, or oversight needs, including:
    - Program impact and costs
    - Utilization rates for services and benefits by underserved groups
    - Obstacles to program effectiveness
- o Special considerations in elder justice research and evaluations include:
    - All segments of the population need to be accurately represented in governmental surveillance, epidemiological studies, and needs assessments.
    - New or adapted methods are needed in program evaluations to differentiate the consequences of implementation failures (e.g., lack of resources or truncated timelines) from ineffective approaches or methods.
    - New or adapted methods may be needed to define markers of success in achieving elder justice goals (e.g., how the program is successful in achieving fairness, autonomy, and choice defined and measured).
- Demonstration projects are needed to compare alternative approaches to services and service delivery systems with respect to their effectiveness, efficiency, affordability, replicability, and scalability (e.g., comparisons between nonprofit versus for-profit care, managed care versus fee-for-service plans). Also needed is information about "alternative costs" of service delivery systems (different approaches to service delivery that achieve comparable or better outcomes at lower cost or in more equitable ways).

EXAMPLE: ELDER JUSTICE–INFORMED RESEARCH ON ELDER ABUSE

- Adapt the ecological model of elder abuse to emphasize elder justice, such as paying greater attention to individual rights and equity in service delivery.
- Identify descriptive and epidemiological studies that identify risk factors for abuse that are associated with social determinants.
- Collect prevalence data that can be used to evaluate the impact of systemic interventions such as mandatory reporting, regulations addressing abuse in long-term care facilities, and outreach campaigns.

(continued)

- Build on earlier work. Examples include incorporating recommendations for data collection contained in the American Bar Association (ABA) White Paper (Wood, 2006), which include adding questions about elder abuse to the Centers for Disease Control and Prevention (CDC) Chronic Disease Behavioral Risk Factor Surveillance System (see Chapter 4).
- Evaluate elder abuse prevention interventions to:
  - Identify ageism and practices that are antithetical to elder justice.
  - Compare state responses (e.g., between New York's voluntary abuse reporting and other states' mandatory reporting systems) and diverse approaches within states.
  - Compare national responses, including how the U.S. approach compares to approaches used in other countries as described in Chapter 5.
  - Track utilization and outcomes for underserved groups.
  - Measure outcomes, including client satisfaction, the extent to which interventions achieve clients' goals, and consequences, including retribution or retaliation experienced by victims, those who report abuse, and whistleblowers.
  - Measure compliance by mandated reporters, nonmandated reporters, victims, witnesses, professionals, and others.
  - Identify barriers to program administration, efficiency, and effectiveness, including insufficient funding.

EXAMPLE: ELDER JUSTICE–INFORMED RESEARCH ON HEALTH DISPARITIES AND ACCESS TO CARE

- Build on existing data collection systems (e.g., add age categories to the *National Healthcare Disparities Report*).
- Evaluate the impact of public health practices, including health promotion and disease prevention programs, health education, the use of community health workers and navigators, screenings, and so on, in achieving longer and healthier lives and reducing disparities.
- Track older people's participation in health and public health programs.
- Evaluate programs that focus on harm reduction with respect to disease, chronic conditions, elder abuse, and dementia.

EXAMPLE: ELDER JUSTICE–INFORMED RESEARCH ON THE LEGAL SYSTEM

- Engage legal scholars, law school faculty, advocates, and stakeholders in developing guidelines and metrics for measuring the impact and implications of laws, government actions, and legal services and interventions on older people's constitutional rights.
- Collect data on lawsuits, guardianships, advance directives, prosecutions, restraining orders, and other legal interventions and remedies that can be used to measure outcomes, utilization rates, underserved groups, and gaps.
- Collect data on public policies and court decisions that have implications for older people's individual rights and social equity.

EXAMPLE: ELDER JUSTICE–INFORMED RESEARCH ON PUBLIC AWARENESS AND ENGAGEMENT

- Engage advocates for the rights of elders, adults with disabilities, human rights, nursing home residents, consumers, and others in developing markers and measures of success and progress.
- Build on existing research, including the FrameWorks Institute's studies, to better understand the attitudes of older people and service providers (see Chapter 3).
- Explore responses to various outreach messages, including the framing of abuse as a human rights issue and calls for the public to take action.
- Studies are needed to measure:
  - Comprehension of messages and reactions to them.
  - Differences among target groups with respect to comprehension and reactions.
  - The extent to which campaigns change attitudes and beliefs and prompt targeted groups to take action. This may include taking steps to reduce personal risk factors or engaging in collective action toward a fairer and more just society for people of all ages.

REFERENCES

California Elder Justice Coalition. (2016). *From blueprint to benchmarks: Building a framework for elder justice.* Retrieved from https://www.elderjusticecal.org/uploads/1/0/1/7/101741090/cejc_blueprint2016.pdf

Connolly, M.-T., Brandl, B., & Breckman, R. (2014). *The elder justice roadmap: A stakeholder initiative to respond to an emerging health, justice, financial and social crisis.* Washington, DC: U.S. Department of Justice. Retrieved from https://www.justice.gov/file/852856/download

United Nations Department of Economic and Social Affairs. (2009). *Report of the expert group meeting "rights of older persons."* Retrieved from https://www.un.org/esa/socdev/documents/ageing/reportofegm.pdf

Wood, E. (2006). *The availability and utility of interdisciplinary data on elder abuse: A white paper for the National Center on Elder Abuse.* Retrieved from https://ncea.acl.gov/resources/docs/archive/Availability-Utility-Interdisciplinary-Data-EA-White Paper-NCEA-2006.pdf

Index

ABA Commission on Law and Aging
(COLA), 187, 188
ACA. *See* Patient Protection and
Affordable Care Act
accountable care organizations (ACOs),
152
ACED. *See* Assessment of Capacity for
Everyday Decision-making
ACL. *See* Administration for
Community Living
ACLU. *See* American Civil Liberties
Union
ACOs. *See* accountable care
organizations
ADA. *See* Americans With Disabilities
Act
ADEA. *See* Age Discrimination in
Employment Act
Administration for Community Living
(ACL), 16
Administration on Intellectual and
Developmental Disabilities (AIDD),
16
Adult Protective Services (APS), 17–19,
87
  block-granting, 197
  bystander interventions, 94
  confidentiality restrictions, 94
  lack of coordination, 93
  lack of sufficient resources, 92–93
  patterning, 197
  self-neglect, 95
  service response evaluation, 93
  utilization, 93
Adult Protective Services/Mandatory
Reporting Model, 81

adultism, 26–27
advance directives
  for emergency and end-of-life care, 180
  limitations, 181–183
  powers of attorney, 180
  trusts, 181
  wills, 179–180
Advocacy Model, 82
advocacy programs, 13
affirmative action, 68
Affordable Care Act. *See* Patient
Protection and Affordable Care Act
age
  as an international public health issue,
  76
  as a human rights issue, 70–75
  in sustainable social and economic
  development, 76–78
Age Discrimination in Employment Act
(ADEA), 14, 33
ageism
  and adultism, 26–27
  Butler's view, 3–4, 23
  and cross-generational antipathy, 23
  disaster preparedness, 35–37
  discrimination, 27, 39
  elder abuse, 28–30
  equity indices, 28
  Gray Panthers' solidarity, 24
  in healthcare, 30–33
  history, 25–26
  institutional, 27
  intentional, 27
  media and marketing, 37–38
  positive ageism and sageism, 28
  public policy and politics, 39, 40

227